REVIEWER PRAISE OF BOO

Making Money in Real Estate

"Gray delivers the goods. It is all-Canadian, and not a retread book full of tips that are worthless north of the U.S. border. It's chock-full of practical streetsmart strategies and advice, pitfalls to avoid, samples, what-to-look-out for, checklists and information."
— *Business in Vancouver*

"...provides consumer insights into securing the best deal and avoiding the pitfalls... Gray's legal background has given him valuable insights."
— *The Edmonton Journal*

"Outstanding...peppered with practical no-nonsense tips...invaluable information throughout."
— *Calgary Herald*

The Complete Canadian Small Business Guide (with Diana Gray)

"This guide is truly a gold mine...an admirable job...taps into the author's expertise."
— *Profit Magazine*

" Excellent...geared especially to Canadians, unlike most small business guides."
—*Financial Times*

"The most informative and comprehensive guide on this subject matter."
— *The Toronto Star*

Home Inc.: The Canadian Home-Based Business Guide

"Should be required reading for all potential home-basers...authoritative, current and comprehensive."
— *The Edmonton Journal*

" An absolute necessity for your bookshelf...crammed with useful information."
— *Victoria Times-Colonist*

The Complete Canadian Franchise Guide (with Norm Friend)

"Down to earth, comprehensive, easy to read and packed with practical information. A superb guide to buying a franchise. Invaluable samples and checklists. Highly recommended."

— Terry and Fran Banting, Franchisees

The Canadian Snowbird Guide

"...an invaluable guide to worry-free part-time living in the U.S. ...by one of Canada's bestselling authors of business and personal finance books..."

— *The Globe and Mail*

"Gray has written a reference book, thoughtful and complete, and prepared with the authoritative research skills and knowledge of a fastidious solicitor...as practical as a sunhat on a Tampa afternoon, and that alone warrants it a place on every southbound RV's bookshelf."

— *Quill & Quire*

The Canadian Guide to Will and Estate Planning (with John Budd)

"...An informative, practical guide...the authors...cover all the bases."

— *The National Post*

"...A bargain for its price, it should be part of every family's library."

— *The Globe and Mail*

THE COMPLETE GUIDE TO
BUYING
AND OWNING
RECREATIONAL
PROPERTY
IN CANADA

BEST-SELLING BOOKS BY DOUGLAS GRAY

REAL ESTATE TITLES

The Complete Guide to Buying and Owning Recreational Property in Canada

Making Money in Real Estate: The Canadian Guide to Profitable Investment in Residential Property

101 Streetsmart Condo Buying Tips for Canadians

Real Estate Investing for Canadians for Dummies (with Peter Mitham)

Mortgages Made Easy: The All-Canadian Guide to Home Financing

Home Buying Made Easy: The Canadian Guide to Purchasing a Newly Built or Pre-Owned Home

Condo Buying Made Easy: The Canadian Guide to Apartment and Townhouse Condos, Co-ops and Timeshares

Mortgage Payment Tables Made Easy

SMALL BUSINESS TITLES

Start and Run a Consulting Business

Start and Run a Profitable Business Using Your Computer

Have You Got What It Takes? The Entrepreneur's Complete Self-Assessment Guide

Marketing Your Product (with Donald Cyr)

The Complete Canadian Small Business Guide (with Diana Gray)

Raising Money: The Canadian Guide to Successful Business Financing (with Brian Nattrass)

The Complete Canadian Franchise Guide (with Norm Friend)

So You Want to Buy a Franchise? (with Norm Friend)

Be Your Own Boss: The Ultimate Guide to Buying a Small Business or Franchise in Canada (with Norm Friend)

The Canadian Small Business Legal Guide

PERSONAL FINANCE/RETIREMENT PLANNING TITLES

The Canadian Snowbird Guide: Everything You Need to Know about Living Part-time in the U.S.A. and Mexico

The Canadian Guide to Will and Estate Planning (with John Budd)

Risk-Free Retirement: The Complete Canadian Planning Guide (with Tom Delaney, Graham Cunningham, Les Solomon and Dr. Des Dwyer)

SOFTWARE PROGRAMS

Making Money in Real Estate (jointly developed by Douglas Gray and Phoenix Accrual Corporation)

THE COMPLETE GUIDE TO
BUYING
AND OWNING
RECREATIONAL
PROPERTY
IN CANADA

DOUGLAS GRAY
AUTHOR OF BEST-SELLING *MAKING MONEY IN REAL ESTATE*

BICENTENNIAL
1807
WILEY
2007
BICENTENNIAL

John Wiley & Sons Canada, Ltd.

National Library of Canada Cataloguing in Publication Data

Gray, Douglas A
   The complete guide to buying and owning recreational property in Canada / Douglas Gray.

Includes index.
ISBN 978-0-470-83972-0

   1. Vacation homes. 2. House buying. I. Title.
HD1379.G738 2007   643'.12   C2007-900982-4

Production Credits
Cover design: Ian Koo
Interior text design: Natalia Burobina
Wiley Bicentennial Logo: Richard J. Pacifico
Printer: Printcrafters

John Wiley & Sons Canada, Ltd.
6045 Freemont Blvd., Mississauga, Ontario L5R 4J3

Printed in Canada

1 2 3 4 5 PC 11 10 09 08 07

Contents

Acknowledgements   xi

Introduction   1

Part I: The Realities of Realty

Chapter 1: *How the Real Estate Market Works*   9

Chapter 2: *Why Recreational Real Estate Is a Good Investment*   17

Chapter 3: *Types of Recreational Real Estate*   25

Part II: Finding the Right Fit

Chapter 4: *Finding the Right Recreational Property*   49

Chapter 5: *Selecting Your Advisors*   69

Part III: Show Me the Money

Chapter 6: *Mortgages and Other Creative Financing Options*   89

Chapter 7: *Negotiating the Best Deal*   99

Chapter 8: *Investing for Yourself or with Others*   107

Part IV: Planning for Peace of Mind

Chapter 9: *Legal Issues and Strategies*   121

Chapter 10: *Tax Issues and Strategies*   131

Chapter 11: *Insurance Issues and Strategies*   149

Chapter 12: *Will Planning Issues and Strategies*   161

Chapter 13: *Estate Planning Issues and Strategies*   169

Part V: Now That It's Yours

Chapter 14: *Maintaining Harmony with Shared Use and Ownership*   191

Chapter 15: *Vacation Home Exchanges and Bartering Networks*   199

Chapter 16: *Professional or Owner-Direct Rental Management*   213

Part VI: Outward Bound

Chapter 17: *Buying Vacation Property in the United States and Abroad*   231

Chapter 18: *Selling Your Recreational Property*   243

Appendix

Helpful Websites   255

Chart 1: Determining the Real Estate Cycle   260

Checklist 1: Recreational Property Assessment Checklist   261

Checklist 2: Preparing for a Mortgage   273

Checklist 3: Real Estate Purchase Expenses Checklist   276

Checklist 4: Vacation Property Sharing and Use Agreement Checklist   278

Glossary   281

Index   295

Reader Feedback and Seminar   305

About the Author   307

Acknowledgements

I am grateful for the kind assistance and helpful information given me by many parties, including the Canada and Mortgage Housing Corporation, the Canadian Real Estate Association, Genworth Financial Canada, Royal LePage, Century 21, ReMax, and Coldwell Banker. I appreciate all the assistance provided by the Condominium Home Owners' Association of B.C., and particularly the helpful insights from the Executive Director of CHOA, Tony Gioventu. Many thanks to Bob and Lesleigh Hevey, for their invaluable insights on maintaining harmony when sharing ownership and use of a cottage with friends.

I would like to thank Nicole Langlois for the superb quality of editing that she has demonstrated throughout. Her insights, creative suggestions, and positive attitude made the editorial experience a most pleasurable one, for this book and the past books of mine she has edited with such professionalism.

My thanks and appreciation is extended to a number of tax experts and professionals who have given so graciously of their time and talent in reviewing parts of this manuscript. I am indebted to Karen Slezak, C.A., Tax Partner of Soberman, LLP, Chartered Accountants in Toronto, who kindly provided much constructive and helpful feedback on various tax issues and strategies to consider. It was a pleasure working with Karen. I would like to thank Frances Sin, Tax Manager of Soberman, LLP, Chartered Accountants in Toronto, for reviewing the section on GST. My appreciation is also extended to my colleague John Budd, FCA, of Cumberland Asset Management in Toronto. John has always been a source of helpful advice, encouragement, enthusiasm, and a wealth of wisdom garnered from his many years as a highly respected professional advisor. He is also the co-author of a book we wrote called *The Canadian Guide to Will and Estate Planning*, and the author of the bestselling book *Second-Property Strategies*.

I would like to thank the staff of John Wiley & Sons for their ongoing support, professionalism, and insightful feedback.

Last but not least, I would like to express my appreciation to Don Loney, Executive Editor of John Wiley & Sons, for his patience and encouragement in the development of this book. I have had the pleasure of knowing Don for over 15 years. I have indeed been fortunate to work with such a consummate professional in the publishing business.

Introduction

If you are reading this book, you are one of the many Canadians who desire to own a recreational property, and want to learn how to make the right purchase through informed decision making and practical insights.

The term "recreational property" refers to a range of options, including an existing home (chalet, cabin, cottage, etc.), building lot, or hobby farm, with recreational features nearby. It could also consist of resort condominiums.

Recreational features consist of numerous types of outdoor choices for exercise, recreation, or enjoyment, including fields, mountains, rivers, lakes, oceans, ski hills, golf courses, campsites, and recreational vehicle parks. Activities could include snowmobiling, hunting, hiking, climbing, boating, canoeing, sailing, fishing, downhill or cross-country skiing, or other recreational pursuits. Your vacation home could be located in a rural or resort area.

Possibly you want a vacation property for personal use and lifestyle enjoyment, and plan to pass it to your children, and so on down through the generations. Maybe you want it for long-term investment, or for rental revenue purposes, or a combination of personal use and periodic or seasonal rentals. You might plan to have an all-season vacation home as your future retirement home. Alternatively, you might have considered buying a vacation home in the United States or abroad for investment, or to live there part-time during the winter months as a "snowbird."

When you buy your vacation home, your preference could be to buy it on your own, with other family members or friends, or with an independent group of investors.

Possibly you already own a vacation home, or have inherited one, or know you will be doing so in the future. You could be concerned about the tax and estate planning implications of passing the property on to family members or selling it. At the time of your death, your vacation property could be subject to probate taxes as well as capital gains tax. There is a deemed disposition of your assets on death. This could result in a substantial and unexpected financial impact on your estate, necessitating the possible sale of the property to pay the taxes. However, with some highly skilled professional tax advice, you might be able to strategically structure your vacation property ownership to legitimately avoid, minimize, or defer the capital gains tax hit during your life, and on your death.

Why Recreational Properties Are in High Demand

Various trends and other motivating factors are causing a keen interest in buying rural, recreational, or resort property. Here are some of the key influencing factors:

- √ Availability of more leisure time.
- √ Preference for an enhanced quality of life, to provide balance from a hectic urban or metropolitan-based career, or from expense and time involved in commuting.
- √ Combination of best aspects of country and city life.
- √ Desire to have a simpler, less complex existence.
- √ Desire to be close to recreational interests.
- √ Desire to operate a business out of the second home, and only commute to the city as needs require.
- √ Dream of having a family retreat for the immediate, extended, or blended family, which could possibly be passed on to succeeding family generations.
- √ Desire to have a future retirement home.
- √ Intention to buy a lot in the desired area, and build when sufficient funds have been saved; in the meantime, possibly use the land by purchasing a mobile home or recreational vehicle.
- √ Attracted by the fact that recreational properties are less expensive to purchase, in general terms, than urban or metropolitan properties.
- √ Increase in demand (and therefore value) for recreational or rural property that is proximate (within a four-hour driving distance) to a metropolitan or urban population growth area.
- √ A growing number of people anticipate they will inherit funds that will allow them to buy a second home.

There are some potential downsides to purchasing recreational property. These are general comments, however, and there are many exceptions.

√ Lenders are sometimes reluctant to lend money or approve a mortgage for recreational property that is in a remote location, or is raw land.

√ There may be some restrictions on land use, especially if you plan to buy in an area of high agricultural use.

√ If you have a seasonal vacation property, and intend to rent it out, you could have a negative cash flow (shortage in revenue to offset expenses) that you would have to subsidize.

√ Maintenance of the property could be frustrating if you are far from home.

√ Vandalism is more likely if the property is in a remote location or only has seasonal usage.

√ If the economy is in a recession, the value of property can diminish considerably, as the demand for recreational property is generally considered a luxury and not a necessity. This can be problematic if you need to sell during this period.

Most of these issues can be addressed—and even avoided—with advance knowledge and good planning. This book will explain how you can do that.

Highlights of Chapter Contents

To have a contextual sense for the book contents, here is a brief overview. Each chapter is mutually exclusive, but inter-related. The book is divided into different parts with similar themes for the chapters within each part. They are:

Part I—The Realities of Realty

This section gives an overview of how the real estate market works in terms of cycles, and what cues tell you where in the cycle the market is for your geographic area of interest. The section also covers why real estate in general is historically a good investment, and why recreational property in particular has enjoyed attractive appreciation.

Part II—Finding the Right Fit

This section discusses the various types of recreational real estate that you may wish to consider, and how to locate and select the right vacation property fit for your needs and wants. How to establish recreational property investment strategies is also explained, along with the types of professional and other advisors you should use, and how to select your key advisors. This includes lawyers, accountants, realtors, building inspectors, mortgage brokers, and insurance brokers.

Part III—Show Me the Money

This section cover the steps you need to follow to make the purchase happen with the least amount of stress and risk, and the greatest amount of satisfaction with the outcome. Buying or renting a vacation home involves financial issues and options. The chapters in this section cover a range of choices available. One chapter will discuss the key tips you need to know when accessing financing and getting the best deal, as well as creative financing options using your RRSP. Another chapter covers negotiating strategies to get the best deal. There is a chapter on investing in recreational real estate on your own, or with others.

Part IV—Planning for Peace of Mind

This is a particularly important section, to provide you with awareness and knowledge on your decision-making strategic options. These options will save you a lot of money and grief, and provide you with the basis for discussion with your professional advisors. Chapter topics include the type of planning and strategies you need to consider in advance to protect your legal interests and your financial investment, save money on tax, and avoid family squabbles. You will also find advice on how to maximize your capital gain when you come to sell your vacation property, while minimizing the tax you pay for that gain.

Part V—Now That It's Yours

If you are planning to own vacation property with others such as friends or family, or share your home with others, this section will provide some helpful insights and practical suggestions. The chapters cover the topics of buying and owning vacation property, as well as how to maintain harmony when sharing with others. This could include a family cottage that you and your siblings have inherited from your parents, or that you know you will inherit in the future.

Now that you own a vacation property, there are creative options available to expand your enjoyment and possible revenue. One chapter in this section will discuss the process of home exchanging with other property owners throughout the world, on a simultaneous or non-simultaneous basis, as well as the concept of trade or barter exchange. This simply means that you make your vacation home available at times you are not using it, or during a slow period for rentals, for an exchange purpose. The typical exchange format involves you putting a monetary value on the time being used, and getting credit towards other goods and services you may wish from a wide range of other exchange club business members.

There is also a chapter on generating revenue from your vacation home, whether you market and rent it out yourself, or use a professional rental management company.

Part VI—Outward Bound

Have you considered buying a vacation home in the United States, Mexico, or another country for personal use or rental income or a mixture of both? If so, you will find the chapter in this section will provide a reality check of the issues and cautions that you need to know.

At some point, you will need or want to sell your vacation home. When that time comes, you want to make sure that you get the best price for your second home or investment property. This chapter will cover the techniques for doing so.

Appendix

You will find a wealth of resources in the Appendix, including an extensive glossary, helpful websites, and informative checklists.

Seminar Education

This book is a helpful resource for a comprehensive overview of the key issues you need to know. However, to fully enhance your learning experience, you may wish to attend some of the seminars offered nationally by the National Real Estate Institute Inc. There are seminars on recreational real estate, as well as real estate investing, taught by professionals and other experts on the topic areas.

For more information about upcoming seminars in your area, and to be on a mailing list, refer to the website www.homebuyer.ca.

PART I

The Realities of Realty

CHAPTER 1

How the Real Estate Market Works

In order to have a better appreciation of buying your recreational property, you need to understand the basics of how the real estate market operates, the various cycles, and the factors that influence prices. The market is a fluid and dynamic process, and no buying or selling decisions should be made without an accurate and objective market assessment.

The Real Estate Cycle

Real estate is a cyclical industry. As in any such industry, the cycle historically creates shortage and excess, which is related to supply and demand in the marketplace. Too much supply creates a reduction in value. Too little supply creates an increase in value. It is essential to know where you are in the cycle relative to the property you are considering to purchase. Different provinces, regions, and communities are at different points of the economic cycle at any given time. Also, there can be micro economic and real estate cycles within the same community. Timing in the cycle is important when making buying and selling decisions.

One of the reasons for the cycle is that many developers are entrepreneurial by nature and operate primarily by short-term planning. If financing and credit are available, developers tend to build without regard for the overall supply and demand. If a consequent glut occurs and the demand is not there, prices come down as houses and condominiums go unsold. The phases of the real estate cycle will be discussed later in this chapter.

External Factors that Can Affect the Real Estate Market

General Business Economic Cycles

The economy historically goes through periods of increased economic growth followed by periods of recession. In any given cycle, the economic impact is greater, of course, in certain parts of the country than in others. In a recession, people lose their jobs, can't afford their mortgage payments, and have to put their houses on the market. Real estate prices become depressed as potential purchasers decide to wait until the economy is more secure. It is difficult to know for certain when the economy will turn around, but various indicators (which will be discussed later in this chapter) should give you some insight.

If the economy has been in a recession for a sustained period, there could be opportunities to buy property. Once the economy comes out of a recession, prices tend to climb. Conversely, if the economy has been on a buoyant growth trend for an extended period, be very cautious in purchasing because a change in the cycle, and therefore a drop in real estate prices, could be imminent.

Local Business Cycle

Each local economy has its own cycles and factors that affect real estate prices. These factors may not be greatly influenced by the general (provincial or national) business cycles just discussed.

Community Cycle

Certain geographic locations within a community can have their own economic cycles as well as supply and demand, all of which affect real estate prices. A new factory or other industry can inject new life into a local economy, strengthening the housing market in the process. And those properties with very good geographic locations, such as waterfront, may retain their value better, even during recession, than other properties might. In addition, a community has its own life cycle, from growth to decline to stagnation to rehabilitation. Look for areas of future growth.

As you can see, being aware of economic, business, and community cycles is critical to prudent decision making. Before buying or selling real estate in a certain area, determine what external factors are prevalent and how they affect the cycle of the real estate market. Different types of real estate—for example, vacation cottages, winter chalets, resort condominiums—can be at different points within the real estate cycle.

There are four distinct segments to a real estate cycle. Each of these segments has identifiable characteristics and therefore helpful clues for assessing the state of the real estate cycle. Refer, too, to Chart 1 in the Appendix.

Three Types of Real Estate Markets

You undoubtedly are familiar with the common terms used to describe the three types of real estate markets. Using the residential housing market as an example, here is a brief review of the different types:

Seller's Market

In a seller's market the number of buyers wanting to buy a home exceeds the supply or number of homes on the market. In this type of market homes sell quickly, prices increase, and there are lots of buyers for the minimal number of available homes. These characteristics have implications for the buyer, who has to make decisions quickly, must pay more, and frequently has his or her conditional offers rejected.

Buyer's Market

In a buyer's market the supply of homes on the market exceeds the demand or number of buyers. In this type of market, homes need longer selling periods, there are more homes for sale than buyers, and prices decline. Buyers in this type of market have favourable negotiating leverage, more time to search for a home, and better prices.

Balanced Market

In a balanced market, the number of homes on the market is equal to the demand or the number of buyers. In this type of market, houses will take a reasonable amount of time to sell, demand equals supply, sellers will accept reasonable offers, and prices will be stable. For the buyer in this type of market, the atmosphere is more relaxed because there are more homes to choose from.

Factors that Affect Recreational Real Estate Prices

There are many factors that influence the price of vacation real estate. Whether you are a buyer or seller, you need to understand which factors are affecting the market so you can make the right decisions at the right time and in the right location. Many of these factors are interrelated.

The Real Estate Cycle

As described in the previous section, where the real estate market is in the cycle will have a bearing on prices.

Interest Rates

There is a direct connection between interest rates and prices. The higher the rates, the lower the prices; the lower the rates, the higher the prices. When the rates are low, more people can afford to buy a recreational property. This puts pressure or greater demand on the market.

Impact of Baby Boomers

The Baby Boomers (i.e., those born after the Second World War, between 1945 and 1957) have had a dramatic impact on the acquisition of recreational property. As a group, they are motivated by the desire for a high standard of living, and they tend to value physical exercise and the outdoors. Since many of them have paid off their primary home mortgages, and any children have left the nest, they frequently have the disposable income for a second property. In addition, many Boomers are at an age where their parents are elderly and a significant inheritance could be anticipated.

Supply and Demand

The principle of supply and demand is a basic real estate price influencer, of course. Studies show that many people who own recreational property have no interest in selling it, and intend to retire to it, or pass it down through the generations, or hold it for investment or capital gain appreciation. This is causing a reduction in the supply of recreational property. At the same time, there is a sustained and growing trend for many in the 40-plus age range to seek a recreational home. This is having a predicable impact on vacation home prices.

Demands of Retirees and Early Retirees

Many people wish to retire to a vacation, resort or recreational property that can be lived in and enjoyed year-round. With many people taking early retirement, the range of activities they might look for is always growing. An active 50-something population often demands, for example, a nearby golf course and other amenities, as well as proximity to commercial and cultural centres.

Taxes

An area of high municipal property taxes can be a disincentive to a purchaser. A rise in property taxes could cause real estate prices to drop. For example, if you have bought a resort rental investment condo that was originally assessed at the residential tax rate, and was subsequently changed to a commercial use rate, your property taxes could jump three times or more and make the investment unviable or at least unattractive. Provincial taxes, such as a property purchase tax, could limit the number of buyers. Federal tax legislation on real estate, such as an adverse change in capital gains tax, could have a negative influence on investors. All these factors would affect the overall amount of real estate activity, as well as prices.

Rent Controls

Naturally, provincial rent controls and related restrictions could have a limiting effect on investor real estate activity, thereby resulting in fewer buyers in the market for certain types of properties. If you rent out your vacation home short-term or periodically or seasonally for less than a month for any one guest, you are exempted from the rent control guidelines. You can effectively charge whatever the market will bear.

However, if you are renting long-term and don't have a lease that protects the fixed duration of the rental period, then you could be impacted by provincial legislation. For example, if you own a chalet in a resort area, and have a one- or two-bedroom rental suite in the basement for long-term tenants to help cover your annual expenses and to provide a sense of security, you would be affected by rent controls. That is, unless you have your tenants sign a one-year lease that you renew each year, with any changes in rent. In most provinces, if your long-term tenant is governed by a fixed-term lease, there is no limit on how much you can increase your rent each year—other than the limits imposed by the rental market itself. Check with your real estate lawyer in your given situation.

Rent controls are set and governed by provincial legislation. Not all provinces have rent control, but any province can introduce them or modify their existing legislation at any time. To find out whether there are caps on rent increases, check out the landlord/tenant legislation in your province. Go to www.google.ca and then type in the key words "landlord tenant law" and the name of your province. If your province has rent controls, you will see the

criteria for increasing rents, including any special circumstances that may permit additional rent increases.

Economy

Confidence in the respective economy is important to stimulate vacation home
and real estate investor activity. If the economy is buoyant and the mood is
positive, more market activity will occur, generally resulting in an increase in
prices, as people have more discretionary income. Conversely, if the economy is
stagnant, the opposite will occur, resulting in decreased homebuyer and investor activity and lower prices. If real estate purchasers are concerned about the
same problem, a predictable loss of confidence occurs in the market. As recreational property is a lifestyle or investment choice rather than a necessity, in a
depressed market the second home would be the first to go on the market for a
lot of owners in a financial crunch.

A stable economy and attractive recreational property opportunities will
result in an influx of people and consequently increase demand and drive values up.

Location

This is an important factor. Highly desirable locations will generally go up in
price more quickly and consistently. For example, many people rank waterfront
properties (with access to a lake, river or ocean) as their number-one recreational property choice, followed by waterview property as number two.

Availability of Land

A natural shortage of land, municipal zoning restrictions, limits on development, or provincial land-use laws that restrict the utilization of existing land
for housing purposes will generally increase prices. Again, this relates back to
the principle of supply and demand.

Public Image

Public perception of a certain geographic location or type of recreational or
resort property or builder will affect demand and therefore prices. Some areas
or types of properties are "hot" or trendy, and some are not, at any given time.
For example, resort or recreational areas near winter skiing or summer water
activities or golfing tend to be popular draws.

Political Factors

The policy of a provincial or municipal government in terms of supporting real estate development will naturally have a positive or negative effect on supply and demand and therefore prices.

Seasonal Factors

Certain times of year are traditionally slow months for residential real estate sales, so prices decline. For example, November through February is usually a slow time, while the market tends to build again as winter turns to spring. The same seasonal factor affects recreational or resort property. There are ideal seasons for purchase and sale.

CHAPTER 2

Why Recreational Real Estate Is a Good Investment

Whether you are buying recreational real estate as a short- or long-term investment, for personal use or for periodic or full-time rental, or a combination of personal use and rental revenue, the historical patterns and future projections of equity growth are very positive.

In Chapter 1 you became acquainted with the reasons for high demand for recreational real estate. In this chapter, the advantages of owning recreational property as an investment will be discussed. By owning a vacation home, you could benefit three ways: lifestyle and quality of life enjoyment, equity appreciation over time, and a revenue stream from periodic or seasonal rentals. In addition, you could use your second home or investment property for home exchanges around the world, or barter time slots for other services or products of value to you. You don't have all those options with a stock portfolio!

Attractive Return on Investment (ROI)

The potential for an attractive return on your investment is very high in real estate, especially taking into account an increase in property capital gain and positive revenue cash flow income.

Historically, real estate has increased in value greater than inflation and many other forms of investments. Depending on the geographic location and type of property investment, the gains are frequently double-digit and sometimes triple-digit. Through the application of financial leverage, the net returns in cash flow and property appreciation can be considerable.

Example: If the investor puts 10% down and borrows 90% of "other people's money" (i.e., lender financing), the return on investment (ROI) is calculated on the actual amount the investor contributes of their own money. Using this formula, the ROI can be very attractive. For example, if an investor buys a $200,000 house for investment with 10% down payment ($20,000) and a 90% ($180,000) mortgage, and the property doubles in value ($400,000) over five years, the equity increase would be $200,000, or $150,000 net after capital gains tax. This would represent a 750% return over five years or 150% ROI annual average over the original investment of your own money of $20,000. Also, the mortgage debt would have been reduced over the five years, providing even more equity. To many people, this type of potential ROI is more attractive than the modest returns on term deposits or GICs!

In the example above, there would be no negative debt financing required by the investor, as there would be break-even of expenses over income. However, if the investor was astute and well informed, there should be positive cash flow. This would mean that the actual average annual net ROI (after tax) of the investor would be greater than 150% annually on the original investment of $20,000. In addition, the fact that there is a positive cash flow is one factor that automatically increases the value of income-producing real estate, sometimes very substantially.

Tax Advantages

There are numerous types of tax advantages to investing in real estate, whether you have a principal residence or investment income property. It would be difficult to find an investment that has as many financial benefits as real estate.

Example: All the interest you receive from a bank account, term deposit or GIC is fully taxable as income. If you are obtaining interest of 4% (the nominal rate) on your deposit, and the inflation rate is 3%, the "effective" or "real" rate of return is 1%. If you are paying tax at a 35% rate, then effectively you are breaking even, or possibly having a negative return on your money. In practical terms, taking inflation and taxes into account, you have lost on your bank deposit investment. Equity investments in the stock market have a degree of risk, depending on the nature of the investment, of eroding the principal and having no positive return.

Real estate traditionally does not have the above problems. With education and awareness, and applying proven strategies and techniques, the risk is minimal. That is why investing in real estate—starting with a principal residence—is clearly an attractive investment. Take a look at some of the tax benefits of investing in real estate:

- √ Tax-free capital gains on your principal residence; e.g., if you bought many years ago at $50,000 and sold at $550,000, the net gain of $500,000 is yours to keep.
- √ Ability to write off your vacation home rental suite income, if you have a suite, e.g., for year-round security and cash flow, against a

pro-rata portion of your home-related expenses (e.g., mortgage interest, property taxes, utilities, maintenance, insurance, etc.).

√   Ability to write off a portion of your home business income against a portion of your home-related expenses (e.g., mortgage interest, property taxes, utilities, maintenance, insurance, etc.). If you are operating a home office out of your vacation home, part-time or full-time, the same principles apply.

√   Reduced tax rate of 50% of capital gain from investment real estate. In practical terms, it means that you can keep approximately 75% of the capital gain, and the Canada Revenue Agency (CRA) gets 25%. Unless, of course, you have investment capital losses that you can offset against your real estate capital gains.

√   Flow-through of losses from negative cash flow against other sources of income.

√   Deduction of real estate property investment expenses against income.

√   Write-off of depreciation of building against income if the property is strictly an investment property. If you use your vacation home primarily for personal use and periodic or seasonal rentals, you don't want to taint the status of your home in that respect as an investment property, in case you subsequently decide to deem your second home as your principal residence for tax purposes, or utilize any of the other tax and estate planning strategies discussed in this book.

Low Starting Capital Using Principle of Leverage

This concept simply means putting in a small amount of money and borrowing the rest—using "other people's money." Many people have become millionaires by applying this principle.

Example: If you put a down payment of 10% and borrow 90%, this is called high-ratio financing. Basically, the ratio is 9:1; that is, 9 times as much money is borrowed as invested personally. This is commonly done. The risk to the lender is low or non-existent, as the property is the security. In the worst-case scenario, if the borrower defaults and the lender has to sell, the net proceeds after sale should at least cover the amount of the mortgage, especially considering the historical appreciation in value. An example of the power of leverage on return on investment was provided above, in the first point.

A related concept to leverage is the concept of pyramiding. In this strategy, you would borrow on the increasing equity (due to appreciation) of your existing properties, applying the principle of leverage to buy even more properties over time. This compounding effect of equity build-up through appreciation, in a prudently selected real estate portfolio, can result in the accruing of considerable wealth.

Low Risk

Any investment has potential risk, and you can indeed lose money in real estate. However, there are reasons why someone might lose money in real estate. These reasons are generally predictable, and can be avoided or minimized through advance knowledge and applying proven principles.

It is probably timely to outline some of the classic pitfalls to avoid in buying real estate for investment. In most cases, investors who have problems generally succumb to a combination of the following traps.

- √ Not having an understanding of how the real estate market works.
- √ Not having a clear understanding of personal and financial needs.
- √ Not having a clear focus or a realistic real estate investment plan, with strategies and priorities.
- √ Not doing thorough market research and comparison shopping before making the purchase.
- √ Not selecting the right property considering the potential risks, money involved, and specific personal needs.
- √ Not verifying representations or assumptions beforehand.
- √ Not doing financial calculations beforehand.
- √ Not buying at a fair market price.
- √ Not buying real estate at the right time in the market.
- √ Not buying within financial debt-servicing capacity, comfort zone, and skills.
- √ Not understanding the financing game thoroughly, and therefore not comparison shopping and not getting the best rates, terms, and right type of mortgage.
- √ Not making a decision based on an objective assessment but on an emotional one.

√ Not determining the real reason why the vendor is selling.

√ Not having the property inspected by a building inspector before deciding to purchase.

√ Not selecting an experienced real estate lawyer and obtaining advice beforehand.

√ Not selecting an experienced professional tax accountant when selecting real estate property, and obtaining advice beforehand.

√ Not selecting an experienced realtor with expertise in the type of real estate and geographic location you are considering.

√ Not negotiating effectively.

√ Not putting in the appropriate conditions or "subject clauses" in the offer.

√ Not buying for the right reasons—in other words, buying for tax shelter reasons rather than for the inherent value, potential, and viability of the investment property.

√ Not independently verifying financial information beforehand.

√ Not obtaining and reviewing all the necessary documentation appropriate for a given property before making a final decision to buy.

√ Not selecting real estate investment partners carefully.

√ Not having a written agreement with real estate investment partners prepared by a lawyer.

√ Not detailing exactly what chattels are included in the purchase price.

√ Not seeing the property before buying it, but relying on pictures and/ or the representations of others.

√ Not managing the property well, or not selecting the right property management company.

√ Not selling the property at the right time in the market or for the right reasons.

Real estate has traditionally been a secure, stable investment compared to other investments, especially if one buys prudently and with advance knowledge. Today's current low interest rates in fixed-term investments is causing investors to consider other options. An investor might be concerned about the equity stock market risk, recent negative experiences with certain categories or types of stocks, or low returns. A buoyant economy, with the attendant sense of confidence in one's employment, and natural comfort and affinity for real estate, are other factors that contribute to the real estate investment environment.

There are various reasons for the relatively low risk, which naturally will vary depending on the geographic area, desirability of location, stability of the market, and other factors. These factors include: population increases, less land available, a high percentage of renters in metropolitan areas, low interest rates, ease of financing for highly leveraged property, intrinsic need and demand for residential real estate, and consistent history of land value appreciation exceeding rate of inflation. The real estate market is cyclical and, depending on location and other factors, almost any property eventually will increase in value.

Appreciation

The increase in value of your original capital investment in the property over time is the key appreciation factor. The national average has been about 5% per year for real estate over the past 25 years. It should be stressed that this is just an average. Certain geographic areas or locations have had considerably more than the average increases in value, especially for a well-selected and -maintained property in a growing and desirable community.

Example: If the real estate market is in its upward swing in a high-demand area, the appreciation on your property could rise by 20% to 50% or even more in one year. When you apply the ROI calculations in this scenario, as discussed earlier, the ROI on your original personal down payment can be considerable.

Equity Build-up

When you make payments on your mortgage, you are paying down the principal over time. As you are reducing your debt, you are at the same time building up your equity—that is, the portion of your original loan that you no longer owe any debt on.

Example: In practical terms, most people commonly refer to equity as the amount of clear value in the property that the investor owns, free and clear of any debt. In realistic terms, the true equity is what you would net upon sale, after all real estate commissions and closing costs are taken into account. Lenders realize this as well, which is why they generally do not like to lend if 100% of the equity would end up being pledged, in order to minimize their risk and leave a margin of safety for the future.

Inflation Hedge

Inflation means the increasing cost of buying a product or service. In other words, it is the decrease in your purchasing power. For example, something that cost you $5, five years ago, might now be priced at $10. People on fixed incomes that are not indexed (through their pension plans) for inflation are very aware of the eroding purchasing power of the dollar. The inflation rate in Canada varies at different times of the year, and in different regions of the country, and for different commodities.

The appreciation of the value of property over time includes an inflation factor. Historically, land appreciation value for residential properties has been approximately 3% to 5% greater than the inflation rate. Another benefit of real estate is that you are paying off the mortgage in inflated dollars. That is, you are probably getting more money now, in terms of salary increases or rental revenue, to pay off lesser-value money when you took out the original mortgage.

Increasing Demand for Land

Land is a finite commodity. As population increases through birth and immigration, there is an increasing demand for property and a decreasing supply. That's why real estate prices go up. And, with the Boomers creating or inheriting wealth, and wanting to buy investment and vacation properties, there is additional demand. Depending on geographic shifts of the population as a consequence of buoyant economies and job opportunities in certain regions of the country at any given time, there can be further demand.

Many communities have slow-growth or no-growth policies, due to rapidly expanding needs for community services. Other communities have extensive red tape or other bureaucratic delays. This restricts land availability for new development, causing existing land to go up in value. Real estate is a commodity that the public needs. Other investment commodities are not so reliable or predictable, because they don't constitute a public need and therefore demand. In addition, many people want to have a second home as a retreat, vacation property, or place for retirement. This creates further demand on land.

Part-time Involvement and Flexible Options

Investing in real estate does not require more than part of your available time. Once you learn the proper techniques and have a written investment plan, you will be more efficient, selective, and confident. This will save you time. An investor should determine at the outset how much time he or she has available for researching the market, negotiating, buying, managing, and selling. There are many types of real estate options available, some which take more time than others to manage.

Example: If you don't have the time or interest in personally investing in real estate, or feel it would be too stressful, there are options. One could keep it simple, and invest in just one property that is nearby and requires little personal maintenance, such as a condominium. Alternatively, one could be involved in a group real estate investment, for example, with family or friends or other investors. However, there are many pitfalls of group real estate investing that need to be understood and avoided.

There are many types of real estate options dealing with recreational property use available. This flexibility appeals to the individual needs and interests of many types of investors, and can usually ensure a comfortable investment fit.

If you'd like to know more about real estate investing, refer to my two books: *Making Money in Real Estate* and *Real Estate Investing For Canadians For Dummies.*

Also, for more information, refer to the website www.homebuyer.ca, and check out the seminars offered by the National Real Estate Institute Inc., outlined on the above site.

CHAPTER 3

Types of Recreational Real Estate

There are numerous types of recreational property options, from buying in rural areas, to resort or established vacation spots; from buying a house, condo, or fractional ownership, to buying on your own or with relatives, friends, or others; and from buying for personal and family use only, to buying for investment revenue.

Many factors will come into play when it comes to deciding which type to buy, for example, your motivation, your budget, and whether you want to buy the property for personal use, or investment, or both. Perhaps it will be your retirement home. If you are buying the property as an investment, how much risk are you willing to take? What level of return are you looking for and how involved do you want to be in managing the property? Other factors include your past experience (if any) in real estate investment, whether you are buying property with others, and your personal needs and investment goals.

This chapter will discuss the main types of options when buying recreational real estate for personal use or investment purposes. The options include condominiums (apartment or townhouse format), single-family houses (including resale houses, new houses, or buying a lot and building a house), and raw land. Shared ownership and shared use properties will be discussed (fractional ownership or timeshares). Other types of recreational options will also be given. Within many of these main categories, there are several options. For more information, refer to www.homebuyer.ca.

Condominium

One of the most popular types of recreational, vacation, or resort property is in the condominium format.

What Is a Condominium?

Many people purchase condominiums to live in or as an investment. The concept of condominium will not suit everyone, though, as it involves not only individual ownership in the unit and shared ownership in other property, but also adherence to rules and regulations, and shared management. On the other hand, many people prefer condominium living to the alternatives.

The word "condominium" does not imply a specific structural form, but rather a legal form. Condominiums (called co-proprietorships in Quebec) may be detached, semi-detached, row houses, stack townhouses, duplexes, or apartments. They can even be building lots, subdivisions, single family houses, or mobile home parks. Whatever the style, a residential unit is specified and owned by an individual in a freehold or leasehold format. Freehold means that you own the title to the property outright. Leasehold means that you don't have any ownership rights to the land, only the leasing rights. The rest of the property, including land, which is called the common elements or common property in most provinces, is owned in common with the other owners.

For example, an owner would own a share of the common elements in the development. If there were 50 condominium owners, then each owner would own one-fiftieth as a tenant of the common elements. The legislation of each province can vary, but it is always designed to provide the legal and structural framework for the efficient management and administration of each condominium project. Once the condominium project documents are registered, the project is brought into legal being.

The part of the condominium that you will own outright is referred to as the unit in most provinces. You will have full and clear title to this unit when you purchase it (assuming you are buying a freehold, not a leasehold, property), which will be legally registered in your name in the land registry office in your province. The precise description of the common elements, and exactly what you own as part of your unit, may differ from development to development, but in any event it will be provided for in the documents prepared and registered for each condominium.

Common elements generally include walkways, driveways, lawns and gardens, lobbies, elevators, parking areas, recreational facilities, storage areas, laundry rooms, stairways, plumbing, electrical systems and portions of walls, ceilings, and floors, and other items. Part of the common elements may be designated for the exclusive use of one or more of the individual unit owners, in which case these are called limited common elements. In other words, they are limited for the use of only specific owners. Examples would include parking spaces, storage lockers, roof gardens, balconies, patios, and front and back yards.

Condominiums can be built on freehold or leasehold properties. A condominium can also be in a stratified format, where a legal description for the unit is allocated in a vertical dimension. In other words, if you live in a condominium apartment on the thirtieth floor, there is a precise legal description in the land titles office for that specific unit in the complex. Another format is a bare-land condominium. In this example, it would be similar to a building lot subdivision with individual units owned by the unit holders, although the units would appear as detached homes. The rest of the land would be considered common elements.

A condominium development is administered by various legal structures set out in provincial legislation.

Types of Recreational Condominiums

Recreational condominiums can take various formats, primarily in an apartment or townhouse style, but could include mobile home parks where the "pad" with utility hookups is owned in fee simple—that is, freehold or the right to the property—with a share in the common property of the rest of the park. Alternatively, it could be in a leasehold format (e.g., a 99-year lease).

Another option is a bare-land condominium in rural, wilderness, or waterfront areas. In these examples an owner could build a cabin, cottage, or chalet with fee simple ownership to the land underneath and own a partial interest in the common elements, which could include a marina, beach, farm, or forest. Common recreational facilities could include a playground or community centre, and assets could include boats or farm animals.

The development of condominiums in resort areas is extensive, and condominiums are frequently built on lakeshores, riverfronts, seacoasts, island resorts, or in ski country. There are two main types of resort condominiums: those developed for warmer climates and those developed for winter climates.

The warmer-climate type is generally built around a common recreational facility that can be enjoyed throughout the year by the owners, one that includes such facilities as a seashore, lake, marina, or golf course. The buildings tend to range from high-rise apartments to cluster housing to detached houses.

Winter resort areas are often built near popular ski resort developments. Many provide recreational facilities for the summer season as well, such as golf courses, tennis courts, and swimming pools, so that it is a year-round resort. The buildings tend to be cluster housing, modular housing, or attached townhouses, or detached houses.

Here are some of the common condo recreational property options:

√   A condo that you own outright without any requirement to rent.

√   A condo that you are required to rent for a percentage of time each year as part of a rental pool, and that you can use for a percentage of the time if you wish.

√   A furnished condo that is part of a resort hotel building, and has restrictions on personal use since it is part of a rental pool.

√   A condo that you can either rent out yourself directly or find your own property management company.

√   A condo that you rent out through the developer's property management company. The company charges between 30% and 45% of the revenue, depending on the range of services offered.

√   A condo in which you have a fractional ownership (e.g., from 10% to 50%), that may or may not be part of a required rental pool, and that you may or may not be able to rent out on your own, if not part of a rental pool agreement. You share the use proportionally with the other owners.

√   A condo that may be in a one-level, apartment-style configuration; in a townhouse configuration with two, three or more levels; or in a detached house or duplex configuration, with the adjacent property being shared by means of common property.

Expenses Relating to Condo Ownership

Once you have completed the purchase transaction and are now an owner of a condominium unit, you have to plan for ongoing monthly or annual expenses and other potential expenses. People often don't realize the extra expenses involved in owning a condominium, which is very different from owning a single-family home. The most common additional expenses, other than mortgage payments, are as follows:

Property Taxes

The municipality assesses each individual condominium unit and the owner has to make an annual payment to cover property taxes. The common elements are assessed in property tax as well, but that tax is covered in your monthly maintenance payments. Property Tax Caution: If you are considering buying into a hotel condo, or condo development in a resort area that is part of a rental pool, this could have a major impact on your taxes, and therefore bottom line and investment risk. For example, it is not uncommon for the above type of condos to be zoned or assessed as commercial operations for municipal tax purposes. Depending on the area and province you are in, the impact could be taxes that are three times higher (or more) than for a recreational condo that is not part of a hotel or rental pool operation. You need to check this issue out thoroughly in advance, and enlist the assistance of a real estate lawyer.

Maintenance Payments

Maintenance payments or "assessments for common expenses" cover all the operating costs of the common elements and are adjusted for any increase or decrease in expenses. You are responsible for a portion of the development's total operating costs.

Unit entitlement is the basis on which the owner's contribution to the common expenses or maintenance fees of the condominium corporation is calculated. Various formulas are used for the calculation. In some developments the percentage calculated for the unit's share is determined by the original purchase price of each unit in relation to the value of the total property. Another method is to apportion costs on the basis of the number of units in equal proportion, regardless of unit size.

The most common formula is to calculate the unit entitlement by dividing the total number of square feet in all the units by the number of square feet in an individual owner's unit.

The payments for common expenses are made directly to the condominium corporation and generally cover the following items:

√ *Maintenance and Repair of Common Property*: This includes costs for maintenance, landscaping, building repairs, recreational facilities, equipment, and other expenses.

√ *Operating and Service Costs*: This includes expenses relating to garbage removal, heat, hydro, and electricity, and snow removal in winter resort areas.

√ *Contingency Reserve Fund*: This is a fund for unforeseen problems and expenses (e.g., replacing the roof or repairing the swimming pool or heating system). This fund is for expenses that have not been included in the annual budgeted expense calculations for the common property and other assets of the condominium corporation. Owners contribute monthly to this fund on the basis of a portion of the monthly maintenance fee. The condominium legislation in most provinces requires owners to contribute a minimum amount to the contingency reserve fund (e.g., 10% of annual budget). If you are buying an older condominium, you should check to see what percentage of the monthly payments is being allocated toward this fund, as there is a higher risk of needing to use the fund in older buildings than in newer developments. In older buildings, the fund will possibly be 25% or more, depending on the circumstances. In most cases you are not entitled to a refund of your contribution to the reserve fund when you sell your unit.

√ *Management Costs*: These are the costs associated with hiring private individuals or professional management firms to administer all or part of the daily functions of the condominium development.

√ *Insurance*: Condominium legislation requires the development to carry sufficient fire and related insurance to replace the common property in the event of fire or other damage. Condominium corporations generally obtain additional insurance to cover other payables and liabilities. Note: This insurance does not cover damages to the interior of an individual unit.

Special Assessment

There could be situations in which 75% or more of the condominium members want to raise funds for special purposes. These funds would not come from the contingency reserve fund or from the regular monthly assessments. For example, there could be an interest in building a swimming pool or tennis courts, or it may be necessary to cover the cost of repairs that will exceed the money available in the contingency reserve fund. Once the decision is made to assess members, and it has been approved according to condominium bylaws, you cannot refuse to pay the special assessment, even though you may not agree with its purpose.

Condominium Owner Insurance

As mentioned earlier, the insurance on the areas of the building that are covered by the condominium development does not include the interior of your unit. Therefore, you will need to obtain your own insurance to cover your contents as well as any damage that might happen to the inside of your unit (including walls, windows, and doors) through fire, flood, or any other cause. There are several types of insurance, including replacement cost, all-risk comprehensive, and personal liability.

It is also common to get insurance to cover deficiencies in the condominium corporation's insurance coverage in the event of fire so that any damage to your unit could be repaired in full; otherwise, the unit owners would have to pay on a proportional basis any deficiency by means of a special assessment. Many insurance companies have developed a specialized program referred to as condominium homeowner's package insurance. Check the Yellow Pages or Internet under "Insurance Brokers" and compare coverage and costs. You can also review the website for the Insurance Brokers Association of Canada (www. ibac.ca) to obtain a list of local members.

Lease Payments

If you have a leasehold condominium, you will be required to make monthly lease payments in addition to many of the other costs outlined in this section.

Utilities

You are responsible for the utilities you use in your unit, including electricity, water, heat, and cable. In apartment condominiums, these expenses are usually included in the maintenance fee, whereas townhouse condominiums tend to have individual meters. You would be billed directly and individually by the utility companies.

Unit Repair and Maintenance Costs

You will have to allocate a certain amount of your financial budget for repair and maintenance needs relating to the inside of your unit. Your monthly assessment fee would cover common elements outside your unit only.

Rental Management Fees and Expenses

If you are renting out your condo or house, and choose not to oversee the rentals yourself, or are not permitted to by the type of condo you purchased, you could be paying a rental management company. If your condo is part of a rental pool, the developer would have set up a property management company to rent the condos, and you would be paying a commission between 30% and 45% of the gross rental revenue for this service. There are different types of formulas for pooled rentals, so make sure you understand them, and obtain the assistance of a real estate lawyer before you commit yourself to a purchase. If you have the option and choose to hire a property management company of your choice, either periodically, for nightly or weekly rentals, or full time, the commission is negotiable depending on the range of services offered. The fee could range from 10% to 30% of the gross revenue received. Find out more in Chapter 16: Professional or Owner-Direct Rental Management.

Advantages and Disadvantages of Condominium Ownership

In any situation of shared ownership and community living, there are advantages and disadvantages. If you are only renting out the condominium, some of the following points may not be as important to you as if you were living in it.

Advantages

√ Ready availability of financing, similar to getting financing for a single-family home.

√ A range of prices, locations, types of structures, sizes, and architectural features is available.

√ There may be amenities such as swimming pools, tennis courts, health clubs, community centres, saunas, hot tubs, exercise rooms, and sun decks.

√ Gives the benefits of home ownership in terms of participation in the real estate market and potential growth in equity.

√ Individual ownership of your living unit.

√ Enables people of moderate and middle income to own property.

√ Freedom to decorate the interior of the unit to suit personal tastes.

√ Enhancement of security by proximity and/or permanence of neighbours and, in many cases, controlled entrances.

√ Elimination of many of the problems of upkeep and maintenance often associated with home ownership, since maintenance is usually the responsibility of a professional management company or manager.

√ Generally considerably less expensive than buying a single-family home because of more efficient use of land and economy of scale.

√ Investment opportunity for profit if selected carefully.

√ Good transitional type of home between rental apartments and single-family houses for growing families or singles or couples; conversely, good transition for "empty nesters" who wish to give up their larger family house.

√ Potentially lower costs due to responsibilities for repair and maintenance being shared.

√ Enhancement of social activities and sense of neighbourhood because of residents' relative permanence.

√ Elected council is responsible for making many business and management decisions.

√ Owners participate in the operation of the development, such as budget setting and approval; decision making; determination of rules, regulations, and bylaws; and other matters affecting the democratic operation of the condominium community. Note: If you are an investor, you want to make sure that you are notified directly by the property management or condominium council or board of directors, of all meetings, and receive all minutes. You want to make sure you have personal input on any budget, bylaw change, or special assessment meetings and decisions.

Disadvantages

√ Real estate appreciation is generally not as high as for a single-family house, due to the total ownership of land when owning a house; it is the land that goes up in value.

√ May be difficult to accurately assess the quality of construction of the project.

√ May be unacceptable loss of freedom because of restrictions in the rules and bylaws (restriction on the right to rent, restriction on pets, etc.).

√ People live in closer proximity, thereby potentially creating problems from time to time. Common problems include pets, parking, parties, people, and personalities.

√ Flexibility may be affected if circumstances require that the condominium be sold in a limited time, as condominiums generally sell more slowly than single-family houses. This is not always the case, of course, and in many instances condominiums sell faster than single-family houses.

√ One could be paying for maintenance and operation of amenities that one has no desire or intention to use, or those amenities could be expensive to maintain.

√ Management of the condominium council is by volunteers, who may or may not have the appropriate abilities and skills.

√ Owners might be apathetic, so that the same people continually serve on council.

√ Some elected councils behave in an autocratic fashion.

Investing in a Condominium

If you are considering investing in a condominium, it is important to consider the advantages and disadvantages of the different types of condominiums—for example, an apartment, townhouse, or hybrid mix, or a conversion of a former rental apartment building to a condominium. Check on whether rental units are permitted in the development before finalizing any offer, and get it confirmed in writing in advance. You don't want to buy a condo with the intention of renting it out on a part-time basis only to find out that while the bylaws permit rentals, the quota has been reached. Check on the current mix of tenants and owner-occupiers.

Here are some of the benefits you may wish to consider:

√ Condominiums generally appreciate in value at a rate that is higher than the inflation rate.

√ There is an increasing demand for the condominium lifestyle and the convenience that it provides. This is especially so in resort and recreational areas, due to the desire of many to have a low-maintenance and secure second home retreat.

√ Because a minimal amount of upkeep is involved, the economic benefits are more attractive for the first-time investor.

√ There is the convenience of having many of the management and maintenance problems taken care of by the condominium corporation and the professional management company, if any.

√ Facilities such as tennis courts and swimming pools are maintained by the condominium corporation, thereby freeing the new investor from the responsibilities of upkeep.

√ The owner is protected by the bylaws and the rules and regulations set by provincial condominium legislation, by the original project documents, or by the condominium council. For example, many condominiums do not allow pets in the building because of the potential wear and tear on the apartment. This type of rule protects and benefits the investor.

Additional tips to look for when selecting a condominium are covered in Chapter 4: Finding the Right Recreational Property.

For a detailed discussion of the pros and cons of buying a resale, conversion, new or presale condos, refer to my book, *101 Streetsmart Condo Buying Tips for Canadians.* Also refer to the website: www.homebuyer.ca.

Recreational Single-Family House

Many people prefer to own a recreational cottage, cabin, or chalet, rather than a condo. Land values appreciate much more than a condo over time, and you have the freedom of choice in what you do with your house.

There are various single-family house choices available. You could buy a resale house, a new house, a lot where you can build a house yourself or with a builder, or you can assemble a prefabricated house. There are advantages and disadvantages to each option. Note: The terms "builder" and "contractor" are essentially interchangeable. If you are buying a newly built home, the term "builder" is frequently used. When contracting for someone to build you a house on a lot you bought, the term "contractor" is common.

Buying a Resale House

Many people prefer to buy a resale house when purchasing for personal use or as an investment. Here are some of the advantages and disadvantages of buying a resale house rather than a new house. These are general guidelines and do not necessarily apply in every case.

Advantages

- √   A resale house is generally less expensive than a new house.
- √   Usually has character or a lived-in feeling.
- √   Frequently has architectural details that are unique and generally no longer in common use.
- √   A competent professional building inspector can discern any problems in house design or construction (e.g., settling, cracks in the walls).
- √   Landscaping is mature.
- √   Neighbourhood is established and has developed its own character.
- √   Community services are established.
- √   Properties are available in and proximate to the centre of the city.

√   May include extras not normally included in a new home purchase, such as customized features that previous owners have built or installed.

√   You do not pay GST on the purchase. In some provinces, this is a combined federal/provincial tax, referred to as HST, or harmonized sales tax, which includes the GST and provincial sales tax.

Disadvantages

√   May not have been built according to current building standards, and therefore might not meet electrical or insulation codes (e.g., it might have aluminum rather than copper wiring, lead rather than copper pipes, inefficient insulation or UFFI [urea formaldehyde foam insulation]).

√   Buyers of new homes may be protected by a New Home Warranty Program, but buyers of used homes have no warranties, unless a new purchaser buys the house within the warranty period of an existing policy.

√   May have been renovated by a previous owner or a handyman who may have done the work without obtaining a building permit and inspection; therefore the safety or functional aspects of the house could be deficient.

√   May not have an attractive or functional design (e.g., layout may be poor, rooms may be too small, low basement ceilings may make the basement impractical for everyday use or as a rental suite, house itself might be sited poorly on the lot, either too close or too far from front of property line). Renovating an older house can be expensive and time consuming.

√   The mechanicals (i.e., furnace, plumbing, electrical) and appliances may be outdated and need repair.

Buying a New House

You may wish to purchase a new house for your second home or investment needs. Here are some of the advantages and disadvantages of buying a new house rather than an older resale house.

Advantages

√ New houses tend to be better designed for modern lifestyles (e.g., larger kitchens, bathrooms, existence of en suite bathrooms), more diverse functions (e.g., family rooms, patios, higher ceilings in basements), and brighter atmosphere (e.g., more windows, skylights).

√ A builder often offers several house models. You can generally select certain features to customize your needs—such as carpet colour and material, kitchen appliance colours, kitchen and bathroom floor coverings, paint colours—if you contract the builder yourself or if you buy before the house is fully completed.

√ New houses are constructed in compliance with current building code standards (plumbing, electrical, heating, insulation, etc.), which gives more peace of mind around safety, and may give you better insurance rates.

√ It looks clean, modern, fresh, and smells new.

√ You are the first occupant in the house, which is an advantage because you can personalize the house to meet your own or your family's needs rather than remodelling.

√ Market valuation of the house is usually easier because there are likely to be comparable houses built in the same area.

√ The price of the house could be lower or the house could be larger (compared to a similar resale house) if a new house is built in a recreational area with lower land costs.

√ Many new homes are built by builders who are registered with the New Home Warranty Program in their respective province, so if problems occur after the sale is completed, the builder or the New Home Warranty Program will correct them if the specific problems are covered by the program. Check with your provincial New Home Warranty Program and read the fine print of the coverage, which can vary from province to province.

Disadvantages

√ The builder may not be registered with the New Home Warranty Program, thereby creating a potentially high risk for the purchaser if problems occur.

√   It is not uncommon to have construction delays (e.g., in paving drive-
    ways, landscaping, finishing touches) and defects, both of which cause
    frustration and possibly extra expense.

√   Many new houses are purchased prior to construction and are selected
    based on an artist's sketch or various model plans. Frequently a model
    home is not constructed at this stage. Conceptualizing how the final
    house will feel compared to the reality is difficult, and your expectations
    may not be consistent with the results.

√   Purchase documents prepared by the builder tend to be more complex
    and detailed than resale house contracts. (This will be discussed more
    later.)

√   You might lose the deposit funds you pay to the company if the builder
    ceases to operate. In some provinces there is consumer protection leg-
    islation that protects these funds. Unless you put the funds in a lawyer's
    or realtor's trust account, though, you could lose your deposit. It is
    particularly important that you check the builder's reputation.

Checking the Builder's Reputation

If the builder is registered with the New Home Warranty Program, in some
provinces the deposit funds are protected up to a maximum amount. If the
builder is not registered with a NHWP, be very cautious and don't pay any
money or sign a builder's contract without your lawyer's advice. The NHWP is
similar from one province to the next, but there are some differences.

The builder adds the fee for NHWP coverage onto the house price or
builds it into the price. NHWP coverage generally includes buyer protection for the deposit, incomplete work allowance, warranty protection up
to a year, basement protection for two years, and major structural defect
protection for five years. Although the NHWP was designed to protect purchasers of newly constructed houses (condominiums can also be covered)
against defects in construction, there are limitations in coverage. These
limitations and exclusions could cost you a lot of money. That is why you
need to check out the NHWP and builder thoroughly. Refer to the Appendix for contact information.

√   The local or provincial home builders' association will be able to
    confirm whether a contractor is a member or not.

√   The local Better Business Bureau will have a record of any complaints
    against the contractor.

√   Purchasers of houses from other developments the contractor has built are good sources of information. Ask the contractor for names and locations of previous development projects. You can then knock on doors and ask the owners if they would give you their candid opinion as to the quality of the house and responsiveness of the builder in correcting any problems. Ask if they got what they bargained for. A key question to ask is: "Would you buy from the same builder again, and why?"

√   The local (municipal) business licensing office can verify if the contractor is licensed.

If the contractor has no previous history in the industry, be very cautious. The contractor could have been operating under a previous company name but gone under, and is now operating under a different company name. Alternatively, the contractor could be a first-timer and be learning at your expense. Take the time to check out the contractor's background and reputation. It will save you time, frustration, and money later on.

Make sure that you take the contract supplied by the builder to your lawyer before you sign it. Builders tend to have contracts that are customized and designed primarily for the benefit of the builder. Sometimes you can negotiate changes to the contract, but at other times you cannot. It depends on the builder, the changes you're requesting, and the market. A builder must occasionally be flexible in terms of the contract, especially if an experienced lawyer who is acting on behalf of the purchaser finds certain clauses or conditions to be unfair. The builder generally would not insist on retaining these clauses if it were to stop the deal from proceeding.

You should have your lawyer advise you in general about any builder's contract, as well as about other issues that may arise if you decide to build a new house.

Buying a Lot and Building a House

Some people prefer this arrangement and want to hire a contractor to build their house, build it themselves, or buy a prepackaged type of house (e.g., log cabin, ski chalet) and have it constructed.

If you are building your own house, make sure that you know what you are doing; otherwise it could be very time consuming, frustrating, and expensive. An alternative is to take a school board or college course on building your own house, and then hire a trustworthy contractor on an hourly basis to advise you. However, there are very few people with the skills, aptitude, and time to do this.

Check with your municipal planning department on the steps, building codes, permits, and inspections required. There are many regulations involved. Read how-to books on building your own house. There are lots of vacation home magazines and vacation home plan guides for building cottages, cabins and chalets. You could save money and obtain personal satisfaction by doing it yourself, but don't overestimate your abilities or the amount of time you have available.

Do-it-yourself construction almost always turns out to be more complicated, time consuming, and expensive than initially expected or budgeted for.

Many of the problems that owners have in their dealings with contractors are due to misunderstanding of the rights, responsibilities, and functions of the various people who are involved in the work, the lack of detailed and clear written agreements in advance, or the lack of due diligence background checks on the contractor before a commitment is made.

Raw Land

Possibly you are buying raw land so you can build a year-round house or a vacation cottage. If so, you have to take into account many factors, including the cost of servicing the land (with electrical lines, septic system or connection to an existing municipal sewer, etc.) in order to prepare it for construction, assuming the land is not already in a subdivision.

If you are buying raw land with no buildings on it, however, for the purpose of holding it as an investment for the future, you should be aware that this is one of the most speculative and risky types of real estate investment. On the other hand, if you are purchasing the land at a reasonable price and you can afford (preferably with cash or a large down payment) to reduce any monthly debt servicing, or if the land is attractive to you and is purchased as a long-term investment without any expectation of profit in the near future, then a raw-land purchase might be an appropriate option to consider. In addition, if the land area is large enough and has good soil, you may be able to generate some revenue by leasing it out to a nearby farmer.

Those who buy raw land and profit from it tend to be sophisticated investors who tie up the property with an option-to-purchase agreement (with a nominal amount paid for the option), spread the risks by going into the purchase with a group of other investors, do their research beforehand, know that the property will increase in value due to rezoning or subdivision potential, or plan to hold it for future development or sale.

In other words, you need to be clear and objective about your goals and the degree of risk you are willing to take. There are inherent problems, though, if you are intending to buy raw land for investment purposes. Due to the risks involved, you should expect a higher rate of return on your investment. Here are some of the advantages and disadvantages.

Advantages

√ Raw land could be available at a relatively low cost.

√ There is high potential gain if the land is rezoned, subdivided, developed, or if it increases in value for other reasons such as the building of a road, highway, rapid transit, or if sewers are installed proximate to the property.

√ Diversification of real estate investments—that is, by investing in different types of real estate, you are spreading your risk and therefore minimizing your overall financial and investment risk.

Disadvantages

√ No income will be generated, so there will be a negative cash flow. You have to subsidize the debt servicing of expenses such as a mortgage and interest, unless you paid the entire cost in cash. You will still have to pay property taxes.

√ If the land cannot be converted to a better use or prospects (such as the expansion of the community) do not materialize, the investment could lose money through debt-servicing costs, real estate sales commission fee, reduction in value to other prospective purchasers, or lack of interest by other investors.

√ The municipality may place zoning or environmental restrictions on the use of land, e.g., agricultural use only.

√ The municipality might expropriate the land to expand a highway, designate the land as green space, or request a right of way over part of the land.

√ Financing from banks and other lending institutions to purchase the land is more difficult to obtain because of the speculative nature of raw land and the lack of income to service the debt.

√ Using raw land as security or collateral for raising money for other investment purposes is difficult for the same reasons as noted earlier, so leveraging potential (borrowing on equity of property) on raw land is reduced.

√ The Canada Revenue Agency (CRA) generally considers the profit obtained from the sale of raw land as income from speculation, not as capital gain from an investment. The result is that you will pay more tax. If it were considered a capital gain, you would be taxed on only 50% of the gain (that is, 50% of the net profit). There are exceptions, and your intent at purchase (i.e., speculation or development), and the facts that support that intention, is a key test. Make sure you obtain strategic tax advice in advance.

√ If you buy a lot in a subdivision, the developer could have conditions that you must build within a certain time period, for example, three to five years, as a condition of your purchase.

Mobile Home

Mobile homes are a very popular form of housing for recreational purposes. The term mobile home can be confusing. It is not an RV and has no wheels, though it is designed to be moved by a large truck and set up on a permanent foundation, referred to as a pad. It is meant to be like any other house, except that it can be readily moved to a new location if desired. In some cases, a basement is built and the mobile home is set on top.

Mobile homes generally come in two widths. The single width is about 10 to 16 feet (3 to 5 metres) wide and sometimes as long as 64 feet (19.5 metres). The double homes are built in two sections and when combined are approximately twice as wide as a single. This type of unit can be very spacious and in many respects will have the layout, features, appearance and fixtures of a regular house. You can either buy a mobile home and have it put on the location of your choice, or buy one already on a site. When selecting a mobile home, you must make sure it meets safety standards. Some older mobile homes contain flammable materials and are poorly designed, and may not even be insurable, so check with your insurance company before you buy.

Most mobile homes are in parks that are set up for permanent communities, even though many of the residents may only live there part of the year, or use their homes only occasionally. These private parks provide water, sewer, and electricity hook-ups and frequently have other features, such as a recreation and social centre, a swimming pool, tennis courts, possibly a golf course and security personnel.

Some parks are restricted to retired people, while others have no restrictions. Some combine seasonal and permanent residents. RVs are permitted in some parks and not in others. There is a variety of different formats for these parks, which are regulated by local bylaws. In some rural locations, there are few restrictions. Some parks have communities that are independent and provide their own facilities, such as showers, laundry, and party room, whereas others use the facilities of the closest community.

Before deciding to buy a mobile home, you may want to rent one for a season to see if you like the concept and the area. Talk to other mobile home owners to get their advice on makes and models. Do a Google.ca search for the keywords of interest.

Finally, before you sign any documents to buy a mobile home, check with a real estate lawyer in the area for your protection. Your lot lease and mobile home warranty and contract can be reviewed for clauses or exclusions that you might not understand or want. Also, if you intend to put a mobile home on your own residential lot, you want to make sure that there are no local bylaws or other restrictions that will prevent you from doing so. Check to see if there is a local mobile homeowners' association and speak to other owners in the mobile home park that you are considering. Do your due diligence research before buying.

Manufactured Homes

Manufactured homes are factory-built housing systems that provide a home in varying degrees of completion, and which therefore will save you time, money, and hassle. These types of homes, whether modular or manufactured format, arrive on your site either virtually complete, or already pre-engineered and panelized, in order to reduce the amount of work required on your site.

There are many types of prefabricated building systems available, including pre-cut cabin and cottage kits, log homes, and prefabricated vacation homes.

Modular homes are built in three-dimensional modules, which provide a high degree of design flexibility, and can fully comply with requirements for energy performance in Canada. Modules can be combined to make one-, two-, or three-storey homes. When the modules arrive on your lot, they are ready for assembly on the foundation. Plumbing, wiring, siding, insulation, air/vapour barriers, and other construction details are mostly completed. Interior finishing is usually well advanced, including drywall, trim, flooring and cabinets. Therefore, if you have a tight time window, or want to save time, you may wish to consider this option.

Completing the home on site can take a builder a couple of weeks or more, depending on the size, style, and features of the home. Some features and custom upgrades are best done on site, such as brick siding and some hard surface flooring.

A manufactured home is the option that is the most complete when it leaves the factory. It is often ready for move-in the same day or a few days after it arrives on your site. Manufactured homes can be installed on surface foundations, and can be relocated, although this is not normally done. These types of homes are available in many designs and layouts, along with a wide selection of standard and customized features.

For more information, check out the Canadian Manufactured Housing Institute. Their website is: www.cmhi.ca. You can also do a Google.ca search on the keywords of interest to enhance your research.

Timeshares

At some time or other you have probably seen the ads: "Luxury Lifestyle at Affordable Prices!"… "Vacation the World!"… "Trade for Exotic Climes!"… "Buy Your Own Vacation Dream Home!" These refer to the concept of timesharing.

Other commonly used terms synonymous with timesharing include: resort timesharing, vacation ownership, multi-ownership, interval ownership and shared vacation plan. The timeshare concept has been applied to numerous other areas such as recreational vehicle and mobile home parks.

Timeshares have grown rapidly, with thousands of resorts throughout Canada and the United States, and around the world. These resorts range from Ontario cottage country, to British Columbia or Alberta ski resorts, to Florida condos, to Mexican beach villas.

There are two main categories of timeshares: "right to use" and "fee simple" ownership.

Right to Use

This concept is much like having a long-term lease, but with limited use for perhaps one, or maybe two weeks per year. It is similar to prepaying for a hotel room for a fixed period every year, 20 years in advance. In other words, you don't have any portion of ownership in the property, you only have a right to use it for a fixed or floating time period every year. The "right to use" concept involves condominiums, recreational vehicle parks, and other types of properties.

The opportunity for return on your money in a "right to use" timeshare is limited or non-existent. This is because there is generally very little demand in the after-sale market, as well as other restrictions on resale or pricing of the resale. In practical terms, timesharing is primarily a lifestyle and convenience choice.

Cautions When Considering "Right to Use" Timeshares

√ If you are interested in RV or mobile home timeshare options in Canada or the United States, ask for free or discount coupons. Most companies will permit you to stay at their locations for a nominal fee, to see if you like them.

√ You may tire of going to the same location every year, as your needs may change over time. Be aware that even the timeshare programs that include an exchange option (i.e., switching for a week in a different location) are not always as anticipated, in terms of availability, flexibility, convenience, or upgrade fee. Sometimes the home timeshare development will discontinue its exchange option, or for various reasons no longer be allowed to participate in the international exchange system.

√ Make sure you know what you are getting. Some people who purchase the "right to use" type think they are actually buying a "fee simple ownership" portion.

√ Be wary of hard-sell marketing. In most instances, you are offered "free" inducements (buffet, cruise, etc.) to convince you to listen to the sales pitch. The dream fantasy is heavily reinforced, and high-pressure sales pitches, given by teams of salespeople, can go on for hours and can be very persuasive—if not aggressive. Furthermore, very manipulative techniques are sometimes used to get you to sign a credit-card slip as a deposit.

√ There is usually an ongoing management fee for maintaining the premises.

√ Timeshare sales in some provinces in Canada and some U.S. states may be covered by consumer protection, in terms of your right to get your money back by "rescinding" or canceling the contract within a certain time period. This is frequently not the case in Mexico and other countries.

√   The legal aspects are generally more complex and expensive when dealing outside Canada.

√   The resale market for timeshares is either non-existent due to developer restrictions, or can be difficult, and can involve a considerable discount in the final sale price, and could also involve developer fees for approving a transfer of timeshare. You need to do your homework in advance.

√   Timeshares are a dream for some but a nightmare for others. If possible, speak to at least three other timeshare owners in the project you are considering in order to get their candid opinion before you decide to buy. Never give out your credit card for any reason as a deposit, or sign any documents without first speaking with a local real estate lawyer. Obtain a lawyer's name from the local lawyer referral service or provincial or state bar association. Don't let yourself be pressured.

√   Check with the local Better Business Bureau. Then sleep on it for some time. If the deal seems "too good to be true," it probably is.

For more details on timeshares in Canada, contact the Canadian Resort Development Association in Toronto. If you are thinking of buying in the United States, contact the American Resort Development Association in Washington, D.C. Refer to the Appendix under Helpful Websites for contact information.

There are other types of recreational property that you may wish to consider such as floating homes, ranches, and farms. You can do a Google.ca search using keywords to obtain further information on these options.

Fee Simple Ownership/Fractional Ownership

There are different formats. One involves owning a portion of the condominium (for example, one-fiftieth of the property). Each one-fiftieth portion would entitle you to one week's use of the premises. Other people would also buy into the property. Normally you would be allocated a fixed week every year. In other instances, it could be a floating time, with the exact date to be agreed upon depending on availability. In some cases, you might purchase a one-quarter, one-half, or one-tenth interest. This smaller group ownership is frequently referred to as fractional ownership. If the property is sold, you would receive your proportional share of any increase in net after-sale proceeds. You would also normally be able to rent, sell, or give your ownership portion to anyone you wished.

PART II
Finding the Right Fit

CHAPTER 4

Finding the Right Recreational Property

Whether you are buying a recreational property for personal or shared use, revenue, capital gains appreciation, or investment, you want to make the selection that is right for you. This chapter will explain the main factors to consider when thinking about the kind of vacation property you want and where to start looking.

Factors to Consider When Selecting a Recreational Property

In general, a combination of factors will determine your decision to buy in a particular area. The first section in this chapter discusses where to get both general and specific real estate information, and the types of issues to consider. Refer to Checklist 1 in the Appendix for an outline of many of the factors you should consider and compare in vacation properties that interest you.

Where to Get General Information

Part of your research to enhance the quality of your decision making is to have a general overview of trends and economic factors that might affect your choice and/or location of investment. The saying that "knowledge is power" is an accurate one. The more general and specific information you have, the better the chance you will have of making the right decision and being aware of opportunities. Here are some sources of general economic and real estate information you may wish to consider. Each market is unique, so general trends may or may not have a direct bearing, but they will give indications. Other factors in your specific geographic area will influence demand and prices.

National Newspapers

There are two main publications—*The Globe and Mail* and *The National Post*—that deal with national financial and economic issues and trends, as well as offering regular features and reports on real estate. Consider subscribing to them. Remember, the subscription fee is a 100% tax-deductible expense against any income from your business or investment.

Regional and Local Business or Real Estate Newspapers

Check with your local newsstand or public library to find out which publications are relevant to your needs. Some publications are free.

Magazines

There are various Canadian magazines on cottage properties and plans for building cottages. Their websites are contained in the Appendix:

- √ *Western Canadian Resorts, Vacation Homes and Investment Properties*
- √ *Cottage*
- √ *Cottage Life*
- √ *The Cottager*

Courses and Seminars

These provide another way to increase your awareness and enhance your decision making. Attend some of the seminars offered nationally by the National Real Estate Institute Inc. There are seminars on recreational real estate, as well as real estate investing, taught by professionals and other experts on the topic areas. For more information about upcoming seminars in your area, and to be on a mailing list, refer to the website www.homebuyer.ca.

There are real estate as well as general business management courses offered from time to time by school boards and college adult-education programs. Also, practical courses for the general public are offered on home buying, home building and renovating, by homebuilder industry associations and the Canadian Mortgage and Housing Corporation. Check out the CMHC site at www.cmhc.ca. Check out the website for the Canadian Homebuilders' Association at www.chba.ca to find out contact information for provincial or local homebuilder association seminars or courses.

Books

Check out your local library and bookstore for books on real estate investing, homebuilding, home buying, landlording, and related topics. Also check the websites of Chapters/Indigo at www.chapters.indigo.ca, and Amazon Books at www.amazon.ca. Some of the real estate books that I have authored or co-authored may also be of interest. See the front pages of this book for a list of them and for more details go to www.homebuyer.ca.

Internet

The Internet is a valuable research tool, as you know. You can find out almost anything you want to know about real estate by using effective search techniques. Google is one of the best search engines currently available (www.google.ca). Other relevant and interesting websites are mentioned throughout this chapter and can also be located in the Appendix under Helpful Websites. Check out www.homebuyer.ca.

Trade Shows

Local home shows or renovation shows, where you can pick up ideas and contacts and attend seminars, are excellent sources of information.

Where to Get Specific Information

The following sources of information will provide helpful assistance for more specific research steps.

Statistics Canada

This federal government department can provide you with invaluable information relating to population movements, general trends, census data, socio-economic profiles, and other demographic data. Contact your local library for Statistics Canada research data and analysis, search their website at www.statcan.ca, or contact Statistics Canada directly by looking in the Blue Pages of your telephone directory under "Government of Canada."

Canada Mortgage and Housing Corporation (CMHC)

This federal Crown corporation compiles historical data, analysis of information, and housing trends and projections, among other things. It has superb sources of information, and can provide personalized research consulting services for a fee if you want specialized information about a specific area. Many of the publications are free and available upon request or found on their website. Other publications are available at market cost. You may want to contact CMHC and ask them to put you on their mailing or e-mail list. To contact the CMHC branch nearest you, look in the Blue Pages of your phone book, or check out their website at www.cmhc.ca. Some of the many CMHC publications available include the following analyses and reports. Obtain a current list of publications:

- √ *The Housing Market Outlook* (semi-annual) covers projections of market activity in communities with a population of 100,000 or more.

- √ *Rental Market Reports* (annual) for all areas with a population of 100,000 or more. Stats are also available for communities of 10,000 or more.

- √ *Local Housing Now* (monthly) covers new and resale home stats for the same type of community populations as noted above.

- √ *National Housing Observer* (annual) for new and resale homes.

Real Estate Company Survey of Recreational Property

There are free annual or semi-annual surveys available online or in publication form on recreational property surveys, prices, and stats in the core recreational property areas in Canada.

- √ Royal LePage (www.royallepage.ca) Publishes the *Semi-Annual Survey of Recreational Home Prices* and the quarterly *Survey of Canadian House Prices*, both available free of charge.

- √ Century 21 (www.century21.ca) Publishes the annual *Survey on Recreational Home Prices in Canada.*

National Real Estate Firms

All of the major national real estate firms have websites with valuable research information available on properties in the location of interest to you. Check in the Yellow Pages of your phone book for real estate company names and websites, or check on the Internet by doing a Google.ca search.

Real Estate Boards

Most boards keep statistics on historical prices in their geographic area. A real estate agent can provide you with helpful data. If the real estate board operates on a Multiple Listing Service (MLS), there will be even more data available through a member realtor or on the MLS website (www.mls.ca). Recent surveys show that about 75% of those buying property do their initial research and shortlist their choices using the Internet, and then visit the location.

Real Estate Agents

Agents are a vital source of information about housing in any geographic area you might be considering. (Refer to Chapter 5: Selecting Your Advisors.) A real estate agent can locate a great deal of information for you through the MLS system that you otherwise would not have access to, such as price comparisons, historical data and trends, complete listing profiles of properties, and more. You can also do your research on the mls.ca website.

Municipal Planning Department

This department should be able to advise you if there is a development planned in the community of interest to you. You could also inquire if there is any potential rezoning that might affect the property you are considering. Check to see if there have been any natural disasters such as flooding or mudslides that might have affected the property, or could affect it in future. Find out how many building permits have been issued for the area. Which areas have the greatest new construction and renovation activities? If you are interested in applying for rezoning, building a new house, or renovating an old house, ask for the following material as your circumstances dictate: zoning maps, zoning regulations, building codes, building permit application forms and instructions, municipal codes, and regional master plans.

Municipal Tax Department

Find out how your property taxes will be calculated. The municipality might have a high commercial tax base, which effectively subsidizes the residential tax base, thereby keeping residential taxes down. Maybe the municipality is growing rapidly and is becoming, in effect, a bedroom community with lots of families. If the supply of schools and teachers in the municipality is low and the demand is increasing, property taxes could go up to finance the construction of schools and the hiring of teachers.

If you are buying your recreational property for retirement purposes, you may not want to pay property taxes for services you will not use. Check to see if there are any major property tax increases planned for the area, and why, and also ask specifically about the property you are considering.

If you are buying a condo in a resort community, depending on the location and type of condo, it might be zoned as commercial rather than residential, and therefore have a much higher tax rate (up to three times or more). This may be the case if you are buying into a condo hotel, or a condo development that requires you to be part of a rental pool for the majority of the year, and be managed by the developer's management company for a commission fee.

Municipal Police Department

Check with the local police department for statistics related to crime in the area that you are considering (e.g., vandalism, break and enter, theft, or arson). Compare the crime rate with other communities. Determine if it is increasing or decreasing, and the nature of the crime.

Municipal or Local Fire Department

Ask the fire department about the frequency of fires in the neighbourhood you are considering, relative to other areas in the general community. If there are a high number of fires, the neighbourhood could be a risk area, especially if arson is suspected. If you are buying in a rural area, ask questions such as what type of fire service is available. Is it a volunteer fire department or municipal fire department, and what is the approximate response time? Where are fire hydrants located?

Municipal Building Inspector

Ask the local building inspector for his or her candid input on the area or home that you are considering, and if they have any cautions. You can also check on the history of the property, in terms of any work orders or other renovations done that received municipal approval, and therefore presumably comply with local bylaws and building codes.

Local Newspapers

These can be an excellent source of information on issues affecting the community in general or a specific location in particular. You can pick up back issues over the past few months from the newspaper office or, in some cases, online. You can also check with the local library. You should also consider subscribing to them to keep on top of issues in the community that could impact on your recreational property in a positive or negative way.

Local Homebuilders' Association

The community you are considering may have a homebuilders' association. Look in the Yellow Pages or check out the website for the Canadian Home-builders' Association at www.chba.ca. You can obtain contact information about provincial or local homebuilders' associations through the site. The association members could tell you which areas of the community have high growth, or about trends that indicate future high growth.

Cottage Associations

Check with local cottage associations to obtain feedback on possible areas of interest to you, and any candid recommendations or cautions, or other advice that would assist your decision process. Refer to the Appendix for a list of associations.

Home Inspector

Check with local home inspectors. You can find them in the Yellow Pages or contact the Canadian Association of Home and Property Inspectors through their website www.cahpi.ca. Ask them which areas of the community are expanding, which areas have had a lot of remodeling done, which have problems such as drainage, pests, etc., and which areas have resale homes in excellent condition. Remember to make any house or condo purchase subject to a satisfactory home inspection that you would arrange.

Neighbours

Don't forget to ask the people in the area you are considering how they enjoy the neighbourhood. Would they buy there again? Which specific features about the neighbourhood do they like or dislike? What is the ratio of owners to renters? Ask for feedback that gives you some feeling for the quality and stability of the community. Whether you are thinking of buying a recreational property as a second home, or for investment purposes, these issues are important for peace of mind as well as resale potential.

Important Factors to Consider

Some of the general features and factors are discussed below. Certain factors might be more important if you are buying for personal use as a vacation home, or as a revenue real estate investment. Remember to refer to Checklist 1 in the Appendix to assist you when making your selection.

Location

One of the prime considerations is the location. If the main local attraction is a body of water, how close is the recreational property to the waterfront? How close is the property to features such as schools, cultural attractions, shopping centres, recreational facilities, work, and transportation? How attractive is the present and future development of the area surrounding the property? You could invest in a property and six months later a building could be built across from you, blocking your view and therefore decreasing the resale value of your property. This is especially a potential risk when buying a condo. The location should have ample access to parking and other attractive features. Check on the amount of traffic on the streets in your area. Heavy traffic can be a noise nuisance as well as a hazard for young children.

Noise

Thoroughly assess the level of noise. Consider such factors as the location of highways, driveways, parking lots, playgrounds, and businesses relative to the property you are considering. If you are buying a condominium, also consider the location of the garage doors, elevators, garbage chutes, and the heating and air conditioning plant or equipment. Depending on the location and type of property, it is a good plan to visit the property at three different times (e.g., morning, evening, and on the weekend). Check to see if the property adjacent to your property is a rental. Are there parties or other noise that would disturb you? If you're considering a waterfront property, is there noise from motorboats or other water craft? Is public access to beaches nearby? If a winter retreat, are there snowmobile trails nearby, or cross-country ski trails? Would any of these factors interfere with your desire for solitude or quiet?

Privacy

Privacy is an important consideration and has to be thoroughly assessed. For example, ensure that the sound insulation between the walls, floors, and ceilings of your prospective property is sufficient to enable you to live comfortably without annoying your neighbours or having your neighbours annoy you. If you have a condominium or townhouse unit, such factors as the distance between your unit and other common areas, including walkways, roads, and fences, are important.

Price

The price of the property you are considering should be competitive with that of other, similar offerings. On the other hand, if you are purchasing a condominium unit, it is sometimes difficult to compare prices accurately without taking into account the different amenities—such as tennis courts, swimming pool, recreation centre, etc.—that may be available in one condominium development but not available in another. You may decide that you do not want these extra facilities in view of your lifestyle needs, in which case paying a premium for the unit would not be attractive. On the other hand, you have to look at the resale potential, so check with your realtor. He or she can obtain accurate information on comparative pricing and cost per square foot for similar properties.

Common Elements and Facilities

If you are buying a condominium unit, review all the common elements that make up the condominium development. Are they relevant to your needs? What are the maintenance or operating costs that might be required to service these features (e.g., swimming pools, tennis courts, fitness centres, party rooms, etc.)?

Parking Facilities

Is the parking outdoors or underground? Is there sufficient lighting for security protection? Is it a long distance from the parking spot to your home? Is there parking space available for a boat, trailer, or second car, and is there ample visitor parking?

Storage Facilities

Check out the type of storage space available, including its location and size. Is there sufficient storage space for your needs, or will you have to rent a mini-locker to store excess items if you are considering the purchase of a condo?

Quality of Construction Materials

Look thoroughly at your building and any surrounding developments, if applicable, to assess the overall quality of the development. If you are buying a condominium, keep in mind that you are responsible for paying a portion of the maintenance costs for the common elements. You should hire a contractor or building inspector whom you trust to give you an opinion on the quality and condition of the construction before committing yourself. An older building will obviously cost money to repair, possibly a considerable amount of money and in a short time.

Design and Layout

When looking at a building, consider your present and future needs.

Right now, a cottage may be exactly what you're looking for. But if you're childless, or your adult children have moved far away from your home and recreational property, will there be someone to help you with the maintenance that's required for a detached building? Will you want to oversee the work that will have to be done by others?

Detached buildings, such as cottages, can also have more than one storey, a fact that may become an impediment as you age.

If you are buying a condominium, although you are entitled to use the interior of your unit as you wish, there are restrictions relating to the exterior of your unit or any structural changes that you may make to the unit. If you intend to add a separate room for an expanded family, in-laws, or an office, if that is possible, you should consider the implications beforehand. Or you may find that the balcony is very windy and for that reason you would like to build a solarium to enclose the balcony. There is a very good chance that you would not be able to do so without the consent of the condominium council because it would affect the exterior appearance of the development.

Neighbourhood Value

Look at the surrounding neighbourhood and determine whether the value of the residences in the neighbourhood will affect the value of your property. For example, are the homes in the area well maintained? Are there children in the same age group as your own children? What is a profile of the people in the neighbourhood? Are they single adults, young couples (with or without children), or older, retired people? Are the properties being rented out full-time, seasonally, or periodically?

Owner-Occupiers vs. Tenants

If you are buying a condominium unit, ask how many tenants as opposed to owners there are or will be in the condominium complex, and the maximum number of tenants allowed. The higher the percentage of owner-occupiers, the better the chance that there will be more pride of ownership and therefore more responsible treatment of common elements and amenities. If you are purchasing a house, the same principle applies. Generally you should be concerned if the tenant percentage in the condominium complex or residential area is 25% or more and is increasing. However, if you are buying a condo as an investment for rental purposes, your selection criteria would be different.

Management

If you are buying a condominium unit, find out whether the building is being operated by a professional management company, a resident manager, or if it is self-managed. As mentioned before, you should check out the condominium unit or property that you are interested in at three different times before you decide to purchase: during the day, in the evening, and on the weekend. That should give you a better idea of noise level, children, or parties, and the effectiveness of the management control.

Property Taxes

Compare the tax levels in the various areas you are considering. Different municipalities have different tax rates and there could be a considerable cost saving or expense. Also, find out if there is any anticipated tax increase and why. Refer to the earlier discussion and cautions about municipal taxes.

Rental Situation in the Area

If you are thinking of purchasing a revenue property, look for an area that enjoys a high rental demand. You want to minimize the risk of having a vacancy. On the other hand, you don't want too much competition. Check the CMHC rental stats in the area that interests you by accessing their website at www.cmhc.ca.

Local Zoning and Building Restrictions and Opportunities

Check for restrictions on use and other matters. For example, is there a community plan? What type of zoning bylaw is there, and is it subject to change? Is there a rezoning potential for higher or different use? Is there a land-use contract? What about non-conforming use of older or revenue buildings? If you want rental revenue to help pay for your annual expenses, or as an investment property, are nightly or weekly rentals to tourists permitted for your house or condo? Are you restricted to seasonal use? Is there a limit on mobile homes permitted on the property at certain times of the year? Are you restricted from constructing other buildings on the property?

Perception of the Area

What perception does the media or the public in general have about a certain area? Is it positive or negative, and why? People's perception of the area may influence rental decisions, and resale potential in the future.

Stage of Development

Areas typically go through a series of stages, phases, and plateaus over time. For example, the normal stages are development (growth), stabilization (maturing, plateauing), conversions (from apartments to condos), improvements of existing properties, decline of improvements (deterioration), and redevelopment (tearing down of older buildings and new construction, with more efficient use of space). As you look in a geographic area, and at specific properties, consider what phase of development the area is in, and what you might expect in the coming years.

Economic Climate

This is a major factor to consider. What is stimulating the local economy? Is there new development, such as housing and condo construction or other commercial activity, that indicates good economic health? Is a major single-industry employer (e.g, a ski resort) the main source of economic activity in the area? In the latter case, you can appreciate the risk involved for resale or rentals if the industry or main employer has financial problems or decides to close down.

Population Trends

Look for the trends in the community you are considering. Are people moving in or out, and why? What is the average age? What types of owners: second property, retirees, rental properties? Income level? Family size? Marital status? Many of these demographic statistics can be obtained from Statistics Canada or from your provincial or municipal government. If the population is increasing, it will generally create more demand for rental and resale housing. Conversely, if it is decreasing, the opposite will occur. If the population is older, people may prefer downsizing to condominiums rather than buying smaller houses. There are many variables to consider.

Size, Shape, and Location of Lot

This factor has to do with subdivision or rezoning potential, resale marketability, and general enjoyment. For example, maybe you have a large lot that has the potential to be subdivided into three building lots, or could be rezoned for higher density than a single family home, for example, a townhouse condo. Possibly you have a lot at the end of a quiet street, or backing on protected green space (e.g., a provincial park) that will not have future development.

Transportation

A prospective tenant or homebuyer will want to have convenient transportation routes. Whether it's a highway, road, ferry, bus, train, or other mode of transportation, the type of transportation in a particular area will have a bearing on your rental or resale price. For example, if your vacation home can only be reached by boat, you may have fewer potential tenants to choose from.

Topography

The layout of the land is an important consideration. If the property is low-lying (i.e., adjacent to a rise or hill), water drainage problems could result. Water could collect under the foundation of the house, thereby causing settling, assuming there is only soil under the foundation. If you are near a river or stream, is there seasonal flooding? If the property is waterfront, is the access easy and safe? These are just some of the many issues to consider.

Appearance

Try to look objectively at the appearance of the property you are interested in. Is it well maintained, or does it need repair? What do the other buildings in the neighbourhood look like? Are they new, renovated, or attractive? Or are they poorly maintained with peeling paint, uncut grass, broken windows, and trash lying about? How will the appearance of the property and its neighbours affect the price you're willing to pay? Would the property be attractive to someone else if you were to resell?

Services in the Community

Different services available in the community—for example, shopping, churches, community and recreational facilities, playgrounds, parks, and schools—will attract different types of tenants or purchasers, depending on their needs. Consider your own needs, and those of buyers in the future.

Climate

If you are buying for personal use and eventual resale or buying as an investment, climate is an important consideration. Certain geographic areas may have more rain, snow, and wind than others, depending on historical climate patterns. There are frequently different micro-climates within contiguous areas. You can check historical weather patterns on the Internet with Environment Canada. You can also check with the local city hall.

Unattractive Features

Look for factors that will have a negative influence on a prospective tenant or purchaser: unpleasant odours (e.g., local pulp mill with the prevailing wind in your direction), a lack of natural light for the home because of overgrown trees, lack of adequate street lighting for safety, inadequate municipal services such as septic tanks rather than sewer facilities, poorly maintained roads, or open drainage ditches. Awareness of these negative factors will also assist you in your decision making and negotiating approach when buying, if you decide to do so.

Convenient Proximity

If you are buying real estate as an investment, it is prudent to purchase within a four-hour drive of your principal residence so you can conveniently monitor and/or maintain your property. This is just a general guideline, of course. There are exceptions, for example, if you can easily take a short flight from where you live, and can afford that luxury.

Reasons for Sale

One of the important factors to determine is why the property is for sale. Maybe the vendor knows something you don't, which will have a bearing on your further interest. On the other hand, maybe the vendor wants to sell for reasons that should not dissuade you, such as wanting to move to a larger home or downsize to a smaller home or condo. Perhaps he or she plans to separate or divorce, has lost employment, needs to relocate for a job, or is seriously ill or incapacitated. Your realtor may know, or be able to find out, the reasons for the property being on the market.

Special Considerations When Assessing Recreational Property for Purchase

There are special considerations when assessing recreational property for purchase. Here are some supplemental issues to consider.

Restrictions on Use

There are various forms of legal restrictions that could affect your land and use of that land. Your lawyer can search the title of the property in the land titles office to see what encumbrances are on title, as a condition of any offer you make. Also have your lawyer check out the local bylaws. You might find, for instance, that you can't rent out your property for "short-term" rentals (less than 28 days), because it is only zoned for single-family use.

Right of Way

This generally means a statutory (legal) right for certain companies, Crown corporations or government departments to use or have access to part of your property. Examples include hydro, telephone, sewer, drainage, dike, and other public access purposes.

Easement

An easement is similar to a right of way, but normally is the term used when one neighbour gives another neighbour the right to use or have access to a piece of land, e.g., permission to reach a waterfront by crossing a neighbour's land. This agreement is put into writing and filed in the nearest land titles office.

Restrictive Covenants

A restrictive covenant limits the use of a property for the benefit of another property, the municipality, or the provincial or federal government (the Crown). These restrictions can include such matters as the number and location of buildings, cutting of trees, septic fields, subdivision of the land, and allowable uses of the land. A builder could also place a restrictive covenant on the property.

Building Schemes

This document is registered by the builder on all lots in the subdivision. It controls such matters as size and location of buildings, and the number of buildings permitted. It can also control the materials used on the buildings (e.g., all shake, shingle, or metal roofs), and sometimes the type of landscaping required. The intent is to have consistency in the appearance of the development.

Under-Surface Rights

This would include rights to minerals, oil, or gas that may be in the ground. They could be owned by either the government or another private party that has previously staked a legal claim to them.

Other Government Restrictions

You need to do your due diligence on this aspect, as not all restrictions on the use of the property are necessarily registered on the title of the property. It depends on the customary approach of the province in which your vacation property will be located. For example, there could be restrictions on the use of the property, on matters such as keeping livestock, heritage conversation, pollution, fishing, damming streams, agricultural use, etc.

Waterfront Boundaries and Restrictions

Properties bordering a water body such as a lake, river, stream, or ocean have special boundary issues you need to research. When you have a survey of land, you have precision. A natural water boundary lacks this type of precision, so there are various tests and formulas used to determine where private property ends and where the government rights begin (i.e., Crown land).

You need to check on what local, provincial, or federal restrictions there are to regulate the use of marine areas adjacent to private property. The purpose of these provisions is to control the construction and use of private floats, breakwaters, docks, sea walls, and the commercial or industrial use of the foreshore.

In these scenarios, the government concern is that the above types of structures or use could impair the aesthetics of the view from the land and sea, or impede the ability of the public to walk along the foreshore.

Water Availability

Check on this critical issue. Is water provided from a public system or from a well? Is the water safe to drink? Is it sufficient for your needs? If a well needs to be drilled, what will be the cost?

Waste Disposal

Is the property connected to a municipal sewer system? If not, does it have a septic tank or another type of system? Is the soil suitable for a septic field? How old is the septic system, how many years can it reasonably be expected to function before needing replacement, and how frequently does it need to be cleaned? What about other types of waste disposal, such as garbage pickup and recycling—are these services available, or will you be required to make your own arrangements?

Land Boundary

Check to make sure that the boundaries of your property have been clearly marked and pegged by a qualified surveyor. This is especially important with acreage or waterfront property. You don't want to have disputes with your neighbours.

Wild Animals

Is the area that you are considering the natural habitat of wild animals such as cougar, deer, bear, fox, etc. Are you comfortable in such an environment? Are there any special arrangements or lifestyle concessions you would have to make in order to live near these wild animals?

Before Starting Your Property Search

There are some preliminary considerations you need to work through before starting your search. First of all, have a strategic plan:

- √ Be clear about what type of real estate you want and which area you are interested in; this will save time and stress.
- √ Target a specific geographic area or areas. This makes your selection process much simpler and gives you an opportunity to get to know specific areas thoroughly. Obtain street maps of the area as well as a zoning map from the town or municipality.
- √ Know the price range that you want to buy in, based on your available financing and real estate needs.
- √ Determine the type of ideal purchase package that you want (i.e., price and terms) as well as your bottom-line fallback position. What is the maximum you are willing to pay and what are the most restrictive

terms that you can live with? Make sure that you don't compromise your own position.

√ Do comparisons and shortlist choices. That way you can ensure you get the best deal, in comparative terms.

√ Be realistic in terms of your purchase conditions in accord with the current market situation.

√ The location of a property is important to maximize your current enjoyment of the property and future resale potential. Location is, of course, also important for investment property, but it has to be balanced against overall investment goals such as tax benefits, appreciation, resale potential, and net revenue.

√ Consider the issue of distance between your prospective property and where you reside. If you are buying a property as an investment, proximity is important to properly manage it.

Where to Find Recreational Real Estate for Sale

There are various methods of finding out about vacation real estate for sale. Here are some of the most common approaches.

Real Estate Agent

An experienced real estate agent is an invaluable asset. A realtor can save you time, expense, and frustration, and provide advice and expertise. Remember that the vendor pays the real estate commission, whether the agent is a listing or selling broker. Check for a real estate agent in the location that you are wanting to buy a vacation home or rural property.

There are many advantages to using realtors. You can use their services to source properties listed on multiple or exclusive listings, or for property being "sold by owner." You can also use them to contact owners of property who wish to sell a property, but who haven't listed it yet. The advantage of using realtors to source unlisted properties is that they might be able to negotiate a better deal for you than you could get yourself.

There are strategic benefits to having an agent present the offer and negotiate on your behalf in non-listed situations. Frequently, the owner will agree to pay a commission to the realtor if you buy, although the commission in an unlisted sale would generally be less. This is because the realtor has not had the expense of time or advertising in actively promoting the listing. Alternatively, you could arrange to pay the realtor a negotiated fee if he or she arranges a sale at a price attractive to you.

If you use a realtor to assist your search, be loyal to him or her if you purchase the property. On the other hand, if the realtor seems uninterested, then find another. Give your agent a list of your requirements so the agent can refine the search for you.

Multiple Listing Service Website

The Multiple Listing Service (MLS) is an excellent source of information. You can research most of the information on the MLS website at www.mls.ca. However, a realtor would be able to assist you in your historical or comparative research by accessing the MLS database, which is not accessible to the general public. If you are viewing the website, look for specific factors that will give you clues as to vendor motivation or the appropriateness of the property. This could assist you in negotiating a lower price. For example, look for the exact area, when the property was listed (how long it has been on the market), if it has been re-listed after a first listing expired, whether the property is vacant, if any price reductions have occurred (how much and when), and whether there has been a previous collapsed sale. Look in the remarks/comments section of any MLS listings: it could say why the property is for sale, such as foreclosure action, order for sale, relocation, vendor ill, the vendor bought another property, etc. All this information is important as you negotiate.

Do a Google Search

Do a search under www.google.ca using keywords for the geographic area or location that you are interested in. For example, "recreational property," "vacation property," "waterfront property," "raw land," together with "Canmore," or "Kelowna," or "Muskoka," etc., and take it from there.

Newspaper Ads

Look in the classified section of the local newspapers under "Vacation Homes for Sale," "Recreational Property," "Homes for Sale," "Condominiums for Sale," or "Revenue Property for Sale." Also, look in the special real estate newspapers that are available free and come out weekly in many major Canadian cities, as well as smaller communities.

Become Familiar with the Area

It is important to become familiar with the area you are interested in. Drive through the area regularly and look for "For Sale" signs, both properties listed with a realtor and "For Sale by Owner." Note addresses, names, and telephone numbers, and other contact information.

Direct Offer to Owner

In the process of becoming familiar with a particular neighbourhood, you might see a property that is not currently for sale but whose owner might be interested in selling, either immediately or some time in the near future. Look for clues that the property is vacant—uncut lawns, peeling paint, etc.

Once you have determined which properties might seriously interest you, you can find out who the owner is by doing a search in the local land titles office. The documents are on public record. You could do the search yourself or through a lawyer or realtor. You would also be able to discover other information in your search, such as when the existing owner bought it and for how much, the nature and amount of mortgage financing, and if there are any legal problems relating to the property such as liens, judgments, foreclosures, or power of sale. If you want to pursue it further, you could contact the owner yourself, or preferably have your lawyer or realtor contact the owner on your behalf.

Word of Mouth

Tell your friends, neighbours, relatives, or business associates that you want to buy property, the type of property you are looking for, and the area you are interested in. They might hear of someone who is thinking of selling.

CHAPTER 5

Selecting Your Advisors

When buying a recreational property, it is important to have a team of experts and professionals to assist you in achieving your goals. The team will likely consist of a realtor, lawyer, accountant, mortgage broker, building inspector, and insurance broker. In this chapter, common selection criteria for each of these professionals will be covered first, followed by more specific considerations. You will also find a list of contact information for the professional associations referred to in the Appendix under Helpful Websites.

Common Selection Criteria

You should be very selective in your screening process. Selecting the right advisors will enhance your prospects for profit and growth; selecting a less knowledgeable or professional advisor will be costly in terms of time, money, and stress.

There are many factors you should consider when selecting advisors. For example, the person's professional qualifications, related experience, and the fee for services are factors you will want to consider. You should prepare a list of such questions, plus other queries relating to your specific needs, and pose these to each of the prospective advisors. Some people may feel awkward discussing fees and qualifications, but it is important to establish these matters at the outset before you make a decision to use that person's services. The most common selection criteria include qualifications, experience, compatible personality, confidence and competence in the area concerned, and fees. Interview at least three candidates before you make your decision.

Qualifications

Before you entrust an advisor with your work, you will want to know that he or she has the appropriate qualifications. These may include a professional degree in the case of a lawyer or accountant, or some other professional training or qualifications relative to the area of work.

Experience

It is very important to assess the advisor's experience related to your needs and requirements. Such factors as the advisor's degree of expertise, number of years of experience, and percentage of time devoted to the service you need are critically important. How much you will come to rely on a lawyer's advice and insights is obviously related to the degree of experience the lawyer has in the area. For example, the fact that a lawyer has been practising law for 10 years does not necessarily mean that the lawyer has a high degree of expertise in the area of real estate.

An accountant who has had 15 years of experience in general accounting and tax advice can certainly provide you with a basic level of service. However, for expert tax advice you want to speak to an accountant who specializes only in tax matters. If that accountant has experience in real estate investment, this is an important factor. Inquire about the advisor's degree of expertise and length of experience in real estate deals. If you don't ask the question, you won't be given the answer, which may make the difference between mediocre and in-depth advice.

Compatible Personality

When selecting an advisor, make certain that you feel comfortable with the individual's personality. If you are going to have an ongoing relationship with the advisor, it is important that you feel comfortable with the person's ability to communicate, their attitude and degree of candour, and their commitment to your real estate goals and interests. A healthy respect and rapport will put you more at ease when discussing business matters and thereby enhance your understanding of the issues and the decisions you need to make.

Confidence

You must have confidence in your advisor if you are going to rely on his or her advice to enhance the quality of your decision making and minimize your risk. After considering the person's qualifications, experience, and personality style, you may feel that you can have confidence in the individual. If you do not, there is a very good chance that you will not use him or her as extensively as you should or when you need to. This could have a serious negative impact on your decision making.

Good Communication Skills

You want an advisor who is a good listener, who knows how to ask the right questions, and who provides feedback in understandable layperson's terms. Any issues and options should be fully disclosed, with pros, cons, and recommendations.

Your advisor should return your phone calls promptly and keep you regularly informed in writing. Some people and situations require more frequent communication than others do.

Accessibility

If your advisor becomes too busy for you, reconsider the relationship. Your needs should be a priority. If you are shunted to a junior advisor against your wishes, your original advisor may be culling clientele to concentrate on more lucrative clients.

Trust

Whether the person is a lawyer, accountant, financial planner, or other advisor, if you don't intuitively trust the advice as being solely in your best interests, never use that person again. You have far too much to lose, in terms of your financial security and peace of mind, to have any doubts whatsoever. You cannot risk the chance that advice is governed primarily by the advisor's financial self-interest, with your interests as a secondary consideration. If advice is tainted in any way by bias or personal financial benefit, obviously it is unreliable and self-serving.

Integrity

Your advisor should have a high standard of personal and professional integrity. The advisor's reputation with other professional colleagues is one reference point. Maintaining the confidentiality of information is another.

Depending on the nature of the advisory relationship, you may disclose your personal needs, wants, hopes, and dreams, as well as concerns. This puts you in a potentially vulnerable position.

References

References and word-of-mouth referrals are particularly important when selecting any advisor who will be taking a holistic approach to your financial affairs. Ask for professional references and then contact those professionals and ask about the advisor's attributes as well as any weak points. Also, ask how long they have been dealing with each other. Don't feel embarrassed to ask the tough questions—candid feedback can provide you with a revealing reality check.

Fees

It is important to feel comfortable with the fee being charged and the payment terms. Are they fair, competitive, and affordable? Do they match the person's qualifications and experience? For instance, if you need a good tax accountant to advise you on minimizing taxes, you may have to pay a higher hourly rate for the quality of advice that will save you several thousands of dollars. On the other hand, if what you require is the preparation of annual financial statements, perhaps a junior accountant can do the job competently at a more affordable rate.

Comparing Candidates

It is a good rule of thumb to see at least three advisors in each category before deciding which one is right for you. The more exacting you are in your selection criteria, the more likely that you will find a good match and the more beneficial that advisor will be to your real estate investment goals. It is a competitive market in the advisory business, and you can afford to be extremely selective when choosing advisors to complement your real estate team.

Selecting a Realtor

There are distinct advantages to having a realtor act on your behalf when buying or selling a property. When buying or selling real estate relating to your business, the right realtor will make all the difference in ensuring a positive purchase or sale experience.

Over the years, a new relationship structure, sometimes referred to as agency disclosure, has replaced the old system. Many people assumed that if they found a realtor and the house was listed on the Multiple Listing Service (MLS), for example, the realtor would represent their interests exclusively when an offer was presented and through negotiation. The agency disclosure system spells out the respective roles and responsibilities of each realtor involved. The seller still pays the real estate commission, which is shared with any other realtor involved. All disclosure of who is acting for whom is spelled out in the agreement of purchase and sale. Some agents working with the buyer may also enter into a buyer agency contract. In other words, each realtor is acting exclusively for the benefit of the buyer or seller. However, if the listing realtor is also the selling realtor (double-end deal), the agent has to enter into a limited dual agency agreement. This is agreed upon and signed by both the buyer and seller. The agent modifies his or her exclusive obligations to both the buyer and the seller by limiting it primarily to confidentiality as to each party's motivation and sharing of personal information.

You can get more information from any real estate agent, real estate company, or your local real estate board.

How to Find a Realtor

There are a number of approaches to finding a good real estate agent:

- √ Ask friends, neighbours, and relatives for the names of agents they have dealt with, and why they would recommend them.
- √ Go to open houses for an opportunity to meet realtors.
- √ Check newspaper ads that list the names and phone numbers of agents who are active in your area.
- √ Check "For Sale" signs for agents' names and phone numbers.
- √ Check the Internet.
- √ Contact real estate firms in your area; speak to an agent who specializes or deals with the type of property you want and is an experienced salesperson.

After you have met several agents who could potentially meet your needs, there are a number of guidelines to assist you with your selection:

- √ Favour an agent who is familiar with the neighbourhood you are interested in. Such an agent will be on top of the available listings, will know comparable market prices, and can target the types of property that meet your needs as you have explained them.
- √ Favour an agent who is particularly familiar with the buying and selling of residential and revenue properties.
- √ Look for an agent who is prepared to screen properties so that you are informed only of those that conform to your guidelines for viewing purposes.
- √ Look for an agent who is familiar with the various conventional and creative methods of financing, including the effective use of mortgage brokers.

√ Look for an agent who will thoroughly investigate properties you are interested in, in terms of background information such as length of time on the market, reason for sale, and price comparisons to similar properties. An agent who is familiar with the MLS can find a great amount of information in a short time, assuming the property is listed on the MLS.

√ Look for an agent who will be candid with you in suggesting a real estate offer price and explain the reasons for the recommendation.

√ Look for an agent who has effective negotiating skills to ensure that your wishes are presented as clearly and persuasively as possible.

√ Favour an agent who is working on a full-time basis rather than part-time.

√ Look for an agent who has financial analysis skills and can clarify the revenue property analysis aspects.

Benefits of a Realtor to the Purchaser

There are obvious benefits to the buyer of using a realtor, as outlined in the previous points. One of the key benefits is that the realtor can act as an intermediary between you and the listing broker. That way, the listing broker may never have an opportunity to meet you and therefore cannot exert any influence on you with aggressive salesmanship, or otherwise make an assessment of you that could compromise your negotiating position. The agent who has the listing agreement with the vendor would know you only through discussions with your realtor and through any offer that you might present. This arm's-length negotiating position is an important strategic tactic that will benefit you.

Another advantage to a buyer is the opportunity for the realtor to access a multiple listing service, which can provide instant, thorough, and accurate information on properties that might interest you. Without an agent searching for you, you seriously minimize your range of selection and the prospect of concluding the deal at a price that is attractive to you.

Benefits of a Realtor to the Vendor

At the moment, you're likely thinking of buying a recreational property, not selling it. But there may come a time when you are ready to sell your recreational property. If and when that time comes, it's good to keep in mind the extensive benefits to listing your property with a realtor rather than attempting to sell it on your own. Some of the key benefits include the following:

√ Realtors can list your property on the multiple listing service as well as the Internet, which provides extensive exposure throughout and beyond your market area.

√ Realtors can pre-qualify and pre-screen potential homebuyers.

√ Realtors can provide information to the purchaser on matters such as financing and other assistance programs that could facilitate the sale of your property.

√ Realtors can suggest methods of improving the appearance of your property in order to maximize the positive impression and therefore the potential buyer's level of interest and sale price.

√ Realtors can knowledgeably discuss the real estate market in their territory with potential buyers, and can provide MLS computer printouts of comparable listings or sales patterns; they can also supply other facts and figures to assist you in realistically establishing a market price.

√ Realtors free up your own time, using all their contacts and marketing techniques in order to effect the sale of your property.

√ As is the case for purchasers, realtors negotiate an agreement on your behalf and according to your instructions, and you remain at arm's length from the negotiations. This improves your negotiating position.

How Realtors Are Compensated

Traditionally the vendor pays the realtor a commission, the amount of which is negotiable. Some are fixed percentages and some are variable, depending on the price involved. Some commissions are a negotiated flat rate, regardless of the sale price. There are different commission structures for residential and commercial properties.

If there is more than one realtor involved, as is usually the case with both a listing broker and a selling broker, then the commission is normally split based on an agreed formula. One common arrangement is 55% to the listing broker because he or she incurs more expenses to sell the property, and 45% to the selling broker.

Selecting a Lawyer

Whether you are the buyer or the seller of real estate, it is essential that you obtain a lawyer to represent your interests—a standard precaution with any real estate transaction. As you will realize by the time you have finished reading this book, there are many potential legal pitfalls for the unwary when buying real estate. Agreements for purchase and sale, and related documents, are complex. For most people, the purchase of a home or other investment property is the largest investment of their life, and the agreement for purchase and sale is the most important legal contract they will ever sign.

How to Find a Lawyer

There are a number of ways to select the right lawyer for your needs:

- √ Ask friends who have purchased real estate which lawyer they used, whether they were satisfied with the lawyer, and why.

- √ Contact the lawyer referral service in your community. Under this service, sponsored by the provincial law society or a provincial division of the Canadian Bar Association, you can have a half-hour consultation with a lawyer for a nominal fee (usually $25), which lawyers generally waive to facilitate bookkeeping and PR. To obtain contact information for the lawyer referral service in your province, look in your phone book or check the Internet. Go to www.google.ca and then type in the key words "lawyer referral service" and then the name of your province. Make sure you specify that you want a lawyer who specializes in real estate. Contact the law society in your province for further information.

- √ Look in the Yellow Pages under "Lawyers" and check the box ads, which outline the areas of expertise.

- √ Check the Internet for specialty lawyers in your area. For example, do a Google.ca search.

- √ If you are arranging mortgage financing, speak to the lawyer who is preparing the mortgage documents on behalf of the lender. If the lawyer you choose is also preparing the mortgage documents, you could save on some duplicated disbursement costs and negotiate a package price. Be careful, though, to avoid conflict of interest; ensure that the lawyer provides you with a full explanation of the mortgage terms and conditions that might affect your interests. Keep in mind that the mortgage is being prepared on behalf of the lender, but at your expense. If you have any concerns in this area, retain a separate lawyer to do the non-mortgage legal work and explain the contents of the mortgage to you. Alternatively, ask the lender to let you see a lawyer of your choice from the lender's list of approved lawyers.

Once you have contacted the lawyer over the phone, ask about the areas of his or her real estate interest and expertise. Tell the lawyer that you are looking for a person with expert knowledge in property law. If the lawyer cannot offer this, ask for a recommendation.

If you did not obtain the referral through the lawyer referral service, ask the lawyer over the phone what a half-hour initial consultation would cost. In many cases it is free.

Have all your questions and concerns prepared in writing so that you won't forget any. If you wish to make an offer to purchase, bring your offer-to-purchase document with you, and the details about the new, resale, or revenue project you are considering. Ask about anticipated fee and disbursement costs. If you are not pleased with the outcome of the interview for any reason, move on to another lawyer.

Selecting an Accountant

An accountant's chief role is to monitor the financial health of your real estate investment and reduce the subsequent risks and tax payable, either when you sell it, rent it, or bequeath it. Along with your lawyer, your accountant will complement your real estate team to ensure that your real estate investment decisions are based on sound advice and good planning. Some accountants have also obtained their CFP (certified financial planner) certification, in order to offer their clients more comprehensive consulting advice.

An accountant can help you right from the pre-real estate investment phase. The services that can be provided are wide ranging and include the following:

√ setting up a manual or computerized bookkeeping system that both the investor and accountant can work with efficiently

√ setting up a customized software program for real estate investment and management of the properties

√ setting up systems for the control of cash and the handling of funds

√ preparing or evaluating budgets, forecasts, and investment plans

√ assessing your break-even point and improving your profitability

√ preparing and interpreting financial statements

√ providing tax- and financial-planning advice

√ preparing corporate and individual tax returns.

Qualifications

In Canada, anyone can call himself or herself an accountant. One can also adopt the title "public accountant" without any qualifications, experience, regulations, or accountability to a professional association. That is why you have to be careful when selecting the appropriate accountant for your needs. There are two main designations of qualified professional public accountants in Canada: chartered accountant (CA) and certified general accountant (CGA). Accountants with the above designations are governed by provincial statutes. The conduct, professional standards, training, qualifications, professional development, and discipline of these professionals are regulated by their respective institutes or associations. Rely on the advice of an accountant, therefore, only after you have satisfied yourself that the accountant meets the professional qualifications that you require for your real estate investment needs.

How to Find an Accountant

√ Often a banker, lawyer, or other business associate will be pleased to recommend an accountant who has expertise in real estate investment. Such referrals are valuable since these individuals are probably aware of your area of interest and would recommend an accountant only if they felt he or she was well qualified and had a good track record in assisting real estate investors.

√ The professional associations that govern CAs, and CGAs may be a source of leads. You can telephone or write the institute or association with a request for the names of three accountants who provide public accounting services to real estate investors within your geographic area. You can also check out the provincial association websites. Often an initial consultation is free of charge. Always find out before you confirm the appointment.

√ In the Yellow Pages, under the heading "Accountants," you will find listings under the categories "Chartered," "Registered," "Certified General," and "Management."

√ Search the Internet, beginning with a Google.ca search.

As with your lawyer, a good level of rapport and communication with your accountant will enhance the quality of advice and the effectiveness of your use of that advice. Openly discuss your concerns and questions with your accountant. You may from time to time wish to seek a second opinion on advice you have been given. If you are not satisfied with your accountant for any reason, you should promptly find another accountant who could better meet your needs.

Selecting a Mortgage Broker

Mortgage lending has become very complex, with constantly changing rates, terms, and conditions. Each lending institution has its own criteria that apply to potential borrowers. Some insist on a particular type of property as security, while others require a certain type of applicant. In this latter case, factors such as type of employment, job stability, income, and credit background are weighed. Lending institutions have a broad range of philosophies and policies on the issue of security and applicant qualifications in order for a lender to advance mortgage funds.

Other factors also affect mortgage approval. Availability or shortage of funds, past experience in a specific area, perceived resale market for a particular property, and the attitude of the lending committee (e.g., if it is a credit union) are all factors that could affect approval of a mortgage.

Mortgage brokers make it their business to know all the various plans and lending policies, as well as the lender's attitude on various aspects of mortgage security and covenants. A mortgage broker is in effect a matchmaker, attempting to introduce the appropriate lender to the purchaser.

Mortgage brokers have access to numerous sources of funds, including the following:

√ conventional lenders such as banks and trust companies

√ credit unions

√ Canada Mortgage and Housing Corporation (CMHC)

√ Genworth Financial Canada (a private insurer that insures high-ratio mortgages)

√ private pension funds

√ union pension funds

√ real estate syndication funds

√ foreign bank subsidiaries

√ insurance companies

√ private lenders.

The broker knows the lenders' criteria; the broker is therefore capable of matching each applicant and his or her property with the appropriate plan and lender. Alternatively, the broker can provide a series of mortgage plans from which the borrower may select the one that best suits his or her needs.

Mortgage brokers basically offer two types of services. They can arrange a simple mortgage that will get automatic approval in your particular circumstance, which saves you a lot of time searching. The broker generally receives a commission directly from the lender as a "finder" or "referral" fee. You don't pay any extra money or higher interest. Lenders do this because the mortgage market is so competitive.

Alternatively, they can arrange a more complex mortgage that would not be automatically approved. This takes more time, skill, and persuasion on the part of the broker to source out a lender or number of lenders who will provide the funds you need. For example, if you were unable to come up with a sufficient down payment, had a negative credit rating, were highly leveraged already, or fell short of income qualification, you would probably be turned down by a conventional lender such as a bank, credit union, or trust company.

If a mortgage broker succeeds in arranging your complex mortgage financing, given the above types of factors, you would pay a commission. The commission could be from 1% to 5% or more of the amount of the mortgage arranged, depending on the degree of difficulty, the urgency of the need for funds, etc.

How to Find a Mortgage Broker

To find a mortgage broker, look in the Yellow Pages of your telephone directory, check the Internet, or ask your real estate lawyer or your realtor. You can also obtain names of mortgage brokers from their provincial association, the Canadian Institute of Mortgage Brokers and Lenders (www.cimbl.ca).

Selecting a Home Inspector

One of the most important aspects of purchasing your vacation home or investment property is to know the true condition of the property before you finalize a purchase. It is a small expense for peace of mind. You don't want to have problems after you buy that will cost you money to repair. You could lose all your potential profit and put your investment at risk otherwise.

Make sure when you obtain an inspection that the person doing it is qualified and independent. Ask what association he or she belongs to, if any, and, if not, why not. One of the main associations in Canada is the Canadian Association of Home and Property Inspectors (CAHPI), with various provincial chapters. To become a member of CAHPI, an inspector must meet various professional and educational requirements, successfully complete a training course and write exams, and practise professionally for a trial period before being considered by the association. In addition, there are annual continuing education requirements to ensure that their industry knowledge is kept current.

You can check out the CAHPI website (www.cahpi.ca) to get names of members in your area. The terms "home inspector" and "building inspector" are frequently used interchangeably in terms of independent fee-for-service inspections. These services are different from municipal building inspectors, who approve various stages of a new home construction or renovation as staff of the local government.

Services Provided by a Home Inspector

A home inspector is an objective expert who examines the home and gives you a written opinion of its condition and, ideally, the approximate range of costs to repair the problems. Home inspectors look at the condition of all key parts of the building, such as the roof, siding, foundation, basement, flooring, walls, windows, doors, garage, drainage, electrical, heating, cooling, ventilation, plumbing, insulation, and so on. They should also look for signs of wood rot, mould, and insects.

The older the building, the more potential problems, but new buildings can have serious problems as well. If the new building is covered by a New Home Warranty Program, then you have some protection. However, that program does have some exclusions and limitations, and you don't need the hassle and expense of rectifying a problem. If a new home is not covered by the New Home Warranty Program, or is not a new property, you definitely want a home inspection; otherwise, you might have to pay to repair the problem if the builder refuses to do so or goes out of business. You can have an inspection done of a cottage, house, townhouse, or apartment condominium, or any type of residential type of building.

Older homes present a more challenging inspection process, for example, to check for aluminum wiring, asbestos, urea formaldehyde foam insulation (UFFI), lead-based paint, and termites or carpenter ants. Vacation homes that are exposed to the elements or in remote areas, need particular attention during the inspection.

Quite apart from avoiding expensive surprises, using a home inspector has another potential benefit. If the report shows problems with a quantifiable cost to rectify it, you could use that information to negotiate a reduction in the property's price to reflect the estimated cost of repair. You may not want to buy the home, even if problems can be rectified. At least the report gives an objective professional's opinion on the condition of the home to discuss with the vendor.

If you decide to make an offer to purchase prior to having a home inspection done, make sure you include a condition that specifies your offer is "subject to purchaser obtaining a home inspection satisfactory to the purchaser within X days of acceptance of the offer." This way it will be at your discretion whether you complete the deal or not. In addition to the need for a home inspection, you might also be able to obtain a "vendor's disclosure statement." Real estate boards in some provinces have prepared such a form for vendors to sign, disclosing any known problems with the home. As this is a voluntary program in some cases, ask for the reasons if a vendor refuses to complete the form. Have a professional home inspection done anyway, for obvious reasons. The owner may honestly not be aware of serious problems with the home if they are not visible or obvious.

How to Find a Home Inspector

It is important to obtain a qualified and independent inspector. Avoid someone who has a contractor business on the side and may hope to get the repair business from you. Their advice could be self-serving and biased. Apply the same selection criteria discussed earlier in this chapter. Look in the Yellow Pages of your telephone directory under "Building Inspection Services." Also search the Internet. Ask friends, relatives, neighbours, or your real estate agent for names of inspection companies they know and recommend. Call several inspectors in your area and interview them. Check with your local Better Business Bureau to see if there have been any complaints against the company that you are considering. Ask for references and contact the references.

Home inspection fees range from approximately $200 to $400 or more, depending on the expertise required and the nature of the inspection, the size of the home, its age and condition, your geographic area, the distance away, and other variables. It normally takes a minimum of three hours to do a thorough inspection.

Here are the questions that you should ask when deciding which inspection company to select:

√ What does the inspection include? Inspections should include the areas previously discussed under "Services Provided by a Building Inspector." Always make sure that you get a written report and ask for a sample of a report and what will be covered.

√ How much will it cost? Determine the fees up front.

√ How long will the inspection take?

√ Does the inspector encourage the client to attend the inspection? This is a valuable educational opportunity, since you will have a chance to see the problems first-hand. You will also learn various helpful maintenance tips. If an inspector refuses to have you attend the inspection, this should raise a red flag.

√ How long has the inspector been in the business as a home-inspection firm and what type of work was the inspector doing before inspecting homes?

√ Is the inspector specifically trained or experienced in residential construction?

√ What and where was the inspector's training? Does the inspector participate in continuing education programs to keep his or her expertise up to date?

√ Does the company offer to do any repairs or improvements based on its inspection? This might cause a conflict of interest.

√ Does the inspector carry errors and omission insurance? This means that if the inspector makes a mistake in the inspection and you have to pay to rectify the problem, the insurance will cover it. How much insurance does the inspector have and are there any restrictions or exceptions? Will the inspector confirm all that in writing before you make a decision to have the inspection done?

√ Does the inspector belong to an association that will investigate any consumer complaint? This is an important point and was covered earlier under "Qualifications."

Selecting an Insurance Broker

An insurance broker is not committed to any particular company and therefore can compare and contrast the different policies, coverage, and premiums from a wide range of companies in order to get you the type of insurance coverage you are looking for. Insurance brokers can also obtain a premium quotation for you and coverage availability from insurance company underwriters if the particular investment you have is unique or difficult to cover by other existing policies. Insurance brokers generally have a wide range of types of insurance available. Ensure that the broker is affiliated with a reputable firm.

When selecting an insurance broker, you should ask about the person's professional credentials, expertise, and experience. It is important to have confidence in the broker's background and skills.

Qualifications

Insurance agents are licensed and regulated by the provincial governments. Some agents are tied to a particular insurance company, and will sell only the insurance products offered by that company. However, it has become far more common for property or life insurance agents to operate as brokers and to deal with any number of insurance companies, although officially licensed by one company. If you want a broker for property insurance, make sure they are a member of the Insurance Brokers Association of Canada. If you want life or health insurance, make sure they are members of the Financial Advisors Association of Canada.

How to Find an Insurance Broker

There are several ways to find an insurance broker:

√   Look in the Yellow Pages under "insurance brokers."

√   Ask your accountant, lawyer, business associates, and friends for a recommendation.

√   Ask your business, trade, or professional association whom they would recommend.

√   Search the Internet.

√   Check with the Insurance Brokers Association of Canada (www.ibac.ca) for names of members in your area.

√   Check with the Financial Advisors Association of Canada (www.advocis. ca) for names of members in your area.

Choose an agent you can trust, one who will take the time to listen to you and understand your needs. Ask the agent how long he or she has been in the business, and consider asking for references or a recommendation from one of the agent's other clients.

You could be interested in obtaining two insurance brokers, one for your property protection needs, and the other for life insurance (e.g., term life insurance to cover any mortgage, or to pay off any anticipated capital gains taxes on the property on your death, in terms of a deemed disposition of that asset). There are strategic tax- and estate-planning options available to minimize or eliminate the tax hit, which are discussed in the relevant chapters of this book.

Refer to the Appendix for professional association contact information under Helpful Websites.

PART III

Show Me the Money

6
Mortgages and Other Creative Financing Options

This chapter will help you find the right mortgage for your recreational property needs, in the amount you want, at the best interest rate and terms, and show you how to save money in the process. You will also learn about the types of mortgages, the factors that impact on interest rates, and some alternative creative financing options, such as using your RRSP or business to lend yourself money for your recreational property. It also covers the protections and cautions to be aware of, if borrowing money from friends or family for your real estate purposes.

This chapter is just an overview. For a comprehensive discussion on all aspects of mortgages and home financing, please refer to my book *Mortgages Made Easy*.

Common Types of Mortgages

There are several varieties of mortgages available from banks, credit unions, trust companies, mortgage companies, private lenders, government, and the vendor. Although most homeowners obtain financing through a conventional mortgage, it is helpful to be aware of other alternatives. Later in this chapter, I will discuss creative ways of using your RRSP or business to fund your recreational property.

Conventional Mortgage

The conventional mortgage is the most common type of financing for residential property. It is fairly standard in its terms and conditions, although there can be variations. In this type of mortgage, the loan cannot exceed 75% of the appraised value or purchase price of the property, whichever is the lesser of the two. This requirement is governed by law. The purchaser is responsible for raising the other 25% of the funds necessary, either through a down payment or through other means such as a second mortgage or vendor take-back mortgage. Conventional mortgages are available through most financial institutions, including banks, trust companies, and credit unions. In most cases these mortgages do not have to be insured, but occasionally a lender may require it. For example, if the property is older or is smaller than is normally required by the policy of the lender, or if it is located in a remote or rundown area, then the mortgage may be required to be insured with the Canada Mortgage and Housing Corporation (CMHC) or Genworth Financial Canada. CMHC is a federal Crown corporation, whereas Genworth is a private corporation.

High-ratio/Insured Mortgage

If you are unable to raise the necessary 25% funding to complete the purchase of the home, then a high-ratio mortgage may be available to you. This is a conventional mortgage which exceeds the 75% limit referred to earlier. By law, these mortgages must be insured, and they are available only through approved lenders that are accepted by CMHC or Genworth Financial. CMHC has specific guidelines for qualifying, but the administration is done through the bank or credit union.

High-ratio mortgages are available for up to 90% of the purchase price or of the appraisal, whichever is the lower, and in some cases 95%. The percentage for which you would be eligible depends on various circumstances. Where a borrower is seeking a high-ratio mortgage for a recreational property, there could be other conditions the borrower must meet, such as a guarantee that the property is for personal use and not for investment, minimum size of the home, location, etc. Obtain further information from your realtor, banker, or mortgage holder, or CMHC or Genworth Financial Canada directly.

Collateral Mortgage

In a collateral mortgage the mortgage security is secondary, or collateral, to some other main form of security taken by the lender. This main security may take the form of a promissory note, personal guarantee, or line of credit. A collateral mortgage is therefore a backup protection of the loan which is filed against the property. The payment requirements on the loan are covered in the promissory note, and once the promissory note has been paid off in full, the collateral mortgage will automatically be paid off. You would then be entitled to have the collateral mortgage discharged from the title of the property.

One of the main differences between a collateral mortgage and a conventional mortgage is that a conventional mortgage can be assumed, whereas a collateral mortgage, of course, cannot be, as it is subject to some other form of security between the parties. Otherwise, the terms of the collateral mortgage could be very similar to the debt of a conventional mortgage. The money borrowed on a collateral mortgage could be used to buy your recreational property, or do repairs to it.

Construction Mortgage

If you are building your vacation house, the lender may approve a mortgage for construction purposes but will advance mortgage draws based on the various stages of construction (e.g., foundation, framing, roofing, etc.). There could be three or more stages, depending on the nature of the construction and the policy of the lender. Once the building has reached substantial completion and received an occupancy permit, it is normally at that time that the construction mortgage is discharged, and replaced with a conventional mortgage.

How the Terms of the Mortgage Are Connected to the Interest Rate

The interest rate is affected by such factors as:

√ The amortization period (that is, the length of time over which the mortgage is paid out in full—usually from 20 to 35+ years). The longer the amortization period, the lower the rate, in most cases.

√ Whether the mortgage is insured by CMHC or Genworth Financial Canada (if there is a lower risk, there is a lower rate).

√ The length of the term before the mortgage is due for payment or renegotiation (e.g., six months, five years, or longer). Generally speaking, the longer the term, the more the risk of uncertainty about interest rates for the lender over that extended period; therefore, the rate is higher, as a protective buffer. This is not always the case, however.

√ Whether the mortgage is open or closed. If it is open, it can be paid at any time before the end of the term without penalty. If closed, it cannot be repaid, or can only be repaid with a penalty (usually three months' interest or the interest differential for the balance of the term, whichever is greater). Open mortgages have higher interest rates; closed mortgages have lower interest rates.

√ Whether the interest rate is calculated and compounded annually, semi-annually, or monthly. The more frequent the interest calculation and compounding, the higher the effective rate of interest that you will be paying.

√   The frequency of your payment schedule (e.g., weekly, bimonthly, monthly, etc.). The more frequent the payment, the greater your savings on interest.

Recreational Property Interest Rates Might Vary

After the lender has appraised the property you're interested in, assessed the type of location and the resale potential of the property, and determined the amount of equity the borrower has, the lender will set the mortgage rate. Depending on where the recreational property is located, and whether you intend to use it personally and exclusively, or rent it out strictly as an investment, it might have a competitive rate or higher rates. For example, if it is rural property that is serviced by a volunteer fire department, the risk is higher that a fire would be catastrophic and consequently the rates would be higher. Frequently, in this type of situation, the lender will require higher owner equity, to lessen the lender's exposure.

Conversely, if the place you are buying is a house or condo in an economically stable resort or vacation community, you would probably obtain a competitive rate.

But you have other options. For example, depending on how much equity you have in your principal residence, you could place a mortgage on that residence as well as the recreational property for added security to the lender, or borrow all the money required using your principal residence as security. There are pros and cons of the various options available.

Be Aware that Recreational Properties Are Eligible for High-Ratio Insurance

Over the past few years, Canada Mortgage and Housing Corporation (CMHC) has modified its lending criteria to enable owners of second properties in recreational areas to be eligible for insurance coverage on high-ratio (over 75% financing) mortgages. This is due to its analysis of the marketplace, customer demand, and analysis of lifestyle trends that show a significant part of the population wants to purchase recreational property. The private-sector high-ratio insurance company, Genworth Financial Canada, has recreational property coverage that is similar to CMHC.

Know the Mortgage Hierarchy

If you need to borrow from more than one institution in order to make up your purchase price, you need to know how the "mortgage hierarchy" works. Basically, the security of the mortgage is greater depending on its date of registration relative to any other mortgages on the property. A mortgage that is registered first is referred to as a first mortgage, a mortgage that is registered second in line is referred to as a second mortgage, and so on. In the event that the borrower defaults on a mortgage and the property must be sold, the first mortgage gets paid out first from the proceeds, followed by the second, etc. Therefore, the lower the mortgage ranks in terms of priority, the higher the risk to the lender if there is a shortfall on the sale price.

There is a direct relationship between risk and interest rate. A first mortgage could be at 6%, a second at 8%, and a third at 10%. How much equity the owner has is also a factor. If the owner has lots of equity, no matter how many mortgages on the property, the lower the risk to the last lender of losing money on a forced sale.

How Getting a Pre-approved Mortgage Can Help You

You have probably heard about pre-approved mortgages. This concept is fairly popular with most conventional lending institutions and credit unions, and through mortgage brokers and online mortgage companies. The purpose is to commit to you in writing the precise amount of money that you can rely on for mortgage purposes when you are out searching to buy a home (or recreational property) and negotiating a purchase. For example, you might qualify for a $200,000 mortgage with an interest rate that would be guaranteed for 60, 75, 90 or 120 days, depending on the market conditions. If the prevailing rate goes up in the meantime, you are protected. If it goes down, you get the lower rate.

You should definitely get a pre-approved mortgage. It will provide a reality check of what you can really afford, plus provide you with negotiating leverage when submitting an offer, as you don't need to put a "subject to mortgage approval" condition in the offer.

Be aware, though, that even though you know you have approval for the funds, the lender always reserves the right to be satisfied that the value of the property is appraised at what you are offering for it. This is often done through an appraisal that the lender will pay for. This gives the lender some assurance that the property is indeed a suitable form of security for the money they are lending you. In most cases, this is just a formality, and few mortgages are refused following appraisal.

Using a Mortgage Broker

As discussed in the previous chapter, mortgage lending has become very complex. Mortgage brokers make it their business to know all the various plans and lending policies, and which lenders are most likely to be aggressive in their lending policies. Their services can be very helpful when you're trying to finance the purchase of a recreational property. Recall that mortgage brokers have access to numerous sources of funds, including conventional lenders such as banks and credit unions, as well as:

√   CMHC

√   private pension funds

√   union pension funds

√   real estate syndication funds

√   foreign bank subsidiaries

√   insurance companies

√   private lenders.

Refer to Chapter 5: Selecting Your Advisors for a discussion of how to find a mortgage broker.

Using Your RRSP to Invest in Your Own Recreational Property Mortgage

There are two options that could be available to fund your recreational property through your RRSP.

Making Your RRSP Payments Pay Down Your Mortgage

Let's say that you want to obtain a $100,000 mortgage and you contribute approximately $10,000 each year into your RRSP. If you deal with a lender who offers this option, you would take out the mortgage with that lender and each time you make your RRSP contribution, the lender will use these funds to purchase $10,000 of your mortgage. When you make your monthly mortgage payments, then, part of the interest you are paying on your mortgage will go into your RRSP and part to the lender. The next time you make a contribution to your RRSP, more of your mortgage will be purchased by your RRSP. Eventually, it is possible that your entire mortgage will be owned by your RRSP. From that point on, you would be making payments directly to your RRSP, in other words to yourself, rather than the lender. The set-up and administrative fees charged by a lender for this plan are fairly nominal.

Depending on the interest rates, in this hypothetical example, you could own your own mortgage within seven years or less. The reason is that the interest in your RRSP is compounding tax-free every year, thereby permitting more money to be available to pay off the mortgage.

In most cases, there is a stipulation that the mortgage be insured by CMHC or Genworth, and that all the other conditions of the plan are complied with.

Using a Self-directed RRSP to Fund Your Mortgage

Another option is simply to use funds from your existing RRSP by means of a self-directed RRSP that you would set up. You can then fund your recreational property purchase by means of a mortgage held by your RRSP, either by means of a first mortgage if you have sufficient funds, or by means of a second mortgage if you are borrowing most of the first mortgage from a conventional lender. There are various conditions required for this type of strategy.

As in any unique plan, there are advantages and limitations. It is not for everyone. Make sure you comparison shop, receive answers to all your questions, obtain detailed written information to review, and obtain professional advice from your tax accountant.

Lending Money for Your Recreational Property Mortgage from Your Own Business

If you have a small business that you control, and retained earnings that you have paid business tax on sitting in your business bank account, you might wish to consider lending yourself money for the purpose of a housing loan for your recreational property. Of course, you need to get professional tax advice on the strategy of having your business provide a loan for the amount of your needs. This loan would be documented in writing, like any other loan your business would do, with an interest rate factor, and structured to comply with CRA regulations for this type of non-arm's-length loan. Normally Canada Revenue Agency (CRA) permits a company to provide a shareholder loan for housing purposes, with an interest rate that is competitive when the loan is set. In a low-interest-rate environment, this rate could be very modest.

You don't need to actually pay interest to your company personally, but your company has to annually account for the amount of interest as income. There is a time frame within which the housing loan needs to be paid back in full. Each year the company needs to show a minimum of 5% of the principal loan amount as being paid back, with the money offset against any payment that your company owes you as a shareholder, whether by means of salary or dividends.

One of the attractive features of this option is that you get the full amount of the funds immediately, and only have to pay back a minimum amount each year against earnings. Normally, if you paid out the full amount of the funds in the year of receipt, you would pay tax on them, which would of course result in a larger tax hit. By spreading the amount deemed to have been received yearly, over 20 years, for example, you will be in a lower marginal tax rate category.

This option is worth considering if you anticipate having difficulty getting funding from conventional lenders for the type of recreational property you had in mind for whatever reason (for example, you are overextended financially and don't comply with CMHC high-ratio mortgage insurance criteria for recreational property, etc.). Alternatively, maybe you would need to make a down payment of 50% of the purchase price, and could use this type of business financing option for that purpose.

"Love Money" Financing: Borrowing from Family or Friends

Have you considered borrowing or obtaining money from people you know best, who are closest to you, people who believe in you, and whose most natural inclination is to want to help you be happy and successful? This type of financing is frequently referred to as "love money."

Love-money financing, although a seemingly attractive option for some borrowers, is not without its perils. It is most important to consider all the implications for you and your family and friends before approaching them for investment monies or loans, especially for vacation rental real estate investment. It is a cruel fact of life that relationships are almost always damaged when money is lost. Even when the prospective investor or lender has confirmed in advance that he or she can afford to lose the money, and is willing to take the risk of doing so, when it actually happens it is quite another thing.

In a complex, frenetic, and impersonal world, our family and friends are the safe refuge with whom we can seek comfort, solace, and sanity. You may feel extremely confident and enthusiastic about your vacation real estate investment potential, but go slowly and thoughtfully before bringing your family and closest friends into your investment plans. How will you feel if you let them down? Or if permanent estrangement occurs, or you cause them serious financial hardship and stress in a negative investment outcome? While people can forgive, few will ever forget. Parents are generally the most forgiving of financial loss, while friends tend to be the least.

If you are determined to access financing from family and friends, temper the outcome in a worst-case scenario. You should provide security for the loan and always put the terms of repayment in writing and give a promissory note. It shows good faith, responsibility, and concern. Security could be in the form of collateral security (mortgage) on your vacation rental investment property. By securing the loan, your family or friends would be secured creditors and would be paid off from the sale of the property before any unsecured or general creditors.

CHAPTER 7

Negotiating the Best Deal

Understanding the art and science of negotiating will be important for you if you want to make money in real estate. Whether you are buying recreational real estate for personal pleasure or investment rental revenue, you will benefit from the practical tips and insights explained in this chapter.

Most interactions with people—personnel, professionals, business associates, suppliers—involve some dynamics of the negotiation process. If you are attempting to sell, persuade, convince, or influence another person's thinking or feelings to accord with your own wants and needs, you are using negotiating skills. If, at the same time, you have defined and satisfied the other person's needs, you have attained an optimal or "win-win" type of negotiation. This is not always possible, and in real estate negotiations you may not satisfy the seller's or buyer's needs, as his or her needs and expectations may be unrealistic in the circumstances.

Different players in the real estate market frequently use psychological negotiating games and techniques. You will learn some of the key concepts. This will help you save more money and therefore make more money on any type of real estate purchase or sale. You will learn how to obtain the best price and terms, how to buy low and sell high.

This chapter will cover the necessary steps to follow to prepare for real estate negotiation, understanding the reasons why the property might be for sale, and what to put in the offer.

Preparing for Real Estate Negotiation

There are various preliminary steps you should go through to maximize your success before any offer is made:

√ Determine the amount of mortgage that you are entitled to, the maximum price that you are prepared to pay, and the terms that you would prefer. If possible, approach your property search, and any eventual negotiations, with pre-approved financing.

√ Have alternative properties that you find attractive so that you have fallbacks.

√ Have your realtor thoroughly check out the property. The services a realtor can offer in this regard were covered in Chapter 5: Selecting Your Advisors. Find out such factors as how long it has been for sale, why it is for sale, how the vendor determined the asking price, recent market comparables in the area, and any vendor deadline pressure. The following section in this chapter discusses in more detail why a property might be for sale.

√ Be thoroughly prepared with all your financial information at hand.

√ Stick to your purchase or investment plan so that you don't offer more than you can reasonably expect to finance, or buy a type of property or in a location outside your comfort zone or original plan.

√ Ideally, use a realtor as a negotiating buffer between you and the vendor.

√ Obtain legal and tax advice on the implications of your purchase.

√ Don't get emotionally involved with the property. Be as objective and realistic as possible; otherwise it could taint your judgment.

√ Train yourself to appear patient and unemotional to the vendor or vendor's agent. Appearing anxious, nervous, or extremely excited about the property will work against you.

√ To increase your bargaining leverage, look for negative features of the property in advance. All properties can be found to have something negative. For example, you could be looking at a cottage on a large lot. Some people would like a large lot. However, others would look at it from a negative perspective in terms of maintenance (cutting grass) and cost (high property taxes). Write down a list of the positive and negative features, and be prepared to mention the negatives in your dealings with the vendor or vendor's agent.

√ Establish a relationship with a building inspector and contractor in advance; you might need their services on short notice if there is a particularly attractive property on which you want to make an offer. Especially in a competitive situation, where there are other bidders, you'll want to have an inspection done quickly, and discuss the costs of repairs or renovations with your contractor so that you can put together a realistic offer.

Typical Reasons Why Recreational Properties Are Put up for Sale

It is important to determine the owner's real motivation for selling the property. This will assist you in knowing how to negotiate in terms of your offer price and terms and general strategies. The motivation for sale could be a positive or negative one. If the vendor is selling in a buyer's market, which is clearly disadvantageous in terms of the negotiating climate and eventual sale price, be particularly thorough in finding out why the vendor is selling at that time.

Some of the most common reasons for sale of a recreational property include the following:

- √ Separation or divorce
- √ Death of owner or co-owner
- √ Principal wage earner's loss of job, or loss of job for one wage earner in a situation where two wage earners are necessary to pay for operating a second home
- √ Falling-out in family
- √ Falling out with friends who co-own the property
- √ If two or more joint owners, one has to sell for health or financial reasons, and the other owners cannot afford to buy out his or her equity interest because the property value has increased substantially since the property was initially purchased
- √ Job relocation
- √ Ill health of owners
- √ Retirement of owners and therefore relocation, downsizing, or desire to take some of the equity out of the property for retirement purposes
- √ Owner has lost money in a business or other investment venture and needs to sell the property to pay off the debt
- √ Owner has not made payments on the mortgage due to personal or financial problems, so the lender has started court proceedings
- √ Owner wants to sell in a seller's market
- √ Owner is concerned that the market is changing and could become a buyer's market
- √ Owner is testing the market to see what the market will pay without making any serious attempt to sell

√ Children of owner have moved away and no longer will be using the
vacation home, or have their own vacation homes, or have lost interest

√ Owner wants to trade up to a nicer vacation home or better
neighbourhood

√ Owner knows of problems with the recreational property that would
detract from a sale (e.g., water damage from flooding, wood rot,
insect infestation, settling, substantial repairs or renovations needed,
vandalism, noisy neighbours, pollution in an adjacent lake or stream,
taxes being increased substantially, wild animals nearby that pose a
safety risk to small children or pets).

Typical Reasons Why Vacation Investment Properties Are Put Up for Sale

There are many reasons why a vacation investment property could be listed for
sale. It does not necessarily mean the property has serious problems or is a bad
investment. Possibly the property is poorly managed, poorly maintained, or has
excessive vacancies. In many cases, an astute investor could turn the property
into an attractive investment by identifying the exact problems and opportunities, devising a plan for turnaround, and buying at below-market value. Explore
to find out the real reasons why the property is for sale.

Here are a few of the common reasons for sale:

Inexperienced Owner: Possibly the owner was a first-time investor who
bought beyond his or her skills, resources, and comfort zone, and feels intimi-
dated by the responsibilities, time, and risk involved. The owner may now have
changed his or her mind and wish to sell due to the associated personal stress.

Partnership Disputes: Many business partnerships at some point break
up or have conflict. Maybe the property is for sale due to unresolved disputes.
Another possibility is that some investors needed to get out for financial reasons or changed investment goals; others wanted to keep the property for a
long-term hold or until the market became more attractive, and therefore the
partnership has split up, triggering the sale.

Tax Benefits: Maybe the owner has depreciated the building as much as
possible and wants to sell because the land value has increased substantially.
The owner has capital losses from other investments that went sour, and wants
to off-set those against a substantial capital gain on the property sale.

Settling of an Estate: If the owner of the property has died, the executor of
the estate may want to settle the estate reasonably quickly. The property could
therefore be priced at fair market value or below in order to effect a quick sale.

Run-down Properties: Due to management or financial difficulties, the property could visibly deteriorate, causing the owner to want to sell. This could be because the owner is attempting to self-manage, but lacks the skills, knowledge, or personality to do it profitably. Maybe the owner has hired the cheapest management firm and they do the least amount possible. If an owner lives outside the city, province, or country, possibly the management company is indifferent and allows the property to deteriorate. Another reason for poor management is that the owner is draining the revenue property by taking out too much money personally. This could result in a shortfall of the revenue required to meet necessary expenses.

Expensive Management: Maybe the vacation property is a condo in a resort community that requires the owner to put the condo in a rental pool for the majority of the time, with a designated property management company charging 40% or more in rental commissions. The numbers may not work for the investor.

Excessive Vacancies: If a condo or cottage or chalet suffers from ongoing short-term rental vacancies, it could be because the building is run-down or has poor management, there is more attractive or better priced accommodation in the same area, or the rental rates are too high. Whatever the cause, the vacancy situation is probably causing serious cash-flow problems for the owner, especially if property taxes and expenses have gone up.

Zoning Restrictions for Nightly Rentals: Possibly the owner bought a condo or house on the assumption that it could be rented out to tourists for nightly, weekly or short-term accommodation, then found that the condo management company does not permit these types of rentals. The buyer had not done their due diligence in this scenario. Possibly the local municipality could have zoning restrictions that restrict rentals of residential properties, such as houses or condos, to fewer than 28 consecutive days. The owner is therefore not able to make ends meet, since there might be little market demand for "long-term rentals" of 28 days or more.

Financing Problems: For various reasons the owner could have, or anticipate having, difficulty refinancing the property.

Distress Sale: This means that the owner is forced to sell, generally due to legal action by the mortgage company in the form of a court order for sale or foreclosure litigation. The reason for legal action would be due to breach of the payment terms or other conditions of the mortgage by the owner. The practical effect is that the lender requires that the property be sold. Due to the circumstances of sale, a buyer might be able to pick up the property for less than fair market value. It really depends on the circumstances, market demand, nature of the price and terms, and other factors.

   In practical terms in Canada, most properties that are forced sales by lenders either have to be court-approved sales or otherwise have to pass the scrutiny of fairness if the lender sells it. Otherwise, the owner could later take the lender to court, alleging that the sale price did not reflect fair market value. In other words, the court or lender wants to make sure that they have received top price for the property in the circumstances and in the market at that time.

   Personal Problems of Owner: The owner could be having personal, marital, health, employment, or financial problems. This could result in the owner wanting to sell the investment property.

   Change in Property Tax Classification: The owner could have originally bought a condo in a resort area that was classified for tax assessments as residential. Property taxes were therefore lower than commercial assessments. Subsequently, the local or provincial property tax assessment authorities re-classified the condo as commercial, and taxes increased substantially, making the investment unviable or unattractive, so the condo owner wants to sell. The reason for this re-classification could have been because the condo was part of a hotel or met other criteria established to determine it should be assessed as commercial.

   Change in Investment Strategies of Owner: The owner could have revised his or her personal investment strategies and goals, and decided to change the nature of the real estate investment or get out of real estate altogether.

   More Attractive Investment: The owner may be interested in purchasing a different real estate investment property that is a more attractive investment package in every respect.

   Seller's Market: Possibly the market is an attractive one for selling revenue property and there is more demand than supply, hence sale prices have gone up. The owner could decide to take advantage of the increased market activity.

   Concern That a Downturn Might Be Coming: The owner could foresee that the real estate cycle could soon be taking a downturn, and that property values could drop. This concern could result in the property being listed for sale.

Negotiating Tips and Techniques

After you have gone through the preparation steps, the next negotiating stage is the presentation of your offer to the vendor. Here are some guidelines to consider about various aspects of your offer. Some of these examples relate to buying a vacation rental property.

Name of Purchaser: Depending on the nature of your purchase, you may want to put your name and the words "or assignee" in the offer if it is your intent to sign over the agreement to someone else. However, you need to get legal advice on this issue as there could be legal implications as to who actually is the purchaser. Alternatively, if you are purchasing an investment with a degree of risk, you may want to incorporate a company and put the offer in the corporate name. If you back out of the deal before closing, your company could be sued for breach of contract and damages (losses) by the vendor, but not you personally. Presumably your new company does not have any assets at that stage. You would need experienced legal advice on these matters in advance.

Deposit: Put down the smallest possible deposit. You don't want to tie up any more money than you have to. This also protects you if you back out prior to closing, since your deposit funds could be at risk of being kept by the vendor. Whatever deposit money you put down, never pay it directly to the vendor. Always have it paid to a realtor's or lawyer's trust account. Make sure you write in the offer that your deposit funds are to accrue interest to your credit, pending the closing date.

Price: Attempt to offer the lowest possible price the market and circumstances allow. Always start with your ideal price and terms. You never know what the vendor will find to be acceptable or not, so don't anticipate disfavour. Think positively. If the vendor counter-offers, you may want to extract concessions from the vendor due to the variation of your original offer. You should always have a property inspection done as a condition before you commit yourself, whether you are buying a house or a condo. The report should state if there are problems, and which are "must do," "should do," and "might want to do" priorities. Those in the first two categories should have an estimate of repair costs, if possible. You could then use this objective third-party inspection report as the basis for negotiating further price concessions. Otherwise, to be realistic about what you are actually paying for the vacation property, you will have to add the cost of repairs to the purchase price.

In addition, if you are buying a rental vacation home, ask to see all the financial statements for the past three to five years to see the pattern. If there is a declining net revenue, it could be because there are increasing expenses, e.g., increased property taxes, and/or reduced revenue, e.g., rental competition and price-cutting. This could make the purchase of the property unattractive to you for rental purposes. It would also give you leverage to attempt to negotiate a discounted price.

Closing Date: Depending on your objectives, you may want to have a long closing date such as three or four months. Maybe you will be receiving funds by then. Maybe the market will have gone up in an escalating market, and you would be entitled to a higher mortgage on closing.

Financing Terms: You may want to ask the vendor for vendor take-back financing for a first or second mortgage. Depending on your objectives, you may want to ask for a long-term open mortgage (say, five years) with an attractive interest rate, and assumable without qualifications. This latter provision would make it easier for resale. The vendor may be willing to provide such favourable terms, especially if the market is slow and he or she is anxious to sell.

Conditions: Conditions are sometimes referred to as "subject" clauses. You should include as many conditional clauses as you feel are appropriate for your needs, such as subject to financing or satisfactory building inspection. Also include any warranty confirmations from vendor. Examples may include the vendor's assertion that "the furnace is functioning properly and still covered under a manufacturer's warranty" or "the condo was built under the New Home Warranty Program," if such a program exists in your province. Refer to Chapter 9: Legal Issues and Strategies for more "subject clause" examples.

CHAPTER 8

Investing for Yourself or with Others

There are lots of good reasons to buy recreational property: for many people, relaxing by the water or having a quiet escape near a great golf course is reason enough. For others, buying recreational property is part of an investment strategy. For yet another group, that investment strategy will involve buying recreational property with others.

If you're among either of the latter groups, you need to have clearly defined goals and objectives, and a plan for achieving them, in order to attain the maximum financial benefit with a minimum of risk. There are various steps in the process of determining your plan: completing a self-assessment, determining your current financial needs, assessing your future personal and financial needs, and planning your investment strategies. And if you are considering being part of a group investment, you should understand the key factors and cautions to consider when investing with others, which this chapter will outline for you.

If you would like a more detailed discussion, refer to my books *Making Money in Real Estate,* 2nd edition and *Real Estate Investing For Canadians For Dummies.* Also refer to the website www.homebuyer.ca.

Where to Begin

Personal Self-Assessment of Skills and Attributes

Your success in real estate investment has a lot to do with the qualities you bring to the process. It is important to know your strengths and weaknesses so that you can capitalize on your strengths and compensate for your weaknesses. This self-assessment is particularly important if you are considering group investments or owning several properties.

Your self-assessment will identify your areas of interest as well as skills, attributes, and talents that are relevant to the business of real estate investing. What do these categories mean? A skill is a degree of specific expertise acquired through experience or training, e.g., website design. An attribute relates to your personality and character, e.g., outgoing or reserved, flexible or rigid, etc. Talents refer to a combination or mix of talents and attributes that make for a particular strength in a given area.

To assess your suitability for a particular type of investment, determine what is necessary for the investment to be successful one, and seeing if it is a good fit for your personal style and objectives. For example: do you feel stressed by the concept of debt or do you take it in stride? How does your partner (relationship partner) feel about debt or the type of investment you are considering? Do you have a high or low risk tolerance? Do you work well with others in a team approach, or are you very independent? Do you have good research, marketing, sales, negotiating, management, or financial skills, or do you lack confidence or expertise in those areas? What are your personal investment goals, needs, and wants?

Determine Your Current Financial Status and Needs

This means doing a personal cost of living budget and personal net worth statement. Your personal cost of living budget should project at least six months ahead, and have columns for projected expenses, and actual expenses, so that you have a reality check. Monitor it monthly to see how accurate your projections are. Your personal net worth statement is simply a list at a given period of your assets, minus your liabilities.

Determine Your Future Personal and Financial Needs

This is an essential step, as it gives you an idea of the degree of risk you are prepared to take. It will also clarify your time commitment, financial involvement, and realistic short-, medium-, and long-term goals and objectives. For example, maybe you want to be financially independent, primarily through real estate investment, in 10 or 15 years.

Plan Your Investment Strategies

Take the time to develop your investment program thoroughly. Like any plan, you will need to monitor and possibly modify it regularly due to changing circumstances. The safest way to make money in real estate is through prudent and cautious investment.

Key Investment Strategies to Consider

Here are some of the key vacation real estate investment strategies to consider:

√ Thoroughly research the market before making any decision. Consider at least three potential investment opportunities, if possible.

√ Give yourself a realistic time frame to achieve your investment objectives. For example, normal real estate cycles are five to eight years and in some cases 10 to 12 years.

√ Buy specific types of vacation revenue property that are in demand and are easy to maintain and/or manage, and rent.

√ Attempt to make a low down payment (for example, 5% to 10%) unless, of course, you can only obtain a maximum of 75% financing. If you can make a purchase with a low down payment, this frees up your available cash for the purchase of additional properties, if that is part of your plan. Refer to Chapter 6: Mortgages and Other Creative Financing Options.

√ Strive to have a break-even cash flow. In other words, try to avoid debt servicing the property because of a shortfall of rental income over expenses. Make sure you cover all expenses from cash flow such as mortgage payments, taxes, property management, condominium fees, insurance, repairs and maintenance, and allowance for vacancies.

√ Ensure that you have competent property management, whether you do it yourself or hire an expert. Refer to Chapter 16: Professional or Owner-Direct Rental Management.

√ Rely on carefully selected professionals—including a lawyer, accountant, building inspector, appraiser, contractor, realtor, property manager—for peace of mind, enhanced revenue potential, reduced risk, and realistic budgetary projections.

√ Never pay more than fair market value unless there are other collateral benefits to you that you have identified. Refer to Chapter 7: Negotiating the Best Deal.

√ Use all the tax-planning strategies available to you after receiving expert tax advice. These options are explained in Chapter 10: Tax Issues and Strategies.

√ Use all the estate-planning strategies available to you after receiving expert tax and legal advice. There options are explained in Chapter 13: Estate Planning Issues and Strategies.

√   Use all the legal-planning strategies available to you after receiving legal advice. These options are explained in Chapter 9: Legal Issues and Strategies.

√   Keep rents at market maximums and manage expenses to keep at market minimum.

√   Buy when no one else is buying and sell when everyone else is buying. This is the so-called contrarian view of investment, which is the opposite of conventional wisdom.

√   Always view and inspect property before you buy. Verify all financial information. Obtain your advisors' guidance.

√   Have a minimum three-month contingency reserve fund for unexpected expenses (repairs) or a reduction in cash flow (vacancies).

√   As a general rule of thumb, buy vacation investment properties within four hours' driving distance of where you live, so you can easily monitor your investment. There are exceptions to this general principle, of course.

Investing with Others

Most people prefer to make real estate investments on their own. Occasionally, however, people may choose to buy in a group. When they do, they should be aware of the pros and cons. On the one hand, investing with a group may provide mutual support, shared (and therefore reduced) risk, pooled skills and expertise, greater investment opportunities, shared responsibility and time, and collective energy, synergy, and momentum. These factors can be reassuring, especially for beginning investors.

On the other hand, if you do not select your investment group or investment wisely, it could be a financial and emotional nightmare. The key is to know the benefits and limitations of the various group investment options and the pitfalls to avoid. Never go into a real estate purchase with others without obtaining prior professional advice from your lawyer and accountant. Always make sure that you have a written agreement in advance.

Factors to Consider When Buying Real Estate with Others

It is important to remember that many investment partnerships don't work out. The statistical odds, therefore, are very high that any real estate group relationship in which you are involved may not survive. There are lots of reasons why the dynamics of relationships can cause potential conflict, for example, differences in investment philosophy, different or changing priorities or goals or objectives, personality conflicts, unrealistic expectations, or ego or control issues.

By cautiously assessing the individuals who will make up a potential group, you can minimize the risk immensely. Here are some key factors to consider.

Goals and Objectives

Ensure that your goals and objectives are consistent with those of the rest of the group. For example, some members may want a long-term investment (e.g., five years) with positive cash flow from rents; others may want a medium-term investment (e.g., three years) and be prepared to subsidize the negative cash flow in the hope that the property value will appreciate due to rezoning or subdivision potential; still others may want to flip the property within a few months of purchase because of its desirability or because of a rapid increase in property values in a hot market.

Expertise

You've done a self-assessment and you know what skills you can bring to an investment partnership. If your partners are friends and relatives, you probably have a clear idea about the skills they bring to the table. But if you are joining an investment group of strangers or people you know only casually, it is important to clarify exactly what, if any, skills they will bring to the group investment. It may not matter if they are silent investors (sometimes called passive investors)—that is, if the investors are just putting their money in and are not actively involved.

If they are active investors and it is a small group, you need to determine what skills they will contribute and in what form. If you are buying into an investment group that will be totally managed by one of the group members, make sure you know the person's credentials and track record. Before you enter into any investment relationship, make sure you put the nature of the relationship and dispute-resolution procedures in writing, and have your own lawyer approve the document to protect your interests. If you are going to rely on someone else to manage or control your investment, it would be prudent for you to be careful and cautious.

Compatibility

Look at the other people in your investment group. Are there similarities in personality, age, financial position, and investment objectives? What do the other group members think about issues such as control, management, and liability? What contributions, if any, are the other people making to the success of the investment? If the people in the group have diversified skills, this could save the group money and make the investment more secure. In general, people you know are safer than people you don't know. Ego, power, greed, arrogance, and unrealistic expectations are common causes of group stress or disintegration. You can't afford the risk, so be selective with your investment partners.

Management

How will the group investment be managed? Will it be managed by a professional management company, a resident manager, a group of investors, one of the investors, or the original promoter? How confident do you feel about the issue of management? What are the management fees? Are they reasonable under the circumstances? Can you select the property management company, or are you required to deal with the developer's or project's selected management company?

Liquidity

Basically, this means how easily and quickly you can get your money out of the investment. Your financial resources and needs will determine your liquidity needs. If you need to get your investment capital back quickly, for example, in just a few months, then you probably won't want a long-term investment. If you are buying shares in a real estate investment on the public stock exchange, you may have liquidity, but not necessarily at an attractive price. You should hesitate before making any investment if you would suffer by having your money tied up or put at risk. You should not invest money you cannot afford to lose. You therefore should be cautious about investing retirement money or contingency reserve funds, especially if you need immediate liquidity.

In practical terms, most investments are tied up for the duration of the deal—however long that deal may be, as agreed upon in the investment group's goals and objectives. Consider having a buy-out clause in the investment group agreement. Such clauses allow for any of the investors to be bought out by the others within a fixed period. Normally, though, the buy-out would be at a discounted price, to discourage investors from leaving the group early.

Legal Structure and Liability

There are several types of legal structures—a general partnership, limited partnership, corporation, or joint venture agreement. Group investments fall into these categories or variations of them. Some legal structures allow more flexibility than others. The degree of personal liability exposure varies depending on the structure and the group investment agreement. This issue is, of course, a critical one to consider.

Make sure, if at all possible, that your risk is limited to the amount of your investment. You want to avoid personal liability for any financial problems that occur, either to mortgage companies, other investors, or the investment group as such.

If you are investing, for instance, in a corporation that is holding the property for the group and the corporation has taken out a mortgage with a lender, the lender may require personal guarantees from the shareholders of the corporation. You minimize the risk by limiting the amount of the guarantee to be within your risk tolerance, rather than having the guarantee open-ended. Alternatively, simply back out of the deal. Another example of risk would be a partnership. If you went into a general partnership with two other investors whose actions resulted in financial problems, you would still be liable for the full amount of the debt if the other two couldn't pay. A third example of risk would be if you signed an investment group agreement and it stated that any shortfall of funds would have to be paid by the investors on a basis proportional to the percentage interest. A last example of risk would be in a limited partnership. If you went from an inactive partner to actively managing the investment, you could be liable. Some limited partners are also asked to sign personal guarantees up to a certain limit. Avoid this scenario.

You can see why you need a lawyer to look at the agreement and advise you of the implications and ways of limiting or eliminating personal liability risk.

Control Issues

Certain types of investment groups allow for more investor control than others. Control relates to the degree of influence that you have on the management of the investment and related decision making. Obviously, smaller groups tend to allow more individual control than others. For example, in some cases, unanimous consent is required for major decisions; in other cases, 75% consent is required; and in still other cases, a simple 51% majority vote of investors is required. In some instances you do not have any vote at all: you simply put your money in and hope for the best. If you are buying into a limited partnership or other form of investment that is being touted to you, make sure you thoroughly check out the promoter's previous history, experience, and reputation. You can see why management and quality of management are so important.

Contribution

Find out what contribution is expected of you in terms of money, time, expertise, management, personal guarantee, and contingency backup capital. Do you feel comfortable with others' expectations of you?

Percentage of Investment

Do you feel comfortable with the percentage of investment that you are getting, relative to the contribution you noted in the above point? For example, let's say that there are four people in an investment who incorporate a holding company. One is an active partner and finds and manages the property, and the other three are silent investors. The active partner has 55% of the investment, but did not invest any money, and did not sign any personal guarantees. The three silent partners invested all the money equally, signed personal guarantees to the bank for the mortgage, and hold 15% of the investment each. Would you feel comfortable with that investment percentage if you were a silent partner? What if you were the active partner?

Tax Considerations

One of the main reasons for investing in real estate would be for the tax benefits in your given situation. Certain types of investments are more attractive than others from a tax perspective. Be very wary of salespeople or financial advisors who attempt to induce you into buying a tax shelter. That area is fraught with potential pitfalls and risks for the unwary. You need objective and impartial advice from your lawyer and professional tax accountant—well in advance of making your investment decision. The property should be inherently viable from an investment viewpoint first, with tax benefits then taken into account.

Risk Assessment

As discussed throughout this chapter, you need to look objectively at the potential risks—the nature of the investment, the potential for profit, the degree of potential personal liability, the type of legal structure, the nature and degree of control, the quality of management, and the compatibility of other investment group members.

Profits and Losses

Determine how these aspects are to be dealt with. For example, what about excess revenue from the income property? Will that be kept in a contingency fund, or will a portion of it be paid to the investors? What about decisions such as selling the shares of a corporation holding the property or the property itself? How will those decisions be made and who will make them? These decisions have tax implications that will affect you. What about losses? Will the shortfall be covered by a bank loan, or by re-mortgaging the property, or by the group investors? In practical terms, how will that be done?

Getting Out or Buying Others Out

One of the important things to consider when investing with a group is getting out. What if you want to leave for any number of reasons? Is there a procedure to follow—a buy-out clause, as mentioned above in the section on liquidity? What penalty do you pay, how is it calculated, and how long will it take to get your money? Conversely, what if you want to buy out the other investors because of a personality conflict or some other reasons? Can you do so? If there is nothing in the agreement outlining how an investor can leave the group before the property is sold, you could have a problem.

Now that some of the key factors have been discussed, you can see why you have to be careful and selective before going into a group investment.

Types of Group Investments

There are many options available in terms of group investing. The most common options are co-tenancy, general partnership, limited partnership, joint venture, syndication, and equity sharing. For a detailed discussion of these types of options and pros and cons, refer to my book *Making Money in Real Estate*, 2nd edition. Also refer to the website www.homebuyer.ca.

Putting the Arrangement in Writing

After you have considered all the factors when buying with others, and have decided which type of group investment you prefer, the next step is to set out a written agreement. As mentioned earlier, make sure that your lawyer prepares the agreement or reviews an agreement prepared by someone else. Each type of investment group requires a different form of agreement.

The agreement you sign should be customized for the specific type of investment in which you're involved, and it should take into account the factors discussed earlier. The main points and procedures that are common to, although not necessarily included in, group investment agreements consist of the following:

√   type of legal structure

√   name and location of investment group

√   goals and objectives of group

√   duration of agreement

√   names and categories of investors (e.g., general, limited, active, silent)

√   financial contribution by investors

√   procedure for obtaining additional capital

√   role of individual investors in the investment management

√   authority of any investor in the conduct of the investment group

√   nature and degree of each investor's contribution to the investment group

√   how operating expenses will be handled

√   how operating income will be handled

√   debts of investment group separate from individual investor

√   separate bank account

√   signing authority for cheques and other legally binding documents

√   division of profits and losses

√   books, records, and method of accounting

√   draws or salaries

√   absence and disability of an investor

√   death of an investor

√   bringing in other investors

√   rights of the investors

√   withdrawal of an investor

√ buying out other investors

√ management of employees

√ sale of investor interest

√ restrictions on the transfer, assignment, or pledging of the investor's interest

√ release of debts

√ settlement of investor disputes and arbitration procedures

√ additions, alterations, or modifications to investment group agreement

√ non-competition with the investment group in the event of an investor's departure.

Pitfalls to Avoid

It is probably timely to outline some of the classic pitfalls to avoid in buying recreational real estate for investment purposes. In most cases, investors who have problems have succumbed to a combination of the following traps. Being aware of these problems at the outset will help you place the discussion and cautions in the rest of the book in context. All these issues are dealt with throughout the book.

√ not having an understanding of how the real estate and recreational property market works

√ not having a clear understanding of your own personal and financial needs

√ not having a clear focus or a realistic real estate investment plan, with strategies and priorities

√ not doing thorough market research and comparison shopping before making the purchase

√ not selecting the right property, considering the potential risks, money involved, and specific personal needs

√ not verifying representations or assumptions beforehand

√ not doing financial calculations beforehand

√ not buying at a fair market price

√ not buying real estate at the right time in the market

√   not buying within your financial debt-servicing capacity, comfort zone, and skills

√   not understanding the financing game thoroughly, and therefore not comparison shopping and not getting the best rates, terms, and right type of mortgage

√   not making a decision based on an objective assessment but on an emotional one

√   not determining the real reason why the vendor is selling

√   not having the property inspected by a building inspector before deciding to purchase

√   not selecting an experienced real estate lawyer and obtaining advice beforehand

√   not selecting an experienced professional tax accountant when selecting real estate property, and obtaining advice beforehand

√   not selecting an experienced realtor with expertise in the type of real estate and geographic location you are considering

√   not negotiating effectively

√   not putting the appropriate conditions or "subject clauses" in the offer

√   not buying for the right reasons—in other words, buying for tax shelter reasons rather than for the inherent value, potential, and viability of the investment property

√   not independently verifying financial information beforehand

√   not obtaining and reviewing all the necessary documentation appropriate for a given property before making a final decision to buy

√   not selecting real estate investment partners carefully

√   not having a written agreement with real estate investment partners prepared by a lawyer

√   not detailing exactly what chattels are included in the purchase price

√   not seeing the property before buying it, but relying on pictures and/or the representations of others

√   not managing the property well, or not selecting the right property management company

√   not selling the property at the right time in the market or for the right reasons.

PART IV
Planning for Peace of Mind

CHAPTER 9

Legal Issues and Strategies

Every aspect of a real estate purchase for personal use or investment will have legal implications. To avoid legal problems, you need to discuss the appropriate matters clearly with your lawyer and then make the correct decisions. To start with, it is important to understand the legal issues and terminology.

This chapter explains different kinds of property ownership, the legal documents involved in the purchase and sale of real estate, the implications of backing out of an agreement, services provided by a lawyer, types of listing agreements, and legal structures to hold revenue property.

Types of Sole Ownership of Property

There are various types of ownership options available. The most common types of ownership (sometimes referred to having an interest in land, though this includes any buildings on the land) are freehold and leasehold.

Freehold

This type of ownership entitles the owner to use the land for an indefinite period and to deal with the land in any way desired, subject to legislation (e.g., municipal bylaws, hydro utility easements or rights of way, provincial mineral rights), contractual obligations (e.g., subdivision restrictive covenants), and any charges that encumber the title of the property and are filed in the provincial land titles office (e.g., mortgages, liens, judgments). Another term for freehold is "fee simple."

Leasehold Interest

In a leasehold interest, the holder of the interest in land has the right to use the land for a fixed period, e.g., 50 or 99 years. The owner of the property (the landlord or lessor) signs an agreement with the owner of the leasehold interest (tenant or lessee) that sets out various terms and conditions of the relationship. The leasehold interest can be bought and sold, but the leaseholder can sell only the right to use the land for the time that is remaining in the lease, subject, of course, to any conditions contained in the original lease.

Both freehold interest and leasehold interest can be left in your will as an asset of your estate, or specifically bequeathed in your will.

Types of Joint Ownership in Property

You may wish to have shared ownership in the property with one or more other people. There are two main types of legal joint ownership: joint tenancy and tenancy in common. For other types of joint real estate investment arrangements, refer to Chapter 8: Investing for Yourself or with Others.

Joint Tenancy

In a joint tenancy, an owner has an undivided but equal share with all the other owners. No one person has a part of the property that is specifically his or hers because all the property belongs to all of the owners. At the time of purchasing the property, all the people who are joint tenants will be listed on the title of the property equally and each of the joint tenants has the right in law to possession of the whole property. These are the essential conditions involved in joint tenancy, and if any of these conditions are not met, then the ownership is deemed to be a tenancy in common and not joint tenancy.

One of the main features of a joint tenancy is the right of survivorship. This means that if one of the joint tenants dies, the others automatically and immediately receive the deceased person's share, equally divided. In other words, the deceased person's share in the joint tenancy is not passed on as an asset of his or her estate to beneficiaries, whether or not a will exists. It is fairly common for a couple to hold the legal interest in the property by means of a joint tenancy. Thus, you should consider tenancy in common if you do not want to have your interest go automatically to other parties.

Tenancy in Common

In this form of ownership, the tenants (owners) can hold equal or unequal shares in the property; in other words, the proportional ownership is divided. Each party owns an undivided share in the property, but is entitled to possession of the whole property. For example, there could be five people who are tenants in common, but four of them could own one-tenth of the property each, and the fifth person could own six-tenths of the property. An undivided share means that the property is not "sliced up" and designated like a piece of pie. The proportional ownership is relative to the whole of the property.

If the holder of a tenancy in common wishes to sell or mortgage his interest in the property, that can be done. If a buyer cannot be found and the tenant in common wants to get his money out of the property, he can go to court and, under a legal procedure called partition, request that the court order the property to be sold and the net proceeds of the sale distributed proportionately.

Tenancy in common does not carry an automatic right of survivorship in the way that joint tenancy does. In other words, if one of the tenants in common dies, the interest does not go to the other tenant(s), but to the estate of the deceased. If there is a will, the interest is distributed under the terms of the will. If the deceased person does not have a will, there is provincial legislation to deal with that type of situation, and the person's assets, which would include the tenancy interest, would be distributed to relatives according to the legislation.

There are various reasons why some people prefer tenancy in common to joint tenancy.

√ If you are purchasing property for investment purposes with people who are not relatives, you may not want them to automatically have your interest in the property in the event of your death.

√ If you have been previously married, have children from a previous relationship, and have since remarried, or are living in a common-law relationship, you may want to specify in your will that a certain portion of the value of the estate goes to those children individually or collectively. The only way this can be dealt with is in a tenancy-in-common situation because the interest would be deemed to be an asset of one's estate.

√ If you are putting unequal amounts of money in the property, a tenancy-in-common structure would reflect those different contributions in terms of the percentage interest in the property.

Written agreements should be signed by tenants in common, setting out the procedures if one of them wants to get out of the situation. This is a prudent procedure that can be accomplished by giving the others the right of first refusal on a proportional basis to buy out the interest, or there could be a clause requiring the consent of the other tenants in common in approving a potential purchaser, or there could be a provision requiring a certain period of notice to the other tenants before the property is sold.

Another case when tenancy in common might be preferable would be when one of the owners of the property wishes to have the personal independence to raise money for other outside interests, e.g., a business. In many cases the tenancy-in-common portion could be mortgaged without the consent of the other parties.

Understanding the Purchase-and-Sale Agreement

The most important document you will sign will be the offer to purchase, which, if accepted, becomes the agreement of purchase and sale. It sets out the terms and conditions between the parties and, as in any contract, it is legally binding if there are no conditions in the contract that have to be met before it becomes binding. Of course, there can be verbal contracts, but all contracts dealing with land must be in writing to be enforceable. That includes a purchase-and-sale agreement or a lease, which, of course, is also a contract.

There are many common clauses and features contained in the purchase-and-sale agreement, many of which vary from contract to contract according to various circumstances—whether one is purchasing a new or a resale property, type of property, revenue property, etc. Here is a brief overview of some of the common features of the purchase-and-sale agreement:

Amount of Deposit

A deposit serves various purposes. It is a partial payment on the purchase price, a good-faith indication of seriousness, and an assurance of performance if all the conditions in the offer to purchase have been fulfilled. The deposit is generally 5% to 10% of the purchase price. If there were conditions in the offer, and these conditions were not met, then the purchaser is entitled to receive a refund of the full amount of the deposit. This is one reason why it is important to have conditions or "subject to" clauses in the offer to protect one's interests fully. Most agreements for purchase and sale have a provision that gives the vendor the option of keeping the deposit as "liquidated damages," in the event that the purchaser fails to complete the terms of the agreement and pay the balance of money on the closing date.

When making a deposit, it is very important to be careful to whom you pay the funds. If you are purchasing on a private sale and no realtor is involved, never pay the funds directly to the vendor; pay them to your own lawyer in trust. If a realtor is involved, the funds can be paid to the realtor's trust account or your own lawyer's trust account, as the situation dictates.

If you are purchasing a new property from the builder, do not pay a deposit directly to the builder. The money should go to your lawyer's trust account, or some other system should be set up for your protection to ensure that your funds cannot be used except under the specific conditions that are clearly set out in the agreement. The risk is high in paying your money directly to a builder because if the builder does not complete the project and goes into bankruptcy, you could lose all your money and, in practical terms, could have great difficulty getting it back. Although several provincial governments have brought in legislation dealing with new property projects to protect the public on the issue of deposits—as well as many other property risk areas—legislation provides only partial protection.

Another matter you have to consider is interest. If you are paying a deposit, you want to ensure that interest at an appropriate rate or based on an appropriate formula is paid to your credit. In many cases, deposit monies can be tied up for many months, and that could represent considerable interest.

Conditions and Warranties

It is important to understand the distinction between conditions and warranties, as it is very critical to the wording that you would use in the agreement.

A condition is a requirement that is fundamental to the very existence of the offer. An inability to meet a condition allows the buyer to get out of the contract and obtain a refund of the full amount of the deposit. A buyer's inability to meet the condition set by a vendor permits the vendor to get out of the contract, which can be desirable to the vendor if a better offer has come along.

A warranty is a minor promise that does not go to the heart of the contract. If there is a breach of warranty, the purchaser cannot cancel but must complete the contract and sue for damages. Therefore, if a particular requirement on your part is pivotal to your decision to purchase the property, it is important to frame your requirement as a condition rather than as a warranty. Both vendor and purchaser frequently insert conditions into the agreement. These conditions are also referred to as subject clauses and should:

√   Be precise and clearly detailed.

√   Have specific time allocated for conditions that have to be removed, e.g., within 2 days, 30 days. It is preferable to put in the precise date that a condition has to be removed, rather than merely refer to the number of days involved.

√   Have a clause that specifically says that the conditions are for the sole
    benefit of the vendor or purchaser, as the case may be, and that they
    can be waived at any time by the party requiring the condition. This is
    important because you may wish to remove a condition even though it
    has not been fulfilled, in order for the contract to be completed.

Here is just a sampling of some of the common subject clauses. There are
many others possible that you or your lawyer may feel it appropriate to insert.

For Benefit of Purchaser

√   title being conveyed free and clear of any and all encumbrances or
    charges registered against the property on or before the closing date
    at the expense of the vendor, either from the proceeds of the sale or by
    solicitor's undertaking

√   inspection being satisfactory to purchaser by relative, spouse, partner,
    etc. (specify name)

√   inspection by house inspector/contractor selected by purchaser being
    satisfactory to purchaser

√   completion of sale of purchaser's other property

√   confirmation of mortgage financing

√   deposit funds to be placed in an interest-bearing trust account with the
    interest to accrue to the benefit of the purchaser

√   approval of assumption of existing mortgage

√   granting of vendor take-back mortgage or builder's mortgage

√   removal of existing tenancies (vacant possession) by completion date

√   existing tenancies conforming to prevailing municipal bylaws

√   interim occupancy payments being credited to purchase price

√   review and satisfactory approval by purchaser's lawyer of the contents
    of the agreement of purchase and sale

√   warranties, representations, promises, guarantees, and agreements
    shall survive the completion date

√   no urea formaldehyde foam insulation (UFFI) having ever been in the
    building

√   vendor's warranty that no work orders or deficiency notices are out-
    standing against the property or, if there are, that they will be complied
    with at the vendor's expense before closing.

Additional Clauses if Purchasing a Condominium

√ receipt and satisfactory review by purchaser (and/or purchaser's lawyer) of project documents, such as disclosure, declaration, articles, rules and regulations, financial statements, project budget, minutes of condominium corporation for past two years, management contract, estoppel certificate, etc.

√ confirmation by condominium corporation that the condominium unit being purchased will be able to be rented.

Additional Clauses if Purchasing a Revenue Property

√ review and satisfactory approval of financial statements, balance sheet, income and expense statement, list of chattels, list of inventory, names of tenants, amount of deposits and monthly rents, dates of occupancy, list of receivables and payables, list and dates of equipment safety inspections, list of repairs and dates, service contracts, leases, warranties, property plans, and surveys.

For Benefit of Vendor

√ removal of all subject clauses by purchaser within 72 hours upon notice in writing by vendor of a backup bona fide (legitimate) offer

√ confirmation of purchase of vendor take-back mortgage through vendor's mortgage broker

√ satisfactory confirmation of purchaser's creditworthiness by vendor or vendor's mortgage broker

√ issuance of building permit

√ builder receiving confirmation of construction financing

√ registration of a subdivision plan

√ deposit funds non-refundable and to be released directly to the vendor once all conditions of the purchaser have been met

√ review and satisfactory approval by vendor's lawyer of the contents of the agreement of purchase and sale.

Risk and Insurance

It is important that the parties agree to an exact date when risk will pass from the vendor to the purchaser. In some cases the agreement will state that the risk will pass at the time that there is a firm, binding, unconditional purchase-and-sale agreement. In other cases the contract states that the risk will pass on the completion date or the possession date. In any event, make sure that you have adequate insurance coverage taking effect as of and including the date that you assume the risk. The vendor should wait until after the risk date before terminating insurance.

Fixtures and Chattels

This is an area of potential dispute between the purchaser and vendor unless it is sufficiently clarified. A fixture is technically something permanently affixed to the property; therefore, when the property is conveyed, the fixtures are conveyed with it. A chattel is an object that is moveable; in other words, it is not permanently affixed. Common examples of chattels are washer and dryer, refrigerator, stove, microwave, and drapes.

A problem can arise when there is a question of whether an item is a fixture or a chattel. For example, an expensive chandelier hanging from the dining room ceiling, gold-plated bathroom fixtures, drapery hardware, or television satellite dish on the roof might be questionable items. One of the key tests is whether the item was intended to be attached on a permanent basis to the property and therefore should be transferred with the property, or whether it was the vendor's intention to remove these items and/ or replace them with cheaper versions before closing the real estate transaction.

In general legal terms, if it is a fixture and it is not mentioned in the agreement, it is deemed to be included in the purchase price. On the other hand, if it is not a fixture and no reference is made to it in the agreement, then it would not be included in the purchase price. To eliminate conflict, most agreements for purchase and sale have standard clauses built into them stating that all existing fixtures are included in the purchase price except those listed specifically in the agreement. In addition, a clause should list any chattels specifically included in the purchase price, and they should be clearly described.

Merger

This is a legal principle to the effect that if the agreement for purchase and sale is to be "merged" into a deed or other document, the real contract between the parties is in the document filed with the land registry. To protect you, it should be stated in the agreement for purchase and sale that the "warranties, representations, promises, guarantees, and agreements shall survive the completion date." There are exceptions to the document of merger in cases of mistake or fraud, technical areas that require your lawyer's opinion, but it is important to understand the concept.

Commissions

At the end of most purchase-and-sale agreements there is a section setting out the amount of the commission charged, which the vendor confirms when accepting an offer. A discussion of the various types of agreements for listing and selling real estate through a realtor is discussed in Chapter 18: Selling Your Recreational Property.

Title Insurance

This type of insurance protects you in the event that pre-existing property "defects," such as claims or charges, show up after you buy the property. Title insurance could also cover you for mortgages that were discharged and paid out, but still remain on title, and certain construction liens. You would be covered up to the amount of your policy for as long as you are still the property owner.

Other types of risks that are usually covered include: claims due to fraud, forgery, work orders not complied with; zoning and setback non-compliance or deficiencies; survey irregularities; forced removal of existing structures; and unregistered rights of way or easements. You need to comparison shop, and read and understand the terms of your coverage. Refer to the discussion in Chapter 11: Insurance Issues and Strategies.

For a more comprehensive discussion of insurance issues and strategies, refer to my books *Making Money in Real Estate,* 2nd edition and *Real Estate Investing For Canadians For Dummies.* Also refer to the website www.homebuyer.ca.

10 Tax Issues and Strategies

The information and tips suggested in this chapter will save you money, or at least help you to understand the key options open to you to save money. As income tax provisions can change at any time, before making any recreational real estate purchase plans for personal use or investment purposes, make sure you contact a tax accountant to obtain current income tax advice. Chapter 5: Selecting Your Advisors gives guidelines on how to find a professional tax accountant.

The following discussion highlights the main categories of local, provincial, and federal government taxes that could affect you. It also includes tax-planning strategies, tax-saving tips, and ways of maximizing your deductions.

There is additional discussion of tax strategies in two other chapters, relevant to the topics of those chapters. Refer to Chapter 13: Estate Planning Issues and Strategies and Chapter 17: Buying Vacation Property in the United States and Abroad.

Local Taxes

Municipalities assess taxes for various purposes. Some municipalities include all taxes within one assessment. Others separate out the taxes. The main taxes are as follows:

Property Taxes

These are generally due on an annual basis, with assessment of value determined within six months prior to the property taxation year. For residential property, a "mill rate" is generally determined annually and multiplied by the assessed value of the property, including the building on the property, to determine the actual tax due. In many provinces there is a homeowner's grant that is subtracted from the gross taxes assessed for your property to determine the net payable tax you owe. As you might assume, this annual grant is for a principal residence only, not a recreational second home or investment property. The grant amount can vary depending on the age of the homeowner.

If you believe your property taxes are unfair because they are based on an artificially high assessment of property value, you can appeal the assessment notice. For example, when a real estate market has gone down, it is not uncommon for property assessment appeals to increase because of the lag time before the assessment reflects the reduction in value. Make sure you don't miss the appeal deadline, as the time frame can be tight.

Property taxes are generally assessed for municipally supplied services such as schools, education, roads, and hospitals. If your personal use vacation property is in a more rural area, you might have lower taxes because there are fewer people and fewer schools, as most of the homes could be second homes. If your property is a personal use or investment property in a resort area, there could be many young families of people who work in the resort. Over time, this could cause higher rates on the school part of your property taxes.

Utility Taxes

These taxes tend to be for services such as water, sewer, and garbage pickup.

Further Information

To obtain further information about the taxes noted above, and other taxes, contact your lawyer, City Hall, or regional assessment authority.

Provincial Taxes

Many provincial governments charge a property purchase tax when you purchase a property.

Property Purchase Tax

Basically this tax is assessed and paid at the time of purchase based on the purchase price of the property. The formula for determining the amount payable varies among provinces.

In addition, provinces also tax the capital gains and income arising from a sale. On your personal income tax return, you pay provincial tax in addition to federal tax. In Quebec, individuals file separate personal tax returns. Refer to the capital gains tax comments on the next page, under Federal Taxes.

Further Information

To obtain further information about provincial taxes, contact your lawyer or the local branch of your provincial government land titles office.

Federal Taxes

There are two main federal taxes: the goods and services tax (GST) and income tax.

Goods and Services Tax

The GST is a federal tax that applies to every "supply" of real property, both residential and commercial, unless the "supply" can fit within one of the exemptions set out in the legislation.

The term "supply" has broad meaning. It includes not only sales and leases of real property but also transfers, exchanges, barters, and gifts. Most services dealing with the real estate transaction are also covered by the GST. In other words, whenever you consume a "good," e.g., buy a product or use a service, you will be required, in most cases, to pay the 6% tax. Those in the Maritimes pay HST (Harmonized Sales Tax), which is a combined GST and PST (Provincial Sales Tax), at a rate of 14%. For the purpose of this book, we will just deal with the GST format.

The following overview discusses how certain types of real estate purchases are affected by or exempted from the GST, and how the GST rebate system operates. Check with your accountant to make sure that you are aware of any changes. Governments tend to modify legislation over time.

How the GST System Works on Property Purchases

The purchaser pays the GST to the vendor at the time of purchase. The vendor then remits the tax to what is colloquially and historically referred to as Revenue Canada. It is now technically referred to as the Canada Revenue Agency (CRA). Sometimes the vendor includes the GST within the purchase price, and other times it may be added on separately. There are also several categories of GST exemptions relating to real estate. Although the basic rate of the GST is currently 6%, it could be changed at any time, of course.

If you are the purchaser who has to pay GST, you may be able to receive a partial or full rebate or offset the GST tax paid against GST tax received. It depends on whether you purchased the property as a principal residence, for investment purposes, or are in the business of buying and selling properties.

Resale Home or Other Type of Residential Dwelling

If you buy a resale residential property as a principal residence, there is no GST payable on the purchase price. In other words, it is exempt. CRA defines "used residential property" to include an owner-occupied house, condominium, duplex, vacation property, summer cottage, or non-commercial hobby farm.

The "residential property" definition requires that the vendor must not be a "builder" as defined in the legislation. A builder is someone who builds or substantially renovates the property as a business. Used property can also mean a recently built house that is substantially complete and has been sold at least once before you buy it.

If you purchase a resale home that includes a room used as an office, and the vendor was self-employed, the entire house still qualifies for the GST exemption if the vendor used the house primarily as his residence. However, if you purchase a home that was used primarily for commercial business purposes, and it is zoned for that type of operation, at the time of purchase you will be considered to have acquired two separate properties. The GST will not apply to the portion in which the owner lived; however, it will apply on the remaining portion.

When purchasing a resale home, you can request that the vendor provide you with a certificate stating that the property qualifies as "used" for GST purposes.

New Home

When you purchase a newly constructed home from a builder as a principal residence for yourself or a relative, the entire purchase price, including land, is taxable. The word "home" refers to a residential dwelling and includes a single family house, condominium (apartment or townhouse format), or mobile home. If the home will be your principal residence, it may qualify for a partial GST rebate, depending upon the sale price. When the home is purchased, the builder can either pay the rebate directly to you or deduct it from the GST you owe on the purchase price.

Purchasers of homes priced up to $350,000 will qualify for the maximum rebate of $7,560 or 36% of the GST paid on the purchase price, whichever is less. Since the $7,560 amount is 2.16% of $350,000, a purchaser is really paying the GST at a rate of 3.84 % on a $350,000 home instead of 6%.

If you are purchasing a home priced at more than $350,000 but less than $450,000, the rebate is gradually reduced, in other words declines to zero on a proportional basis. On a home priced at $450,000 for example, the full GST of $27,000 is payable without rebate. There is no rebate for homes selling for $450,000 or more.

If you are purchasing the home for investment purposes and you intend to rent out the property to tenants, the full 6% GST will be charged to you on the purchase price. Subject to some conditions, 36% of the tax you pay will be eligible for rebate.

Owner-built Home

If you build your own home or hire someone to build or substantially renovate a home for you as a principal residence for yourself or a relative, you will qualify for a GST rebate if all of the following applies:

√ you paid the GST on the land and/or construction materials and contracting services; and

√ you or a relative are the first occupants of the home.

The amount of the rebate will depend on the fair market value (FMV) of the home and whether or not the GST was paid on the acquisition of the land. FMV must be under $450,000. If you owned the land when the GST started, you will not have paid the GST on this purchase.

Renovated Home

Under the GST, sales of substantially renovated homes are treated in the same way as sales of new housing. "Substantial renovations" mean that all, or substantially all, of the house except the foundation, external walls, interior supporting walls, floor, roof, and staircases are removed or replaced.

For example, if a person in the renovation business buys an older home, there is no GST on the purchase price as the GST does not apply to resale homes. The person then completely guts and replaces the interior with new walls, railings, floor, kitchen, wiring, and plumbing. At least 90% of the items on the CRA guidelines must be removed to constitute a substantial renovation. For GST purposes, this substantially renovated home, when sold, will be treated like a new home. If you purchase this substantially renovated home, you will pay the GST on the purchase price and be entitled to claim the GST new housing rebate if the price is under $450,000. Refer to the "New Home" section discussed earlier.

If there are other renovations or improvements to a home, such as replacing a kitchen or building an addition, these are not considered substantial renovations. If you buy an older home that has only been partially renovated, with a remodeled bathroom, for instance, an additional bedroom, or a new roof, you will not have to pay the GST on the home.

You can see the importance of making sure that the renovations do not fall under the "substantial renovation" category if possible when you buy a home from a builder in the business of renovating older homes. It will mean you pay less for the house at the outset if you can avoid the GST on a resale home.

A substantially renovated home is considered a resale home if the renovator owns it and lives in it, even for a short time. That is an important point to keep in mind, especially if you are buying from another homeowner or renovating it yourself, and in both instances the renovations are substantial. You should be able to get more money on resale if the purchaser does not have to pay GST.

Land

There is no GST on the sale of vacant land or recreational property, such as a hobby farm owned by an individual or by a trust for the benefit of individuals. Certain sales and uses of farmland are also exempt.

If you paid GST on the land because the previous use of the land was such that GST was applicable, the rebate would be the same as for a new home. See the "New Home" section.

If you build on the land and sell it, refer to the GST discussion in the "Owner-built Home" section.

Income Tax

There are many tax considerations you should be aware of when buying real estate for personal use or for investment purposes. The following discussion highlights only the common areas to consider. It is not intended to be complete or go into detail. As cautioned before, it is important that you obtain advice from a professional tax accountant familiar with real estate issues before you make a decision on real estate investment. Laws and regulations dealing with taxation matters are complex and constantly changing. Also, you need specific advice based on your personal circumstances. In addition, there are forms, guides, information criteria, and interpretation bulletins available from Canada Revenue Agency (CRA). Make sure you obtain the *Rental Income Guide* for further tax details. Look in the Blue Pages of your telephone directory under "Government of Canada" departments. Check the website of the Canada Revenue Agency for information, and forms, at www.cra-arc.gc.ca.

Principal Residence Exemption

Most people start their first real estate investment by purchasing their own home to live in. Your principal residence may be a house, apartment, condominium, duplex, trailer, mobile home, or a houseboat.

A property will qualify as a principal residence if it meets various conditions:

√ It is a housing unit, a leasehold interest in a housing unit, or a share of the capital stock of a cooperative housing corporation.

√ You must own the property solely or jointly with another person.

√ You, your spouse, your former spouse, or one of your children ordinarily inhabit it at some point during the year.

√ You consider the property your principal residence.

Tax Benefits of a Principal Residence

One of the key benefits is that the gain you will realize on the sale of your principal residence is not usually subject to tax. For example, if you bought the property originally for $50,000 many years ago and sell it for $500,000, you would not pay tax on this increase in value of $450,000. Refer to Chapter 17: Buying Vacation Property in the United States and Abroad for a discussion on one-half hectare of land if that applies to you.

Key Tax-planning Strategy: The Principal Residence Exemption

Chapter 13: Estate Planning Issues and Strategies details additional tax-planning options when selling or transferring property to family members for will- and estate-planning purposes. The purpose of these techniques of course is to reduce, defer, or eliminate taxes.

Surprisingly, a cornerstone of the tax-planning strategies for your vacation property is the *principal residence* exemption. Probably, more Canadians make use of this exemption than any other, and yet it is also the most misunderstood. The term "principal residence" implies that the particular property must be your primary, or main place of residence; in other words, the place where you make your home. However, this is not the case. In fact, the definition of principal residence in the *Income Tax Act* is quite broad, and will allow even a seasonal residence, a recreational second home, a mobile home, or a houseboat to be claimed as a person's principal residence if so desired.

This section will try to clear up some of the misconceptions, and outline how you may be able to maximize the tax benefit of this exemption.

Your Principal Residence Versus Your Home

If you and your spouse own more than one residential-type property (such as a house as well as a cottage), it is generally not necessary for you to decide which property is to be designated as the principal residence for capital gains tax purposes until the year that either property is sold or disposed of. The fact that you show your home address on your income tax return does not mean that you are designating your house as your principal residence.

A Seasonal Residence Can Qualify as Your Principal Residence

A principal residence, by definition, is a dwelling place that is owned by you, or in which you have a part ownership interest, and it must be *ordinarily inhabited* by you, your spouse, or a child, *during the year*. A vacation home (whether you call it a second-home or seasonal residence, or what have you) that you use for weekends or vacations can therefore qualify, because you will meet the test of having occupied the property for some period or periods of time during the year. You are not required to inhabit the property throughout the year.

You Don't Have to Move to Your Vacation Property

You do not have to move to your cottage or vacation home on a permanent or year-round basis in order to qualify it for the principal residence exemption. The "183-day rule" that is sometimes used in determining whether a person is a resident of Canada has no relevance whatsoever in this context. As long as you, your spouse, or at least one of your children occupy the vacation property for some period or periods of time during the year, that is enough to bring you within the principal residence definition.

When to Disclose Your Principal Residence to the CRA

Even if you have made up your mind that you will treat your vacation home as your principal residence for capital gains purposes, there is no need to disclose this when you file your income tax return. You would continue to show your home address and the mailing address of your permanent residence, if that is what you have been doing all along. As far as the CRA is concerned, you need not work through the principal residence exemption formula until the year that you dispose of a property. At that time, you can make your final decision on whether to designate the property as your principal residence for some or all of the years of ownership.

Principal Residence Exemption Is Calculated Under a Formula

It is not simply a matter of establishing a property as your principal residence at the time that you are about to sell it, in order to claim a full exemption from capital gains tax. Instead, the exemption is calculated by reference to the number of years that you owned the property, and the number of years that you are able to *designate* it as your principal residence for capital gains tax purposes. The exemption formula is as follows:

$$\frac{\text{Number of years after 1971 designated as your principal residence, plus ``1''}}{\text{Number of years after 1971 that you owned the property}} = \text{Exemption fraction}$$

The Principal Residence Exemption Formula

It is worth spending a few minutes now to understand how the exemption formula works, in order for you to be able to estimate how much tax will arise in the future. Upon an actual disposition during your lifetime, or a deemed disposition on death, you or your executor(s) would need to do the following:

√ First, calculate the capital gain in the usual way. This means taking the actual proceeds of disposition (or the fair market value in the case of a deemed disposition) and subtracting the selling expenses, if any, and the adjusted cost base (ACB). This simply means the original base cost for acquisition of the property, adjusted for any closing and other carrying and professional advisory costs.

√   Next, you would apply the exemption fraction described on the previous page to determine how much of the capital gain is exempt.

√   The remainder is the capital gain that you would have to report in your tax return, and one-half of that amount would be included in your taxable income.

For pre-1971 properties, the starting point is the value on December 31, 1971. Many people don't realize this. If they elected in 1994 to utilize the $100,000 capital gains exemption (no longer available), there may be a bump in the cost base (ACB).

Doubling Up the Exemption for Vacation Property Acquired Before 1982

In the case of properties that were acquired by a married couple before 1982, it has usually made sense from a tax-planning viewpoint for the husband to be the sole owner of one property, and the wife to be the sole owner of the other. This is strictly for technical reasons because of peculiarities in the principal residence definition, and in the income tax rules relating to spousal transfers. Thus, it is only the post-1981 appreciation in the value of one of the properties that would eventually be subject to capital gains tax. This assumes that the principal residence designations after 1981 are allocated entirely to one property.

Jointly-owned Vacation Property Owned Before 1982

In the case of jointly-owned properties that were acquired before 1982, it may not be possible to *double up* on the principal residence exemption up to the end of 1981. In some cases, it may be desirable from a tax-planning viewpoint for the husband to make a gift of his half-interest in one of the properties to his wife, and for the wife to gift her half-interest in the other property to the husband. If you are in this situation, you should get professional tax advice to determine whether it is necessary to go through the red tape of creating separate ownership for each property. You should also speak with your lawyer to find out whether there are any family law or other legal implications of making such ownership changes.

Real Estate Investment Property

It is important to understand the concepts and options outlined in this section. It will save you time when discussing the issues with your accountant and enhance your decision making. The following is only a brief overview to high-light some of the key areas. By the time you finish reading this section, you will appreciate the need and benefit of using professional advisors to maximize your tax savings and net after-tax profit.

For a very comprehensive discussion of the tax aspect involved in investment real estate, refer to my book *Making Money in Real Estate*, 2nd edition.

Capital Gains or Income?

Many investors assume that when property is sold for a profit, the profit will be treated as a capital gain for income-tax purposes. This would result in a lower tax rate than other types of income. You have to be very careful, though, as CRA could consider the profit as regular income, at regular tax rates.

Capital gains are taxed at 50% of the capital gain. In other words, if you bought a property for $100,000 and sold it for $225,000, but after all expenses were taken into account you net $200,000, the net profit (gain) would be approximately $100,000. You would normally have to pay tax on 50% of the net gain, i.e., on $50,000. If the profit were deemed to be income instead of a capital gain, you would have to pay tax on 100% of the amount; that is, on the full $100,000.

CRA applies various types of criteria to determine whether the profit is a capital gain from a real estate investment, or income from a business of speculating in real estate without any investment intent. Each situation depends on the individual circumstances, so make sure you get tax advice from a professional accountant in advance.

For example, if you purchased a property with the intention of selling it as soon as possible in a "hot" real estate market, the profit from that could be deemed to be income. In other words, you "flipped" the property or sold your rights under an agreement of purchase and sale. Another example would be a situation in which a person bought vacant land with the intention of selling it quickly. The key tests are what your original intent was when you purchased the property, the facts and the circumstances, and how quickly you sold it.

There are many credible and logical reasons to refute the income theory and argue that it should be considered a capital gain. It would be very frustrating to plan on specific after-tax money from a sale, and then find that you owe more money to Canada Revenue Agency than you had planned. That is why you need good tax planning and advice from a professional accountant, a point that is reinforced throughout this chapter.

Capital Expenses

These expenses are usually outlays that provide a lasting benefit beyond the current year. This would include such expenses as purchasing or improving your recreational property. Generally, capital expenditures are not fully deductible in the year they are incurred. Instead, you may deduct a portion of their cost each year as capital cost allowance (CCA). This percentage may vary between 4% and 100% each year. In effect, you are depreciating the value of the item according to the CCA classification table, and writing off the depreciated amount against your rental income.

You cannot claim CCA on the cost of land, as it is not a depreciable property. On the contrary, as an investor, it is your hope and intention that the property will appreciate!

Canada Revenue Agency considers the following types of expenses to be capital in nature:

√   the purchase of rental property

√   legal fees and other costs in connection with the purchase of property

√   the cost of furniture and equipment rented with the property

√   major repairs and expenditures that extend the useful life of your property, or improve it beyond its original condition.

Current Expenses

These types of outlays are usually ones that benefit the current year only, e.g., repairs made to maintain the rental property in the same condition it was in when you originally bought it. You may deduct current expenses from your gross rental income in the year you incur them. Current expenses are also referred to as operating expenses.

The following is a list of typical costs associated with renting a vacation property. These are general guidelines only. You may deduct these expenses from your gross rental income in the year they are incurred unless otherwise stated. As mentioned previously, tax rules can change, so obtain current tax advice. In addition, there may be various tax-planning options on which your accountant can advise you.

Accounting Fees

Accounting fees include amounts paid for bookkeeping services, auditing books and records, and preparing financial statements.

Advertising

Amounts paid for advertising that you have space available to rent. This would include all costs relating to your vacation rental website listings, your own website, etc.

Capital Expenditures

Capital expenditures, as discussed earlier, are not fully deductible in the year they are incurred. This could include computer equipment and digital or video cameras for taking photos of your property for website marketing purposes. Discuss this with your accountant, as only a portion could be deducted, if you are also using it for personal usage.

Commissions and Fees

Amounts paid or payable to agents for collecting rents or finding new tenants. This would include any fees you pay for property management or referrals of renters for your vacation home.

Computer-related Expenses

As you are probably using a computer to manage your properties, doing research on the Internet, or doing letters or e-mailing, all related directly or indirectly to your business, investment, or landlord activities, you should be entitled to deduct all, or a portion, of the related ongoing expense costs, for example, copy paper and toner, high-speed Internet connection, and computer repairs.

Electronic Communication Expenses

If you are using a cell phone, pager, or any other means of communication relating to operating your investment rental business, these would be legitimate deductions.

Condominium Expenses

If you earn rental income from a condominium unit, you are entitled to deduct any expenses that are normally deductible from rental income. These may include condominium fees representing your share of the upkeep and maintenance of the common property, and other rental expenses you incur for the upkeep and maintenance of the unit.

Education

If you are spending money to remain current with your landlord and invest-ment activities and to protect your investment and risk, you would be able to write off those legitimate expenses. Taking seminars or courses; attending con-ferences, conventions, and trade shows in town or out of town; subscribing to newspapers, magazines, newsletters; buying books and CDs, related directly or indirectly to your investment activities, would all fall into the category of edu-cation. For example, the cost of taking the recreational property seminars we offer would be tax deductible against any income you generate from your vaca-tion home. Please refer to the website www.homebuyer.ca for more information.

Finder's Fee

A finder's fee is an expense incurred for arranging a mortgage or loan for the purpose of purchasing or improving the rental property. The expense is deduct-ible in equal portions over five years. However, if you repay the mortgage or loan before the end of the five-year period, you can deduct any un-deducted balance in the year of repayment.

Insurance

Premiums for current insurance coverage on your rental property are deduct-ible in the year. If your policy provides coverage for more than one year, you may deduct only the current-year premiums.

Interest

Interest on money borrowed to purchase or improve your rental property is deductible. You may also deduct interest paid to tenants on rental deposits. However, if you refinance your rental property to obtain funds for purposes other than the acquisition or improvement of your rental property, you may not deduct the interest against your rental income.

Landscaping

The cost of landscaping the grounds around your rental property is deductible in the year of payment.

Legal Expenses

Fees incurred for legal services such as lease preparation or collection of over-due rents are deductible. However, legal fees incurred for the purchase or sale of your rental property are not deductible against your gross rental income. Instead, legal fees you incurred to acquire your rental property are treated as part of your cost of the property. When you sell the rental property, any legal fees you incurred in connection with the sale may be deducted from the pro-ceeds of disposition when calculating your gain or loss.

Maintenance and Repairs

If you do the repairs yourself, you can deduct the cost of the materials. The value of your own labour is not generally deductible unless you structure your services with the advice of a professional accountant. There are various creative and legitimate ways for you or your family to be paid for services.

Mortgage Payments

Repayments of the principal portion of your mortgage or loan to purchase or improve your rental property are not deductible. See "Interest" regarding the interest portion of your mortgage.

Motor Vehicle Expenses

Travel expenses you incur to collect rents are considered personal expenses and are usually not deductible. However, reasonable travelling expenses may be deductible if incurred in certain circumstances. For example, if you receive income from only one rental property that is located in the general area where you live, you may deduct motor vehicle expenses to the extent you personally do part or all of the necessary repairs and maintenance on the property, and incur the expenses transporting tools and materials to the rental property.

If you own two or more rental properties, you may deduct reasonable motor vehicle expenses incurred for the purpose of collecting rents, super-vising repairs, or generally providing management of the properties. This is the case whether your rental properties are located in or outside the general area where you live. However, technically the properties must be located in at least two different sites away from your residence for your motor vehicle expenses to be deductible.

Office Expenses

Expenses for items of stationery such as journals, receipt books, and photo-copying, pens, printer paper and toner and stamps, are deductible.

Penalties

Amounts paid for early retirement of your mortgage (even on its renewal), for example, could be deductible. For example, if a penalty or bonus is paid out in respect of the repayment of all or part of the principal amount of a debt obligation before its maturity, this is a legitimate deduction. In certain circumstances, the penalty or bonus is deemed to have been paid and received as a payment of interest, to the extent that it does not exceed the future interest that would, but for the repayment, have been payable on the debt obligation. If the payor is a corporation, trust, or partnership, the deduction is amortized over the term of the original obligation, subject to special adjustments. Penalties for the late filing of your income tax return are also not deductible.

Property Taxes

These are deductible if assessed by a province, territory, or municipality and relate to your rental property.

Salaries and Wages

Amounts paid or payable to superintendents, maintenance personnel, and others employed by you for the operation or supervision of your rental property are deductible.

Tax Return Preparation

Fees and expenses for advice and assistance in preparing and filing tax returns are deductible when the nature of your rental operation is such that it is a normal part of operations to obtain legal and accounting services.

Travelling Expenses

Costs of travel related to your landlord and investment activities are deductible, for example, if you are checking out other potential properties or land to buy, and need to fly to the location. Possibly you want to attend a trade show, conference, or convention out of town, which is related directly or indirectly to your real estate investment and management activities.

Utilities

Utilities are deductible if your rental arrangement specifies that you will pay for the lights, heat, water, or cable used by your tenants.

Vacant Land

If you are holding vacant land for investment purposes, there are various tax rules that may restrict the deduction of interest on borrowed money used to buy the land, and property taxes paid on the land. If you are not earning rental income from the vacant land, CRA will consider your costs as capital expenditures and therefore they would be added on to the original cost of the property on sale. Because of this approach, when the property is sold, the cost for tax purposes is higher than it otherwise would be and therefore the capital gain is lower.

On the other hand, you may decide to rent or lease out the vacant property, e.g., to a farmer, in order to generate revenue. If you earn rental income from the vacant land, there are limitations to the amount you may deduct for interest on money borrowed to acquire the land, as well as property taxes and related land assessments. Your deduction is restricted to the amount of rental income remaining after you have deducted all other expenses from your rental income.

You cannot create or increase a rental loss, nor can you reduce other sources of income by claiming a deduction for the above expenses. However, if you are unable to deduct a portion of the expenses because of the limitation, you may add the un-deducted portion to the cost of the land.

The above are general guidelines. Check with your tax accountant for specific and current advice.

Keeping Records

If you are investing in real estate or are generating revenue from your investment, keeping detailed records is essential. Make sure that you have all the documents necessary to verify money collected and paid out. This includes all receipts, invoices, and contracts. If you don't have the proper documents, your claim could be disallowed by CRA. Also, any future purchaser will want to have them. You do not need to submit these records when you file your return. CRA requires you to report rental income using the accrual method. This means that:

√ Rents are included in income for the year in which they are due, whether or not you received them in that year, and

√ Allowable expenses are deducted in the year they are incurred, regardless of when you actually made the payments.

Insurance Issues and Strategies

Although it is possible to buy too much insurance, many people don't purchase enough or the right type of insurance. You want to minimize the risks you face at your recreational property from fire or theft, for example, by making sure you have adequate insurance protection. This chapter will help you gauge your insurance requirements and determine how to meet them.

Selecting an Insurance Broker

√ Refer to the section on "Selecting an Insurance Broker" in Chapter 5: Selecting Your Advisors.

√ For property and business-related insurance, refer to the website of the Insurance Brokers Association of Canada (www.ibac.ca) for a list of members to obtain comparative quotes.

√ For life and health-related insurance, refer to the website of the Canadian Life and Health Insurance Association (www.clhia.ca) for a list of members and helpful consumer information.

Regular reviews of risk exposure can help avoid overlaps and gaps in coverage, and thereby keep your risk and premiums lower. This is especially important if you are investing in recreational real estate. Reviews can also help you keep current with inflation.

Types of Property Coverage

When you are buying real estate for personal use, investment, or rental purposes, it is important to understand the jargon of the property insurance trade, and how premiums are determined and risk assessed. This will enhance your negotiating skills, save you money, and ensure you get the right protection for your needs. It will also protect you from having inadequate insurance coverage or running the risk that a claim could be denied. Here is an overview of the key concepts.

Inflation Allowance

This coverage protects you against inflation by automatically increasing the amount of your insurance during the term of your policy without increasing your premium. On renewal, the insurance company will automatically adjust the amount of your insurance to reflect the annual inflation rate. The premium you pay for your renewal will be based on those adjusted amounts of insurance.

Inflation allowance coverage will not fully protect you if you make an addition to your building or if you acquire additional personal property. This is why you need to review the amount of your insurance every year to make sure it is adequate.

Special Limits of Insurance

The contents of your dwelling are referred to as "Personal Property." Some types of personal property insurance such as insurance for jewellery, furs, and money have "Special Limits of Insurance." This is the maximum the insurer will pay for those types of property. If these limits are not sufficient for your needs, you can purchase additional insurance.

Your policy automatically includes some additional coverage to provide you with more complete protection. The individual types of coverage that are included are listed in the section "Additional Types of Insurance to Consider."

Insured Perils

A peril is an occurrence such as fire or theft. Some policies protect you against only those perils that are listed in your policy. Other policies protect you against "all risks" ("risk" is another word for peril). This means you are protected against most perils.

All insurance policies have exclusions. Even if you have selected "all risks" coverage, this does not mean that *everything* is covered. It is important that you read the exclusions carefully in order to understand the types of losses that are not covered by your policy. For example, floods and earthquakes may not be covered if you reside in a high-risk location for these types of perils.

Loss or Damage Not Insured

This is the "fine print," the section that tells you what is not covered. They are also known as "exclusions." Exclusions are necessary to make sure that the insurance company does not pay for the types of losses that are inevitable (e.g., wear and tear), uninsurable (e.g., war), or for which other specific policy forms are available to provide coverage (e.g., automobiles).

Basis of Claim Settlement

This section describes how the insurer will settle your loss. It's the real test of the value of your policy and the reason why you purchased insurance.

Replacement Cost

You should purchase replacement-cost coverage for your property. This is particularly important for your personal property (e.g., the contents of your dwelling and personal effects). Otherwise the basis of settlement will be "actual cash value," which means that depreciation is applied to the damaged property when establishing the values. You therefore would get less money, possibly considerably less, than what you originally paid for your property or what it would cost you to replace them at current prices.

"New for old" coverage is available. All you have to do is ask for "replacement-cost coverage" and then make sure that your amounts of insurance are sufficient to replace your property at today's prices.

Guaranteed Replacement Cost

This is one of the most important types of coverage available to a homeowner. You can qualify for this coverage by insuring your home to 100% of its full replacement value. If you do, then the insurance company will pay the full claim, even if it is more than the amount of insurance on the building. Make sure this is shown on your policy.

The guaranteed replacement cost coverage applies only to your building, not your personal property.

There is usually an important exclusion. Many insurance companies won't pay more than the amount of insurance if the reason the claim exceeds that amount is the result of any law regulating the construction of buildings. Check this out.

Bylaws

Some municipalities have laws that govern the height of a house, what materials you have to use, or even where you can build it. These are known as bylaws.

If the insurance company has to rebuild your house to different standards, this can increase the amount of your claim significantly.

Your policy doesn't cover this increased cost because the insurance company has no way of knowing which laws may apply in your municipality, but you can find out. Then make sure that your amounts of insurance are high enough to cover the increased cost, or increase them if necessary, and ask for a bylaws coverage endorsement. It'll cost a bit more now, but it can save you a lot later.

Deductible

There is a deductible and the amount is shown on the coverage summary page of your policy. It means that you pay that amount for most claims, for example, $250 or $1,000. The insurance company pays the rest.

As you can imagine, the cost to investigate and settle a claim can be considerable, often out of proportion when the size of the claim is relatively small. These expenses are reflected in the premiums you pay. By using deductibles to eliminate small claims, the insurance company can save on expenses and therefore offer insurance at lower premiums.

Conditions

This is a very important part of your policy. It sets out the mutual rights and obligations of the insurer and the insured. This section governs how and when a policy may be cancelled, as well as your obligations after a loss has occurred.

Purchasing Adequate Amounts of Insurance

Purchasing adequate amounts of insurance that reflect the full replacement value of everything you own is without a doubt the single most important thing you can do to protect yourself. The penalty is that insurance companies will not pay more than the amounts of insurance you have purchased, so it is up to you to make sure the coverage is adequate and realistic. Review your coverage before the annual policy renewal date.

Establish how much it would cost to rebuild your vacation home from scratch. This is the amount for which you should insure the house or condo, in order to make sure that you are fully covered.

If you put an addition onto the house or carry out major renovations, you should recalculate the replacement value, as your current amount of insurance doesn't take this into consideration. Notify your insurance company representative. The inflation allowance feature of your policy does protect you against normal inflation, but is not sufficient to cover major changes.

You may also want to check with municipal authorities to see whether there are any bylaws that govern the construction of houses in your area, as you may need a higher amount of insurance so that the reconstruction expense of your home will be fully covered.

Contents Coverage

If you are using the home personally, the following discussion relates to personal use. Your policy provides coverage for your contents. You should make sure that this amount is enough to replace all your possessions at today's prices. If the home is rented to a tenant, they are responsible for obtaining tenant's insurance. You should make that a condition of any rental agreement.

If you have a claim, the insurance company will ask you to compile a complete list of everything that you have lost. Ideally, you should maintain an inventory of everything, furniture, appliances, clothes, and other possessions. Estimating what it would cost you to replace them is a good way to check if the amount of insurance you carry is enough.

At the very least you should keep the receipts for all major purchases in a safe place. Another good idea is to take pictures of your contents or make a video of everything by walking from room to room. In addition, most insurance companies will provide you with a checklist, so you can compile a list of your contents. This may seem like a chore right now, but it can really save time and aggravation if you do have a claim.

As you could lose your inventory or photographic evidence in a major loss, you should store your records away from your house. The best place is a safety deposit box. Whatever method you use, remember that you should update it periodically (ideally annually) to make sure that it remains accurate.

How Insurance Companies Calculate the Premium

The pricing of insurance is governed by a principle known as the "spread of risk." This means that the premiums paid by many people pay for the losses of the few.

When more dollars in claims are paid out than taken in as premiums, then the premium paid by everyone goes up.

The premium you pay therefore represents the amount of money needed by the insurance company to pay for all losses, plus their expenses in providing the service, plus a profit factor divided by the number of policyholders.

The potential for loss assessment is based upon a number of risk factors. Most of these risk factors are based upon where your recreational property is located. Here are the three most important ones:

Fire

Although theft losses occur more often, fire still accounts for most of the dollars insurance companies pay out in claims. The potential damage due to fire is therefore based upon a municipality's ability to respond to, and put out, a fire.

If you own recreational property in an area with fire hydrants, your premium will be lower because the fire department will have access to a large water supply. Fires in hydrant-protected areas can be extinguished at an earlier stage than those in less well-protected areas.

If you own recreational property in an area without hydrants or even a fire department close by, or just a volunteer fire department, the premium will be even higher, due to the obvious higher risk.

Theft

Insurance companies track the loss experience caused by theft by area, which is reflected in the premium you pay.

Weather

If the location of your recreational property has a history of severe weather storms, such as windstorms, snowstorms, hail, or flooding, insurance companies obviously look at and rate these risks as well. They will exclude coverage for those risks, limit it, increase the deductible or increase the premium.

Ways to Reduce Your Premiums

Higher Deductible

Many people don't realize there are ways to reduce the premium payment significantly. What exactly do you want protection for? What you are really concerned with is the possibility of a catastrophe or a total loss. If so, you can save money by increasing your deductible. By doing so, you save the insurance company the expense of investigating and settling small claims. That saving is passed back to you in the form of a reduced premium.

You should never reduce your amount of insurance so that you pay a lower premium. If you ever do have a claim, it could cost you a lot more than any amount you might save.

Use Discounts

Always ask what discounts are available and see if you are eligible. Generally, discounts recognize a lower category of risk. Listed below are the most common types of discounts available. They could range from 5% to 10% premium discount each. You could utilize several of them. However, most insurance companies have a cap on the aggregate amount of discounts not being more than about 50% to 70% of the base premium.

√ Mortgage-free discount

√ Loyalty discount (e.g., a customer for more than three years)

√ Community Watch discount (e.g., your community is a member of Block or Neighbourhood Watch)

√ Mature discount (over 50 years of age)

√ Senior discount (over 60 or 65 years of age)

√ New home up to 10 years old discount (with a depreciated premium discount for each year the house is older than new)

√ Monitored fire and burglary alarm (through a central station)

√ Local alarm discount (built into the home that will go off when motion or fire is detected)

√ Multi-line discount (if you have different types of insurance products with the same insurance company or broker, e.g., house, boat, car, etc.)

√ Claims-free discount (you don't usually have to ask for this)

Most insurance companies will reduce your premium automatically if you have been claims free for three or more years, but don't assume this. Ask the question in advance.

Personal Liability Protection

This is the part of the policy that protects you if you are sued. If someone injures himself or herself on your vacation property (e.g., falls on your stairs, slips on your driveway, deck, or dock, etc.) and a court determines that you are responsible and therefore liable, your insurance company should defend you in court and pay all legal expenses and the amount up to the limit of the policy. The normal minimum limit is $1 million. However, you can and should increase this amount. It is recommended that you increase your coverage up to $5 million minimum. The extra premium is normally very reasonable, and it is cheap money for peace of mind.

There are specific exclusions that apply to this section of the policy. They are listed under the heading "Loss or Damage Not Insured." Make sure you read this carefully.

How to Avoid Being Sued

Every year, many people are injured while visiting the premises of others. The last thing you want is to be sued. The process is stressful, negative, uncertain, time consuming, and often protracted. Here are some suggestions to avoid problems. If you are renting to a tenant, your contract should cover hazard reduction and require the tenants to have tenant insurance coverage as a condition of your tenancy agreement. You should receive a copy of the policy.

Maintain Your Premises

Most injuries are caused by "slip and fall." They are usually the result of a lack of maintenance. In winter, you should clear ice and snow from all walkways on your premises. Exterior steps should be kept in good repair and a handrail provided.

Inside your house, carpets should be secured to stairs and floors and kept free of toys or objects that could trip a visitor.

Alcohol and Guests

If you serve alcohol to guests, you could be found responsible, to some extent, for their subsequent actions. Some courts have gone to extraordinary lengths to assign responsibility to a host. Good judgment is required. In particular, never allow an intoxicated guest to drive a car or boat.

Other Hazards

You are potentially responsible for everything that happens on your premises. If you have a swimming pool, you are responsible for the safe use of the pool. If you have a dog, you are responsible for the actions of the dog. The list is almost endless. If you are renting to a tenant, you want to pass on the responsibility and liability as much as possible to your tenant. As mentioned earlier, you should make it a condition of tenancy that the tenant obtain tenant insurance prior to moving in and provide you with a copy of it.

The good news is that most injuries can be avoided by using nothing more than common sense. All you have to do is be alert to the potential hazards on your own premises.

Additional Types of Insurance to Consider

Mortgage Insurance

If you owe money on your mortgage and die, the bank insurance offered by your lender will pay off the outstanding mortgage. However, there are drawbacks and other options available to this type of insurance. The good news about mortgage insurance is that almost everyone is considered insurable. The drawbacks are that the premiums are high and the insurance is not portable. In other words, it is only for the purpose of paying off your mortgage. A better alternative is to get your own private term life insurance coverage. The premiums will be lower, and you can keep the insurance coverage long after the mortgage has been paid off. It gives you that flexibility. Also, if you become uninsurable in the future due to health reasons, at least you will have your own portable life insurance protection.

Life Insurance

Term life insurance insures a person for a specific period of time or term, and then stops. Term life does not have a cash-surrender value or loan value as with a whole-life plan. Term premiums are less expensive than whole-life premiums. If you have a bank loan or personal or business obligations, consider term life coverage. If you could be hit with a capital gains tax on your death, you should consider the benefits of your estate or beneficiaries being protected from that expense with term life insurance. All insurance proceeds are tax-free. This topic is discussed in more detail in Chapter 13: Estate Planning Issues and Strategies.

Home Office Insurance

It is important to recognize the potential risks of working from home and the policies available for protection against them. If you don't have home office insurance protection, your claim could be denied; that is, you could be personally liable for all financial losses. Always advise your insurance agent that you are operating a business from your home. You will need extra coverage for any risk areas involved directly or indirectly with your business operation. The home office coverage is normally an extension endorsement of your regular homeowner insurance policy coverage. Almost all basic homeowner policies exclude home businesses.

Rental Insurance

If you are renting your vacation home out for nightly or weekly rentals full-time, seasonally, or periodically, you need to extend your basic homeowner coverage to include this risk. If a problem and claim occurs and the insurance company does their investigation, and finds out that you were insured for personal use only, your claim will be denied. Premiums are based on insurance risk. The more you rent out the property during the year, the more likely the insurance company will rate your property under their commercial coverage. This would entail higher premiums, due to the higher risk as a consequence of higher turnover and use by renters.

Have your insurance broker get competitive quotes from different companies. You want to make sure you understand the fine print, and know the limitations and exclusions, etc. You want to make sure you have high third-party liability coverage in case anyone is seriously injured. You don't want to be faced with a shortfall in that type of doomsday scenario. If your recreational property is a full-time or significant rental property, make sure you get protection to cover you for lost revenue while your home is being rebuilt. Sometimes it takes a year or so for a house to be rebuilt, and that could constitute considerable lost revenue.

Title Insurance

Your lawyer or lender could also recommend the benefits of obtaining title insurance for your peace of mind. Sometimes lenders require it. This insurance protects you in the event that pre-existing property defects show up after you bought the property. You would be covered up to the amount of your policy for as long as you are still the property owner.

The types of risks that are usually covered include: claims due to fraud, forgery, or work orders not complied with; zoning and setback non-compliance or deficiencies; survey irregularities; forced removal of existing structures, unregistered rights of way or easements; and lack of vehicular or pedestrian access to the property. Do your comparison-shopping of policy rates, features, and coverage.

For more infomation on insurance options, check out the website www.homebuyer.ca.

12   # Will Planning Issues and Strategies

Your will is the most important document you will ever sign. With very few exceptions, everybody should have a will. A will is the only legal document that can ensure that your assets will be distributed to your beneficiaries according to your wishes (instead of by a government formula), in a timely manner and with effective tax, legal, and estate planning. Your will takes effect only after your death and is kept strictly confidential until that time.

There are no estate taxes or succession duties in Canada, but estate planning can minimize the amount that is taxed in other ways. Part of estate planning also includes having an enduring power of attorney, a living will, and health care directive. For a more detailed discussion of estate and tax planning, refer to *The Canadian Guide to Will and Estate Planning* by Douglas Gray and John Budd, and www.estateplanning.ca. You may also be interested in attending a seminar on recreational property that covers all the key issues. Refer to www.homebuyer.ca for more information on seminars offered in your geographic area.

If you have a recreational second property or vacation rental property, it adds another level of necessity to have a will legally prepared, and to keep it current.

This chapter covers: why you need a will, what's in a will, what happens if you die without a will, preparing a will, and key reasons for consulting a skilled lawyer. It also covers other documents that should be completed concurrent with a will or revised will, including enduring powers of attorney, living wills, health care directives, and a personal information record.

Why You Need a Will

About one out of four people dies suddenly, leaving no opportunity for tax or estate planning if such a plan was not already in place. It is estimated that only one out of three adults has a will, which means that when the other two-thirds die, the government has to become involved. Some people just procrastinate by nature or have busy lives and simply do not put a priority on preparing a will. Others do not appreciate the full implications of dying without a will or even think about it. And some people simply resist the reality that they are mortal. Preparing a will and dealing with estate-planning issues certainly involves facing the issue of mortality in a direct way. If you organize your life plan by having a will and estate plan, you will be leaving a legacy of positive and appreciative memories.

Of those who do have a will, many do not modify it based on changing circumstances. People think of preparing a will when they marry, have children, fly for the first time without their children, hear news of a sudden death of a friend or relative, or are leaving on a vacation. Once they complete a will, they forget about it. Yet not updating your will can be as bad as not having one and could cause your beneficiaries much grief, stress, time, and expense. Your marital status may have changed, assets increased or decreased, or you may have started or ended a business, moved to a new province, or a new government tax or other legislation could be introduced that should prompt you to revisit your estate plan. For those who consider writing their own will, there is a risk of serious mistakes and oversight. Don't even consider it, for reasons that will become clear in this chapter.

What's in a Will?

Depending on the complexity of your estate, your will could be either simple or complex. A basic will contains the following:

- √   name and address of the person who is making the will (known in legal terms as "the testator")
- √   a declaration that the document is your last will and testament and it revokes all former wills and codicils (a supplementary document that may change, add, or subtract from the original will)
- √   appointment of an executor (person or organization that will administer your estate) and possibly a trustee (required where you have included trust provisions in your will)
- √   authorization to pay outstanding debts, including funeral expenses, taxes, fees, and other administrative expenses before any gift of property can be made
- √   disposition of property and cash legacies to beneficiaries, or a gift of part or the entire residue of your estate (what is left after all debts, funeral and administrative expenses, taxes, and fees have been paid and specific property gifts and cash legacies distributed)

√ attestation clause that states that the will was properly signed in the presence of at least two witnesses who were both present at the same time, and who both signed in your presence and the presence of each other

√ appointment of a guardian for children under the age of legal majority. Depending on the province, this can be 18 or 19 years of age.

What Happens If You Don't Have a Will?

If you don't have a will, or don't have a valid will, the outcome could be, and almost certainly will be, a legal and financial nightmare and an emotionally devastating ordeal for your loved ones. This is compounded greatly if you have more complex estates, e.g., having a second home or revenue property. Not having a will at the time of death is called dying "intestate." Under provincial legislation, the court will appoint an administrator. If no family member applies to act as administrator, the public trustee or official administrator is appointed. Your estate will be distributed in accordance with the legal formulas of your province, which are inflexible and almost certainly will not reflect either your personal wishes or the needs of your family or loved ones.

While the law attempts to be fair, it does not provide for special needs. A home or other assets could be sold under unfavourable market conditions in order to distribute the assets. Your heirs may be required to pay taxes that might easily have been deferred or reduced. There may not be sufficient worth in the estate to pay the taxes. Your family could be left without money for an extended period, and your assets may be lost or destroyed. There may be a delay in the administration of your estate and added costs such as an administrator bond. This is similar to an insurance policy if the administrator makes a mistake.

If you die without a will appointing a guardian for your young children, and there is no surviving parent who has legal custody, provincial laws come into effect. The public trustee becomes the guardian and manager of the assets that your children are entitled to. The provincial child welfare services assume responsibility for the children's care, upbringing, education, and health. A relative or other person can apply to the court for guardianship, but any awarding of guardianship will be at the court's discretion, and involves ongoing monitoring, red tape, expense, and delay.

Preparing a Will

There are basically two ways to prepare a will: writing it yourself or having a lawyer do it for you.

Do-It-Yourself Will

This is the poorest choice because the inadequacies of a self-written will could result in a legal, financial, and administrative nightmare for your family, relatives, and beneficiaries. How you expressed your wishes may be legally interpreted differently than what you intended. Worse still, a clause or the whole will could be deemed void for technical reasons. Some people draft a will from scratch or use a "standard form" of will purchased in bookstores or stationery stores. It is false economy. You will be missing out on legal, tax-, and estate-planning advice by doing your own will. A do-it-yourself will is almost guaranteed to leave a legacy of frustration, legal expense, possible litigation, and more money paid to Canada Revenue Agency than required. If you have a second home, your estate matters are even more complex, as clearly outlined in the tax- and estate-planning chapters.

Lawyer-prepared Will

In almost all cases, wills should be prepared by a lawyer who is familiar with wills because he or she is qualified to provide legal advice and is knowledgeable on how to complete the legal work. Depending on the complexity of your estate, you may also need to enlist the expertise of other specialists, including a professionally qualified tax accountant or a financial planner. Refer to Chapter 5: Selecting Your Advisors.

The fee for preparing a basic will is modest, ranging from $200 to $300 or more per person. If your affairs are more complex, which would include owning a vacation home or rental investment recreational property, the fee could be higher due to the additional time and expertise required.

Key Reasons for Consulting a Lawyer

To reinforce the necessity of obtaining a legal consultation before completing or re-doing a will, just look at some of the many scenarios in which legal advice is specifically required because of the complex legal issues and options involved:

√   You own or plan to own investment real estate.

√   You currently jointly own investment real estate with others or plan to do so.

√   You currently own or plan to own a vacation property second home.

√ You own or plan to own foreign real estate on your own or jointly with others.

√ You own or plan to own your own business.

√ You own or plan to own a business with partners.

√ You are separated from your spouse but not divorced.

√ You are planning to separate from your spouse or partner.

√ You are divorced and paying support.

√ You are living in, entering, or leaving a common-law relationship.

√ You are in a blended family relationship.

√ Your estate is large and you need assistance with estate planning to reduce or eliminate taxes on your death.

√ You anticipate being a beneficiary of a substantial inheritance.

√ You have a history of emotional or mental problems such that someone could attack the validity of your will on the basis that you did not understand the implications of your actions.

√ You want to have unbiased, professional advice rather than being influenced by or under duress from relatives.

√ You want to live outside of Canada for extended periods of time, for example, retire and travel south in the winter. Your permanent residence at the time of your death has legal and tax implications. For more information, refer to my book *The Canadian Snowbird Guide: Everything You Need to Know about Living Part-Time in the USA and Mexico.*

√ You have a will that was signed outside Canada or plan to have one signed outside Canada.

√ You want to forgive certain debts, or make arrangements for the repayment of debts to your estate should you die before the debt is paid.

√ You want events to occur that have to be carefully worded, such as having a spouse have income or use of a home until he or she remarries or dies, at which time the balance goes elsewhere.

√ You want to set up a trust for your family, business, investment real estate, vacation property, or charity.

√ You want to donate money or assets to a charitable organization during your life or on your death.

√   You want to make special arrangements to care for someone who is incapable of looking after himself or herself or unable to apply sound financial judgment, for example, a child, an immature adolescent, a gambler, an alcoholic, a spendthrift, or someone with emotional, physical, or mental disabilities or who is ill.

√   You wish to disinherit a spouse, relative, or child because of a serious estrangement or the fact that all your children are now independently wealthy and don't need your money, or they were prodigal and reduced your net worth through poor judgment.

√   You have several children and you want to provide one specific child with the opportunity to buy, have an option to buy, or receive in the will a specific possession of your estate.

As you can see, there are many reasons to consult with a legal expert for a will that is customized for your needs. There are many, many more. The list above is just a small sampling. The general factors to look for when selecting a lawyer are discussed in Chapter 5: Selecting Your Advisors.

Enduring Power of Attorney (PA)

Many lawyers recommend a power of attorney (PA), referred to as an "enduring" or "sustaining" PA, at the same time that they prepare a will. The reason for the word "enduring" or "sustaining" is that the document will continue to have force and effect even if you are unable to revoke it. The purpose of a PA is to designate a person or a trust company to take over your affairs (for example, transferring your vacation property or selling it) if you can no longer handle them due to illness or incapacitation. Another reason is that you may be away for extended periods on personal or business matters. A power of attorney is important if you have substantial assets that require active management. You can grant a general PA over all your affairs, or a limited one specific to a certain task or time period. You can revoke the power of attorney at any time in writing. A PA is valid only in your province. You would need to have a separate PA if you own assets in the United States or elsewhere.

If you do not have an enduring power of attorney and become incapacitated, an application has to be made to the court by the party who wishes permission to manage your affairs. This person would be called a committee. If another family member does not wish to perform this responsibility, a trust company can be appointed, with court approval. Committee duties include filing with the court a summary of assets, liabilities, and income sources, with a description of the person's needs and an outline of how the committee proposes to manage the accounts and/or structure the estate to serve those needs.

Living Will

A living will is designed for those who are concerned about their quality of life when they are near death. It is a written statement of your intentions to the people who are most likely to have control over your care, such as your family and your doctor. Have a copy of the living will where it can be readily obtained, such as in your wallet. Give a copy to your spouse and family doctor. You should also review your living will from time to time to be sure that it still reflects your wishes.

The purpose of a living will is to convey your wishes if there is no reasonable expectation of recovery from physical or mental disability. Such a will may request that you be allowed to die naturally, with dignity, and not be kept alive by "heroic medical measures." In some provinces, a living will is merely an expression of your wishes and is not legally binding on your doctor or the hospital. Other provinces have officially endorsed the concept through legislation if your written instructions are correctly done. For further information and to download free living wills and health care proxies for each province, contact the Joint Centre for Bioethics, University of Toronto, through their website: www.utoronto.ca/jcb.

Health Care Directive or Proxy and Representation Agreement

This is a document that sets out who is going to look after your health care and financial decisions if you are unable to do so, for example, deciding that it is timely for you to go into a personal care facility or nursing home, in conjunction with feedback from your family and health care providers. Someone needs to have the authority to make these types of health care decisions. There are different names for this authority that you are granting, depending on the province, e.g., representation agreement, health care proxy, health care directive, etc. Sometimes this document incorporates your wishes as set out in a living will.

Personal Information Record

If you died suddenly, or had a serious head injury or stroke, would anyone have an accurate and current knowledge of your personal, business, and investment matters? For most people, the answer to that question would be no. That is why you need to prepare a personal information record, and update it both annually and whenever any financial matters change. Your family, executor, and trustee will think of you fondly for having the foresight to make the administration of your estate so much easier. It will also save a lot of money and hassle. This personal information record is normally kept with your will, for example, in your safety deposit box, with a copy at your home. Make sure your executor and family members know where you are keeping it.

To obtain a copy of a personal information record template, go to the website www.estateplanning.ca. The types of matters covered in a typical personal information record would include:

√ personal information such as partners, children, dependants
√ key documents and location of documents
√ names of professionals or advisors you deal with
√ details of banking information
√ details of investment information
√ details of personal property
√ details of personal or investment real estate
√ details of ownership in a business
√ details of mortgages and other debts
√ details of insurance
√ funeral information.

Estate Planning Issues and Strategies

Millions of Canadians have fond memories of spending their holidays at a family cottage. In fact, thousands of cottages, camps, and chalets have been in the same family for several generations, and are the magnets that bring far-flung family members back together for family reunions.

This chapter will provide you with some ideas on how you might want to deal with your vacation home under your estate plan. How the capital gains tax rules apply to a second property or investment property will also be discussed. Your will is a core estate-planning document, as discussed in the previous chapter. In order to help you reduce, postpone, or eliminate capital gains taxes on your vacation property, this chapter will show you how to:

√ utilize the principal residence exemption on your vacation home

√ double up the exemption for properties acquired before 1982

√ use the principal residence exemption on the property with the larger gain

√ arrange the ownership so as to capitalize on another family member's unused principal residence exemption

√ transfer ownership to a trust

√ shift the future growth in the value of your vacation property by a direct transfer of ownership to your children or grandchildren

√ create a life interest and a remainder interest

√ create a charitable remainder trust.

This chapter will highlight only some of the key issues for your consideration. If you want a more comprehensive discussion, refer to my co-authored book (with John Budd, C.A.), *The Canadian Guide to Will and Estate Planning*. The strategies involved in estate planning are complex and require expert professional tax and legal advice to ensure your needs are met. Refer to Chapter 5: Selecting Your Advisors and to Chapter 10: Tax Issues and Strategies.

What Is Estate Planning?

Estate planning refers to the process of preserving and transferring your wealth in an effective manner. From a tax perspective, your estate objectives, including a properly drafted will, include:

- √   minimizing and deferring taxes

- √   moving any tax burden to your heirs to be paid only upon future sale of the assets.

There are techniques to attain the above objectives, including:

- √   arranging for assets to be transferred to family members in a lower tax bracket

- √   establishing trusts for your children and/or spouse

- √   setting up estate freezes, generally for your children, which freezes the capital gains tax payable by the person doing the freeze, and shifts the growth in capital gains to the next generation

- √   making optimal use of the benefits of charitable donations, tax shelters, or holding companies

- √   taking advantage of gifting during your lifetime

- √   minimizing the risk of business creditors encroaching on personal estate assets

- √   having sufficient insurance to cover anticipated tax on death

- √   avoiding probate fees by having assets in joint names or with a designated beneficiary.

Keeping Things in Perspective

Keep in mind that there are many important personal, financial, and legal factors that you need to consider before taking any action. Although achieving tax savings now or in the future is a worthwhile objective, the tax considerations should not be paramount. Your cottage or chalet is probably, next to your family home, the most "emotionally charged" asset that you own. If it has been in your family for a long time, you, your spouse, and each of your children probably have a very close attachment to the place.

Unfortunately, all too often the cottage ends up causing family fights over its ownership, use, and the sharing of the annual operating expenses. Often, a parent will leave the cottage to one child, rather than leaving it to all of the children, fearing that joint ownership among siblings and their spouses will lead to family squabbles. But this approach can also cause hard feelings, because the children who are left out may feel that the parent loves the child who received the cottage more than them. This happens even in cases where the parent equalizes bequests by leaving cash, securities, or other assets to the other children.

Whether you decide to do nothing, or to adopt one of the tax- and estate-planning strategies outlined in this book, your decision should "withstand the test of time." Your personal circumstances will change over the years, and there is no way of knowing what your family situation will be in five, 10, or 20 years' time. Therefore, don't back yourself into a corner. If possible, adopt a plan that is flexible and can be revised to reflect changing circumstances.

Will and Estate Planning and Your Vacation Property

It is extremely important that you take the potential capital gains tax on your vacation property into account when designing your will. Since capital gains resulting from the deemed disposition of property at the time of death will one day have to be reported in the final income tax return, your or your spouse's portion of the overall income tax bill for the final year will relate to such capital gains.

Wills are always drafted in such a way that the executors are instructed to pay the deceased's debts. One such debt would be the income tax for the deceased's final year. The typical will then goes on to describe the specific bequests to various beneficiaries, and what is left (the residue) usually goes to one person or is divided equally among various people. Because the capital gains tax on a vacation property has to be accounted for before the specific bequests and the distribution of the residue, inequities among beneficiaries can occur unintentionally.

Estate-planning Strategies for Your Vacation Property

Utilize the Principal Residence Exemption

Some people may find themselves in the situation of owning one or more properties that are worth less than what they paid for them. Therefore, capital gains tax is not a problem—at least for the time being. Or, in the case of a property that has not been held for a long time, the current market value may not be much higher than the original cost. Also, because some locations are more desirable than others, and real estate prices across Canada do not necessarily follow the same patterns of change, the appreciation in the value of a person's house may be quite small compared to the gain on the vacation property.

Every situation is different. It is not possible to cover all of the permutations and combinations in this chapter. You need to carefully consider how your principal residence exemption can be used in the most effective manner because one of the largest elements of the capital gains tax arising in your estate could be related to your vacation property.

Refer to Chapter 10: Tax Issues and Strategies for a detailed discussion of the option and procedures for utilizing the principal residence exemption for your recreational property.

Transfer the Ownership to a Child

One way of preventing a capital gain from arising on the future death of you or your spouse is to transfer the ownership now to one or more children, or possibly a trust. Trusts will be discussed later. Such a transfer (either as a sale, or as a gift) would have the effect of shifting the ownership and the future growth in value to one or more of your children. Since children normally outlive their parents, such a move will generally have the effect of postponing the time at which there will be a deemed disposition at fair market value of the vacation property. Be aware that a transfer of ownership at this time could give rise to an immediate taxable capital gain, because your deemed proceeds of disposition for capital gains purposes would be the current fair market value of the property. However, if you have only recently purchased the property and a small amount of capital gain has occurred, or you have capital losses from other investments available to use, then it could be a timely strategy.

Up to 1994, a straightforward transfer of ownership to a child was one way of taking advantage of a special $100,000 lifetime capital gains exemption, since such a transfer had to be recorded at fair market value for capital gains purposes. Unfortunately, this $100,000 capital gains exemption was eliminated.

The prime motivating factor in transferring ownership to one or more children is that the odds are that the cottage can "stay in the family" for a much longer period of time, before capital gains tax is triggered at the time of someone's death under the deemed disposition on death rule. However, there are a host of personal, legal, and financial factors to consider in deciding whether or not to make such a transfer. Some of the questions you should ask yourself are:

√   How will you decide which child or children to transfer the property to?

√   What type of legal documentation should be signed prior to, or concurrent with any transfer, to protect the family's and parents' interest, e.g., usage, expenses?

√   What happens if a conflict or estrangement occurs with the child or children "owning" the vacation home?

√   If the child or children are under the age of majority in the province, how will you handle the need for their legally binding signatures on a contract?

√   What if a child has a future marriage break-up? Will the applicable provincial family law legislation exempt the vacation home from any marriage settlement, without a marriage contract or pre-nuptial agreement?

√   Should you keep the ownership of the property in your own name as a hedge against inflation? Maybe the time will come when you would want to sell the property in order to be able to invest the sale proceeds so as to have additional investment income to live on during your retirement years.

Refer to Chapter 14: Maintaining Harmony with Shared Use and Ownership for the type of documentation that should be signed whenever a vacation home use is being shared with family or friends.

Sell the Property to the Children with Promissory Note Back

In this option, you would sell the property to your children at fair market value, and obtain a promissory note back in return instead of cash, if that is your preference. You can then collect any portion of that note, or not, as you choose. You can forgive any unpaid portion of the debt with no adverse tax consequences to your children. In this scenario, you would have to declare the capital gains tax in that taxation year, as a deemed disposition of the property.

However, you could defer tax on your capital gain by structuring the promissory note so that you cannot demand payment over a period of less than five years, for example. That way you could spread the tax on the capital gain over a period as long as the five years.

Buying the Property in the Child's Name with Trust Declaration

Based on legal and tax advice, age of child or children, and other circumstances, you may wish to buy a property and put the legal title of the property to one or more children, but have a declaration of trust document signed concurrently. This document gives you the beneficial ownership to the vacation property, even though your child would show up on title as the legal owner. This type of document would be signed by the relevant parties, and include terms such as:

√   the property is held in trust for you, and at any time at your written request and within a certain specific time, the property would be transferred to your name

√   the property cannot be pledged as security for a mortgage or line of credit without your prior written consent

√   the property cannot be financially encumbered with judgments, liens, etc.

√   the revenue, if any, generated from the property (e.g., vacation rentals), is held in trust for you and for your sole benefit

√   the property can only be used for personal use, and not rental revenue (if that is your wish)

It is common for a lawyer to also recommend that, for precautionary reasons and concurrent with the signing of the above declaration of trust, the new title holder sign a transfer of title document to your name, which could be filed at any time of your choosing, if required.

The benefit of the above type of arrangement is that it permits you to indirectly control the ultimate legal ownership of the property, based on your evolving needs and family circumstances. It gives you lots of flexibility in the event that, for example, your child subsequently has a common-law or marriage relationship that dissolves and the partner makes a claim for separation of joint assets. Another example is your children having business or other creditors who want to file a judgment or lien against the property. Or, you need the money from the house, net after capital gains tax if that applies, for your future health or lifestyle needs, and therefore you exercise the provision in the declaration of trust, and file the pre-signed transfer document of the property to your name for that purpose. You need expert tax and legal advice in this scenario first.

Conversely, you may not need the house for financial reasons, and decide to destroy the declaration of trust document and un-filed transfer of title document at some future point. In other words, you have effectively gifted the property to your child or children on title. You are the only one holding the original documents. In this example, you may feel that your children could sell the property and use the funds to pay off student loans and have a financial buffer left over. However, if your children turn out to be prodigal, or never phone you anymore to see how you are doing, you could transfer the property back! This arrangement gives you options.

You need to get expert legal and tax advice on this strategic approach, as there are issues of gifting, whether capital gains applies to the parents who are beneficial owners if they eventually terminate that relationship, or whether the future sale of the house is capital gains tax-free to the children, on the grounds that it is their principal residence. If the parents transfer the property back to their own names, there would obviously be capital gains tax applicable, as it would be a second (or third) property, and not a principal residence.

In terms of the option and scenario of the parents "tearing up the trust documents," there are two possible interpretations about the timing of the gift by the parents to the children. One interpretation is that the trust arrangement never existed. Therefore, the parent made a gift at the time that the property was purchased in the child's name (i.e., a gift of the cash to fund the purchase). No requirement to disclose anything to the CRA would normally be required, as it was a gift of cash. The children would likely assert that it was their principal residence from the beginning, assuming they have been inhabiting the property.

Another interpretation is that at the time the documents are destroyed there is a gift of the beneficial ownership. The parent has deemed disposition at FMV (fair market value), must report the disposition, and will pay the resultant capital gains tax. The child owns the property with the step up in the ACB (adjusted cost base). Thereafter, the property qualifies as the child's principal residence.

You can see why you need expert tax strategic advice in advance, to optimize the financial benefits to all concerned—with the exception of the CRA.

Transfer the Ownership to a Trust

Over the past decade or so, many vacation properties were transferred into family trusts for tax- and estate-planning reasons. In spite of recent tax changes, trusts continue to be extremely effective estate planning tools in many situations. There are several reasons for the popularity of a trust being used as a vehicle for holding the ownership of a vacation property. Many people are reluctant to transfer ownership directly to one or more children for a variety of reasons. For example, how can you know what the relationship will be like with any of your children in the future? You may not want to lose the legal control over your vacation home, as well as the legal right to use the property. A trust is a useful vehicle for dealing with some of these concerns, and for keeping the ownership of the cottage "one step removed" from the children.

Even though a large number of trusts were set up in recent years primarily as a way of taking advantage of the now-defunct $100,000 capital gains exemption, and in spite of recent tax changes relating to the "21-year deemed disposition rule" for trusts, trusts will continue to be a useful device for holding the ownership of vacation properties in many situations.

The trust deed would normally specify that you have exclusive use of the property during your lifetime, and full control of the property as the trustee of the trust. When you are no longer using the property, you can distribute it to the beneficiaries you have selected. On distribution, the property can be moved from the trust to the designated children as the original cost base. Thus, capital gains tax would be deferred until the property is sold by the next generation.

Using a Family Trust

With this type of family trust, you do not need to hire a trust company to act as the trustee. In fact, most trust companies would decline to act as a trustee for the type of discretionary trust that is so often used as a vehicle for holding the ownership of a cottage. There are too many family issues to consider and too many potential conflicts (or lawsuits!) if the trustees were ever to decide to transfer the ownership to one of the capital beneficiaries, to the exclusion of the others.

Under trust law, there is nothing to prevent the *settlors* of the trust (the person(s) who creates the trust), from being the *trustees* (those who hold legal ownership of the trust). However, there may be a tax problem in doing this. Under a particular set of rules that apply to *revocable trusts*, the trust might be forced to recognize a capital gain (assuming the cottage goes up in value) if the cottage were to be transferred to any of the children during the lifetime of the settlor(s) of the trust. The trust should be designed so that it can be terminated, if necessary, prior to its twenty-first anniversary, so as to avoid the 21-year deemed disposition rule.

Ordinarily, a trust can distribute property that has appreciated in value to any capital beneficiary who resides in Canada on a rollover basis, without having to recognize the accrued gain for tax purposes. However, in the case of trusts that are subject to the revocable trust rules in the *Income Tax Act*, a rollover to the capital beneficiaries can generally be done only after the death of the settlor(s).

It is possible to prevent the application of the revocable trust rules in several ways. For example, there could be three trustees of the trust, not two. For reasons too technical to explain here, it would probably also be necessary for the trust agreement to stipulate that any decisions of the trustees do not have to be unanimous, and that a simple majority is all that is required in order to make any decisions or to carry out any transactions for the trust. In other words, two out of three trustees must agree. Furthermore, the majority rule provision in the trust agreement may also need to say that the "third trustee" must always be one of the majority, that is, the third trustee should have a veto on any decisions.

It is not possible to go into all of the technical details of setting up a trust. You should ensure that you fully understand all of the consequences of putting the ownership of your cottage into a trust, and be sure to get integrated tax advice from an accountant or lawyer who is familiar with the special rules relating to the taxation of trusts.

The Joint Partner Trust

If you are age 65 or older, and you wish to leave your assets to your spouse or partner, you can now do this by transferring your assets into a joint partner trust while you are alive. During your lifetime, you would continue to have the use of the trust's assets, and to receive any income or capital gains realized on such assets within the trust. The *Income Tax Act* allows assets to be transferred into a joint partner trust at cost, without triggering capital gains tax.

On your death, the assets that are held by the joint partner trust will pass to your spouse under the terms of the trust, rather than under the terms of your will, or they will remain in the trust until your partner passes away. A joint partner trust achieves a postponement in capital gains taxation on death, since the trust's assets are not deemed to be disposed of at fair market value until the second partner dies. This is no different than if you left assets to your spouse under your will. However, assets being transferred after your death via a joint partner trust may not be subject to provincial probate fees, depending on the province in which you reside.

A joint partner trust can be used for a same-sex or opposite-sex spouse, or for a common-law spouse.

The Alter Ego Trust

An alter ego trust is similar to a joint partner trust, but is for people 65 or older who do not have a spouse or partner. At the time of your death, the trust's assets would be deemed disposed of at fair market value for capital gains tax purposes. This is no different than for assets that you held personally at the time of death, where there is no surviving spouse.

Besides avoiding probate fees, another significant advantage of alter ego and joint partner trusts is that there is no requirement for obtaining court approval after your death, and no requirement to file a list of the assets that are passing to your intended beneficiaries under the terms of the trust. Even if there were no savings in probate fees, many affluent people 65 and older are using joint partner and alter ego trusts as a means of preserving secrecy regarding the level of their net worth and information on how their estates are to be distributed after their death.

Using a Life Interest and a Remainder Interest

Another planning technique that can produce results similar to those achieved with the use of a trust involves the creation of a life interest and a remainder interest in your cottage. If you already own a vacation property, this would mean altering the form of ownership so that one or more of your children would be granted a remainder interest in the property. You and/or your spouse would retain a life interest.

If you are about to acquire a vacation property, you might consider arranging the purchase so that you and/or your spouse acquire the life interest in the property, and one or more of your children acquire the remainder interest. This could be a good way of deferring capital gains taxation, provided that you are absolutely certain about the full ownership ultimately passing to the particular child (or children) who hold the remainder interests, after the deaths of you and/or your spouse.

Under this form of ownership, the person who holds the life interest has the legal right to the use and enjoyment of the property for the rest of his or her life (unless something is done to intentionally terminate the life interest prior to the person's death). The person who acquires the remainder interest does obtain a type of ownership interest in the property, but there are no immediate rights to use the property.

Basically, they must wait until the person who holds the life interest dies, at which time the full rights of ownership and use of the property will pass. The life interest/remainder interest form of ownership can produce similar tax results to those that are achieved with a trust. However, you don't have as much flexibility as with a discretionary trust, because you need to decide now, rather than later, who will ultimately get the ownership of the property.

On the other hand, a distinct advantage over a trust is that a vacation property which is owned by way of a life interest/remainder interest is not subject to the 21-year deemed disposition rule which applies to trusts. Whereas the "useful life" of most trusts is not more than 21 years because of the deemed disposition rule, you could hold a life interest in a vacation property for the rest of your life without there being any deemed disposition for capital gains tax purposes.

Why would you want to utilize this form of ownership? One reason might be that you are absolutely certain about whom the property should go to after your death. By creating the remainder interest now, rather than allowing the property to pass to the intended beneficiary under the terms of your will, no capital gains tax will arise at the time of your death. This is because the termination of your life interest does not attract capital gains taxation, under the present income tax rules, which are always in a state of flux. However, there is a catch.

Unfortunately, the creation of the life interest and remainder interest is treated for capital gains purposes as a deemed disposition for proceeds equal to the fair market value of the property at that time. Therefore, if you currently own a property that has gone up in value, the creation of a remainder interest in favour of one of your children would trigger a taxable capital gain, and income tax would be payable now rather than later. You would need to obtain strategic advice in advance on this plan.

Principal Residence Exemption and Trusts

A personal residence held by a joint partner or alter ego trust will continue to qualify for the principal residence exemption. For other types of trusts, the principal residence exemption may also be available depending upon whether the property is regularly inhabited by a beneficiary of the trust, and certain other conditions are met.

Buying Life Insurance to Cover Future Tax Liabilities

One of the least expensive solutions to the capital gains tax problem on your vacation property may be to purchase enough life insurance to cover the future capital gains tax liability. Therefore, instead of setting up a trust (and possibly paying tax on a taxable capital gain that is triggered on the transfer into the trust), it may be better to acquire some form of permanent life insurance (such as whole life, universal life, or term-to-100 insurance) to provide funds to cover the tax.

Obviously, there is a cost in taking out life insurance, and the older you are, the more expensive it is. If you are in your sixties or seventies, the premiums may be prohibitive on the amount of insurance that would fully cover the future capital gains tax liability. You also may not be medically eligible for life insurance coverage. A further consideration is that the capital gains tax exposure on your vacation property will keep rising, if the property grows in value. Therefore, the amount of life insurance that you take out today may not be enough in five, 10, or 20 years' time. However, it is a common and popular estate-planning option. If the premiums are unaffordable, you could speak to your children if they are going to be the eventual beneficiaries of the vacation property, and arrange for them to pay the premiums.

Using a Corporation to Own Vacation Property

It is almost always a bad idea to utilize a corporation to hold the ownership of a property that is for the personal use and enjoyment of the shareholder of the corporation or members of his or her family. Suffice to say that there can be a variety of adverse income tax implications. In particular, the shareholder may have to report a taxable benefit each year in his or her income tax return, based on an imputed rent calculation of the value of the personal use of the corporate-owned property.

One exception to the rule is where a so-called *single purpose corporation* is used to hold the ownership of a vacation property that is located in the United States. This has been a common practice for many years as a device for avoiding U.S. estate tax. However, recent changes by the CRA have occurred. Properties acquired after December 31, 2004, are now subject to taxable benefit rules if acquired in corporations. Only grandfathered properties escape. Check with a tax expert.

Donating Your Recreational Property to Charity

This option is worth considering if you do not have children to pass your vacation home to, or you don't want to for whatever reason, or the children have all left the nest and moved to other geographic areas and no longer use the family cottage, or the children are no longer interested in using it, or they have their own respective recreational property that they use and enjoy.

If you are considering donating your vacation home to charity, you need specialized tax and legal advice. Most major charities have staff who can explain to prospective donors, without any obligation of course, the benefits your donation would make to the charity of interest to you. They also have access to legal and tax experts who will assist you, without charge, on behalf of the charity, to facilitate your charitable wishes. There are numerous tax benefits to you of donating to charity. For a detailed discussion of charitable giving and the numerous tax benefits, refer to *The Canadian Guide to Will and Estate Planning* or www.estateplanning.ca.

The three main ways of donating a vacation property to charity are discussed below. There are other options and variations available as well.

Charitable Remainder Trusts

In some situations a trust can be used to make a donation of property to a charity. A charitable remainder trust involves the creation of a trust under the terms of which a particular charity is named as the capital beneficiary and the donor is named as the income beneficiary. The donor would then transfer one or more assets to the trust. The trustees of the trust would hold the legal title to the property under the terms and conditions spelled out in a written trust agreement.

As income beneficiary of the trust, the donor could be entitled to all the income that is earned on property within the trust, for example, if you have a vacation home rental property, or use it periodically for rental revenue. The trust agreement would specify that, upon the donor's death, the trust's assets are to be transferred to the capital beneficiary charity.

Alternatively, you could receive an annuity during your lifetime from the proceeds of the sale of the vacation property by the charity.

Such a trust might also be used to hold real estate that is intended to be donated to the charity after the death of the donor. Under the terms of the trust agreement, the donor might retain the exclusive use of the property during his or her lifetime, that is, a legal "life interest." This would allow you to retain possession and continue to have the use and enjoyment of the property during your lifetime. This is a somewhat complex estate-planning technique.

In most situations, a donation tax credit at the current fair market value is allowed at the time that the property is transferred to the trust, provided that the trust agreement contains certain terms and conditions. However, the amount that is eligible for the donation tax credit is not the full value of the property transferred into the trust. Instead, the donation amount is a reduced amount that must be calculated by an actuary, based on the donor's life expectancy. In effect, the donation amount is the value of the property transferred to the trust, minus the actuarial value of the donor's "life interest."

As an estate-planning technique, this option has benefits you may want to consider. You can contribute to a charity or charities of your choice, and provide a benefit to society in that way. There is no capital gains tax on death, as the property is being transferred to a charity. You get the immediate benefit of a charitable donation tax credit that you can use for your financial-planning purposes, including offsetting against future tax owing for your income or capital gains during your lifetime or on your death.

Gifts in Kind

You could provide for a gift of your recreational real estate (referred to as a "gift in kind") under your will, to be made to one or more charities.

Most gifts in kind are eligible for the same donation tax credit as a cash gift, but with a few notable exceptions as outlined below. In the case of a gift in kind, the donation tax credit is based on the fair market value of the property that is donated. Normally, it is necessary to obtain an independent appraisal in order to substantiate the fair market value of such a gift, so as to enable the charitable organization to issue an official donation receipt.

There are also capital gains tax implications of making a gift in kind. When any property is disposed of by way of gift, the donor is considered, for income tax purposes, to have received notional sale proceeds equal to the fair market value of the property. In the case of property that is donated to charity under the terms of a person's will, one needs to look at the combined effect of the usual deemed disposition of the property at the time of death for capital gains tax purposes, as well as the donation tax credit that may be claimed based on the fair market value of the property. The donation tax credit should be 100% of the fair market value.

Charitable Memorial Endowment

You may wish to use the equity in the vacation property as a funding source during your lifetime or on your death for a charitable memorial endowment. You might establish an endowment in memory of a loved one in their name, in honour of a passion or keen interest they had that reflected their joy and love of life, for example, if they had a life-long love of music, and played an instrument or sang. In this example, you could set up during your lifetime a memorial scholarship for students in the faculty of music at your local college or university. The annual scholarship could be for students needing a bursary or based on academic excellence. You would set the criteria.

For most charities in Canada, there is a minimum donation of $10,000 to establish a memorial scholarship. You could then set it up in such a way that your vacation home would be transferred to the charity either during your lifetime or your death. The proceeds of sale would be added to your pre-established memorial endowment with the charity. This type of charitable donation is invested by the charity, and after administrative fees are taken off, the rest is available for the annual scholarships that you have designated.

Most charities will guarantee you a minimum or fixed interest rate on your funds for the charitable use you desire, net after administrative fees have been taken off. If interest rates are fixed by the charity and rates go up, the extra revenue from investments will be added to your endowment fund to increase the capital. Your endowed capital is not at risk, as the allowable investments by charities are controlled. Write down the questions you want to ask to satisfy yourself before you meet with your own advisors to review your wishes.

Should You Pay Capital Gains Tax Now, or Later?

The dilemma you may be facing at some point is whether to "bite the bullet" and pay the capital gains tax based on the current fair market value, or leave things as they are and have your estate bear the capital gains tax burden at the time of your death, based on that fair market value.

When it comes to tax planning, a good principle to follow is that you should never trigger a tax liability any sooner than you have to. Although your arithmetic might show that it is cheaper to trigger the capital gain now and pay the applicable tax, than to pay tax in the future on a much higher gain, there is still no way of knowing when the future "taxable event" (i.e., death) will occur. Therefore, it is usually wise for one to plan his or her affairs so that capital gains taxes can be postponed until the time of death, rather than triggering taxable capital gains on transfers of ownership to a child or grandchild or trust during one's lifetime. However, it is difficult to generalize, because everyone's situation is different.

Taxation of Investment Properties on Death

The deemed disposition of the property may trigger recapture of previous CCA (capital cost allowance, i.e., depreciation) claims, if the value of the property is greater than the un-depreciated capital cost pool. Your accountant can discuss this scenario with you, so you can consider strategic tax-planning options.

Probate Taxes

All provinces other than Quebec have a probate tax on the value of the assets that are part of the deceased's estate. The amount varies depending on the province. For example, Alberta's is the lowest at a maximum of $400. British Columbia has a sliding scale up to $50,000, and 1.4% of the value of the estate over that amount with no maximum cap. Ontario is $5 on each $1,000 for the first $50,000, and $15 per $1,000 thereafter, without maximum.

In order to avoid probate taxes, sometimes people register the vacation property in joint names, or joint tenancy, for example, with one of their children. If one person dies, their equity in the property automatically transfers to the surviving owner, bypassing the will and thereby avoiding probate tax. The intent and fairness of this probate avoidance technique could be challenged depending on the circumstances, e.g., if there were other children not included on title in this scenario. Alternatively, one of the children might have personal or business debts that could result in a court judgment and lien against the property. One could be penny wise but pound foolish.

Never make a tax- and estate-planning decision based on probate taxes. There are far more important issues, strategies, and implications to consider, after you receive skilled tax and legal advice.

Limiting Your Estate Liability Exposure

What if you are currently running your own small business and you die holding personal use or rental investment vacation property? Your business could cease to function, as you are the key person. If the business goes under, creditors will start looking for assets. If you are liable under a personal guarantee or as a director, then creditors could make claims against your estate.

Here are some options to discuss with your professional advisors to minimize the risk to your estate:

√ Make sure you have a will. A current will that has been drafted with your lawyer and accountant is the first step.

√ Make sure you have a shareholder's agreement with a buy-sell clause with all investment or business partners if that situation applies. This enables one owner to buy out the other's interest in certain situations while they are alive or from their estate.

√ Designate beneficiaries of your insurance policies. By designating beneficiaries in your insurance policies, the money bypasses the will completely and is therefore not part of your estate. It goes directly to your designated beneficiaries tax-free. Your personal creditors can claim only from assets in your estate.

√ Designate beneficiaries for your RRSPs and RRIFs. By designating beneficiaries for registered retirement plans, you bypass your will and your estate. The money goes directly to the beneficiary and is unavailable to creditors. You can also designate beneficiaries for your non-registered investments.

√ Consider the use of trusts. If you set up a living trust while you are alive, it bypasses your will and therefore your estate on your death. A testamentary trust is set up through your will, and takes effect after your death. Both types divert assets out of your estate, away from creditors of your estate.

√ For more information on will- and estate-planning, refer to the latest edition of *The Canadian Guide to Will and Estate Planning* by Douglas Gray and John Budd or refer to www.estateplanning.ca.

√ If you own and operate a small business and you want more detail on how to protect your personal assets, refer to my books *The Canadian Small Business Legal Advisor* and *The Complete Canadian Small Business Guide*. Also refer to www.smallbiz.ca.

Estate-planning Tips to Remember

It would be prudent to keep the following things in mind:

√ If you are thinking of selling or changing the ownership of your vacation property in the near future, whatever you do, talk it over with your family before you act.

√ If you are planning to leave your cottage, camp, or ski chalet to one or more children under your will, discuss your plans with all your children now. It may be better to resolve any hard feelings now, rather than causing an irreparable family rift after you have gone.

√ If you are planning to leave the cottage to your children under a joint ownership arrangement, is that really such a good idea? Your hope might be that the cottage will be the "glue" that keeps the family together after you're gone. However, this might be the last thing that the children would want. And they might be unwilling to admit their true feelings about this to you or your spouse.

√ There are thousands of vacation properties that are jointly owned by second- and even third-generation descendants of the original owners. Everybody gets along reasonably well, and they manage to sort out the various problems of sharing the use and financial responsibilities. However, there are also many other situations where the jointly-owned vacation home has become the battleground for siblings, cousins, and in-laws who can't agree on anything. Talk over your plans with your family, and speak to your tax and legal advisors to help you reach a decision.

√ The principal residence exemption does not depend on whether your vacation home is your "main" residence; nor does it matter if you show it as the address on your T1 income tax return. Secondly, the principal residence exemption is based on a formula that takes into account the number of years of ownership, and the number of years the particular property is *designated* as your principal residence (for capital gains purposes only).

√ The principal residence automatically allows one-half hectare of land to be included with the dwelling as a principal residence. This is equivalent to about two acres. The *Income Tax Act* also allows land in excess of one-half hectare to be included under the principal residence umbrella, provided that the taxpayer can demonstrate that the excess land is necessary for the person's "use and enjoyment" of the property as a principal residence.

Keep Current with Canadian Vacation Home Magazines

If you own a cottage, ski chalet, or second residence, consider subscribing to the four main Canadian magazines that specialize in cottage, chalet, and resort properties. They are a constant source of useful information, and often contain articles or letters to the editor that deal with financial, estate-planning, and tax matters. The magazines are: *Western Canadian Resorts, Vacation Homes and Investment Properties; Cottage Life; Cottage;* and *The Cottager*. Refer to the Appendix under Helpful Websites for contact information.

For more information, refer to the website www.homebuyer.ca. Also consider taking one of the seminars on recreational property offered by the National Real Estate Institute Inc. in your geographic area. You can obtain more details form the homebuyer.ca website.

PART V

Now That It's Yours

CHAPTER **14** Maintaining Harmony with Shared Use and Ownership

We have all heard stories of conflict revolving around the use of a cottage owned by family members or friends. Possibly you have personally experienced the pain and frustration that results when disagreements arise, emotions are vented, and negative dynamics are raised.

Maybe you are thinking of buying a vacation home with family members or friends. Maybe you, or you and your siblings, have inherited a family cottage. Alternatively, maybe you anticipate the family cottage will be passed on to the next generation in the near or distant future, and you want to ensure that peace is kept in the family. Chapter 8: Investing for Yourself or with Others went into detail on other issues that need to be reviewed, depending on your circumstances.

Almost all, if not all, of the numerous conflict-causing scenarios that could potentially occur when people are sharing the use or ownership of a recreational property can be anticipated and avoided. In some respects, it is not unlike a marriage, where we bring our own backgrounds, personalities, experiences, expectations, values, habits, and ideas into a relationship. Flexibility, pragmatic compromise, respect, being open-minded, and keeping the bigger and longer picture in perspective are admirable and desirable traits that can go a long way to maintaining tranquility in the cottage environment.

With diligent, prudent, and insightful preparation, you can ensure that harmony and peace reign supreme. The result will be lifelong lingering memories that are positive and nurturing to the spirit and soul. A relaxing lifestyle and quality of life full of laughter, joy, new experiences, and good times shared with friends and loved ones. Life is entirely too short to settle for anything less, is it not?

How do you attain this state of nirvana and vacation home bliss rather than risking a chronic migraine? It all has to do with looking on the management and operation of the cottage as a business—that is, with a logical structure and written framework with rules and regulations and use policies. The goal is to avert all the classic relationship pitfalls and human misunderstandings that can occur.

If you are a parent considering bequeathing the property to your children, it is critically important to get legal and tax advice for your planning, and to openly discuss a lot of key issues with your children, so that there are no misunderstandings and sensitive areas can be respectfully explored long in advance. This book's chapters on Estate Planning Issues and Strategies, and Tax Issues and Strategies, are particularly helpful in considering the options before you meet with your professional advisors.

This chapter will cover some of the tips to follow to maintain harmony when sharing the use and ownership of your vacation property.

Draft a Written Vacation Home Use Agreement

If you have shared ownership and shared use with family or friends of a vacation home, or will have, you should consider the management of the cottage as a business. Like any business that works well, you need to have systems in place, and use policies, and rules and regulations to give structure and to create a framework for the operation of the cottage. You need to clearly and unambiguously define, in writing, the rights and responsibilities of the owners who are sharing the use of recreational property.

Refer to the Appendix for a detailed checklist on Vacation Property Sharing and Use Agreement Checklist. This will stimulate discussion and ideas.

Meet with the other owners over the phone or in person, and establish the guidelines and agenda for discussion. You want to make sure that you are philosophically on the same planet. Have regular annual or semi-annual meetings. Elect the president and secretary, take minutes of the outcome of the meetings, and circulate them in a draft form. Have everyone put all the issues and concerns to be addressed on the table for discussion. Examples of the issues will be discussed now.

Topics to Discuss and Cover in Your Agreement

Here is a sampling of the types of issues that should be addressed. Everyone's situation is different, but there are many core commonalities:

How Property Is Legally Held

Whether you are buying a property with family or relatives, or have inherited it, how the owners are registered is an important consideration. That is, whether it is held in joint tenancy or tenancy in common. If joint tenancy, when an owner dies, his or her legal title in the property is automatically transferred to the remaining owners and bypasses the deceased's will.

If the title is in tenancy in common, it means that each owner is registered as having a proportional interest relative to their equity rights. For example, if there are four owners, two could each own an undivided 25% interest in the property, a third owner could own an undivided 40% interest in the property, and the fourth owner could own an undivided 10% interest. The implication of this legal format is that each owner could pledge their respective legal interest as security to the bank if they wanted to. If an owner dies, their legal interest goes to whomever is named in the will as the beneficiary, e.g., one or more individuals or a charity for that matter. That is, assuming they have a will.

For more discussion, refer to Chapter 9: Legal Issues and Strategies.

Right of First Refusal by Other Owners on Death of an Owner

A key issue to consider is what happens if one of the property owners dies? Who is going to get that individual's portion of the equity ownership? As discussed above, there are many permutations of outcome. The owners should have a written agreement prepared by a lawyer stating that, in the event of an owner's death, the remaining owners have a right to buy out the equity, based on a set formula and valuation criteria that everyone agrees to in advance, as well as payment options. If the owners are business partners, that is one issue. If the owners are family members, that is a more complicated issue. It is possible that the deceased's family want to maintain their interest in the cottage. So lots of issues and implications need to be considered and addressed.

Every Owner Should Have a Will and Enduring Power of Attorney

It should be part of any owner's agreement that every owner has a current will prepared by a lawyer, and keeps it updated annually and when special circumstances occur. The reason is that in the absence of a will, the laws of the state, i.e., the province, take over. Every province has legislation dealing with wills, trusts, and the lack of a will. The distribution is set out by formula. You would have lost the ability to have your wishes met, or have any strategic tax- and estate-planning done to reduce taxes. It will invariably cause stress, expense, uncertainty, delay, and very likely fractious discord among the people you care more about. You don't want to go there.

In addition, every owner should have an enduring power of attorney. This document deals with the right of someone else to act on your behalf on financial and legal matters, if you are not able to do so mentally for whatever reason. You assign who you want to have as your "attorney" or person to act for you. So, if any documents need to be signed dealing with the vacation property, a legal protocol has been set up to do so. The "enduring" word means that the power of attorney will continue, even if you have lost the mental ability to revoke it.

For a more detailed discussion on wills, trusts, and enduring powers of attorney, refer to Chapter 13: Estate Planning Issues and Strategies.

Owners Need to Discuss Long-term Goals

It is important to discuss goals in advance of any purchase, unless you inherited the cottage. If you have inherited a cottage jointly with siblings, it is important to have a meeting and agenda to discuss a range of issues of joint interest or concern. For example, each owner should do a candid self-evaluation of their individual needs, wants, expectations, intentions, attitudes, concerns, and philosophy on the use and enjoyment of the cottage. A good technique is to write down your thoughts on all of these, and reflect on them over time and update them, and before any meeting, so that specific issues can be added to the agenda. For example, possibly some owners want the property for speculation or investment purposes, and a short- or long-term hold and then sale. Others may want it for personal use only, and to pass it down through the generations of their respective families. Still others may want to use the property for generating as much revenue as possible, or a hybrid mix of personal use and rental income during the peak-demand seasonal periods.

Discuss How to Manage a Parting of the Ways

For many different reasons—such as illness, disability, a move, a divorce, financial problems in a business or investments, falling out with other owners, wanting to use the money for other lifestyle interests or to buy one's own vacation property—an owner may want to sell their equity interest. Conversely, one or more of the owners may want to buy out the other owner or owners. A fair formula should be established for these types of scenarios. There are various methods available.

Determine Formulas and Policies for Resolving Disputes

In any joint ownership relationship, there are always potential areas of disagreement or impasse on issues of concern. There should be an objective process to follow, through written procedure and protocol, to find resolutions.

Owners Need to Treat the Property Like a Business with a Budget

An agreement needs to be reached about financial expectations: monies to be spent annually for maintenance/upkeep; need, expectations, and priorities for improvements; how emergency expenses will be handled; contingency buffer for the unexpected; funds for staples and supplies; who is going to perform the work when repairs or improvements are needed, i.e., work party or a hired contractor.

An annual or semi-annual meeting needs to be held over the phone or in person with an agenda circulated in advance for discussion, along with elected "officers" (president and treasurer), and minutes kept and recorded. Two bank accounts should be set up. One would be a chequing account for ongoing operating expenses (e.g., property taxes, utilities, insurance, mortgage interest if applicable, maintenance, supplies, etc.), as well as to receive any revenue received from guests or renters. Another account could be a trust account for future anticipated expenses for repair and improvements and contingency buffer. It is prudent to have two signatures required for each account. Once an annual budget is drawn up for operating and future reserve purposes, the owners could divide the total amount and divide that by the equity interest of the owners. A deadline would be set for the owners to make their contributions to the two accounts. Policy on borrowing money and amount, if required, need to be discussed. Ledgers and bookkeeping need to be maintained, and this responsibility should be clearly defined.

Maintenance Schedule

All properties require regular maintenance and upkeep. A schedule should be determined including who will do it, when, and how the maintenance will be done. Will the work be done by individuals or families, or by work parties with friends? If a contractor will be hired, who will get the competitive quotes and oversee the work?

Policy on Use of the Property and Rules and Regulations

This is an important step that will help you pre-empt conflict. A written policy would cover everything from use of boats or other equipment and replenishing gas and minimum age for use, to whether the cottage can be rented out and for how much and to whom. Booking procedures should be covered (double booking, collection, time limits, reminders, bumping, first-come first-served, etc.) as well as user fees (when and what to charge, security deposit, responsibility for loss or damage, etc.). The use policy should be readily available to the owners, and those using the property or renters. The policy manual should also cover keys, security, storage (shared or non-shared, and closets or rooms allocated for the owners or guests), gardening, laundry, smoking inside house, fire extinguishers and smoke alarms, quiet hours, use of cottage by minors without adults present, first aid kit, emergency phone numbers and contact numbers for trades, garbage removal, recycling, bird feeders, energy savings policy, environment care policy, agreement on how interior decorating will be done, etc.

Prepare Lots of Checklists

Checklists are an effective and organized way of maintaining continuity of approach, and serve as reminders to owners, guests, or renters. Common types of checklists would include: opening-up checklist, closing-down checklist, basic pantry checklist, supply checklist, checking-in checklist, checking-out checklist (including clean-up), meal-planning checklist, care and maintenance checklist, asset checklist (for group or individual owners) for boats, car left at cottage, equipment, other toys, etc.

Obtain Legal and Tax Advice on Your Agreement

After you have prepared a draft agreement, have it reviewed by a lawyer who practices in the area of real estate and contract law. To avoid any perceived conflict of interest, confidentiality concerns, or problems if a dispute occurs in the future, you want to make sure this lawyer is not already acting for one of the other owners. The lawyer should be asked to look for any loopholes or gaps in the content of the agreement, and recommend changes to make the document more legally enforceable.

Once you have the above document draft finalized, take it to a tax lawyer or qualified tax accountant for review. Again, this person should not already be acting for one of the owners. You want this professional to review the agreement and provide feedback on the tax and accounting issues, to make sure that those are taken into account, and have the agreement modified accordingly.

Refer to Chapter 5: Selecting Your Advisors for suggestions on finding the right experts for your needs.

Once the draft agreement has been sanctified by a qualified lawyer and accountant, and agreed to by all the owners, then it is ready to be signed.

15 Vacation Home Exchanges and Bartering Networks

There are many benefits to owning a property in a recreational area. One such benefit that is often overlooked is that you can creatively exchange your home for other lifestyle and monetary options that might appeal to you.

You might occasionally envy those who have a timeshare in a resort area, because they can trade their timeshare allotment of a week or a month in their home location for a timeshare in some exotic or tropical area of the world. You might think this is an attractive feature in case one tires of going to the same location all the time.

Of course, you could rent your home periodically or seasonally and use the money to cover all or part of your travel costs to anywhere you want. Or you could become a snowbird and rent your winter or all-season vacation property, for example, if you are in a ski resort area, while you spend up to six months in the U.S. Sunbelt, Mexico, or some other desirable locale.

If you own your own vacation property, you also have many advantages over the timeshare option when it comes to utilizing your property for other appealing purposes, quite apart from the capital gains appreciation, and the pride of ownership and control over your property.

The main attractive option is a home exchange anywhere in the world. A secondary option is a trade exchange, which is sometimes referred to as a bartering network. This chapter discusses the above options in more detail.

Home or Vacation Exchange

You probably know people who have done home exchanges, or you are familiar with the terminology but not the details of the process.

Home exchanging has become a very established and popular trend over the past 20 years. In simple terms, it means exchanging your vacation home and/or primary residence with other people's homes for a short time, such as a long weekend if they are within easy reach, or a week to a month, or long-term for up to six months or a year. Home exchanges are available everywhere in the world, and can be simultaneous or non-simultaneous. Exchanges frequently include the use of a car.

Home exchanging can be an exciting and rewarding lifestyle experience. It allows you to travel almost anywhere in the world inexpensively, with your accommodation being free, and generally the car available for usage as well. Your only costs are the airfare, tourist activities, fuel for the car, and meals. As you would be eating and driving anyway at home, the net outlay can be very minimal, especially if you are using airline points, or if you get cheap flight deals. So you can easily vacation away from your vacation home and experience new adventures, sights, scenes, people, and culture.

Money rarely changes hands between exchangers. It is almost an unwritten philosophical rule that one exchanger not pay another. Although one type of housing accommodation might be more luxurious than another, this is usually offset by the location or attractiveness of the area; for example, a Whistler chalet for an apartment in the centre of Paris.

Here are some points to consider about the home exchange option:

Profile of Typical Exchanger

Well, there is no typical exchanger profile. They range from 30 years to 80-plus, from retirees with a desire to travel, to parents with young children not old enough for school; from teachers with the summer off as well as Christmas and Easter breaks, to parents with school-age children who want to travel in the summer; from a single person or couple taking a six-month or one-year sabbatical from work with or without kids, to adults who want to experience a year or two in different parts of the world by having a continuous series of sequential exchanges, or a long-term exchange in various countries. Some people wish to travel around the world for many years, and knock off each item on the checklists from the various books on the theme of "places to see before you die" before they pass on to the ultimate extended vacation in the hereafter.

The common denominator is a love of travel and the joy that comes from new experiences and exploring diverse and different parts of the world.

Having a Vacation Home Provides a Flexible and Attractive Exchange Option

You are presumably only using your vacation home part of the year. If it is located in a year-round access location, and particularly a developed recreational or resort area, then it would be in high demand and more desirable for exchange guests any time of the year. This will make your exchanging easier.

It is generally easier to get a vacation home ready for visitors than it would a primary residence, especially if you periodically rent your vacation home and have drawer or closet space already cleaned out to be used by your guests. If you rent, you are accustomed to people you don't know using your property. You probably don't have as many personal possessions and clothing in your vacation home as in your primary home.

You also have flexibility in arranging an exchange with your vacation home, as the timing of the exchange does not have to be simultaneous. This will be explained in more detail in the next point.

Simultaneous and Non-Simultaneous Exchanges

The most common format is a simultaneous exchange where two parties exchange with one another at the same time. The times do not have to be of equal duration. It is whatever is arranged. For example, you might be spending four weeks in Europe and want to spend a week in several different areas. You might exchange two weeks of your primary home and/or vacation property for two weeks in a Tuscan villa in Italy, then trade another two weeks of your vacation home for one week in Paris or Rome, and just have the freedom to roam the remaining week or travel between the above exchanges.

Another format is the non-simultaneous exchange. In this format, you don't exchange at the same time. You can bank—or the other exchangers bank—the use at a future time to be agreed upon or determined at some later date. For example, you might be planning to visit relatives next summer for two months, leaving your vacation home available for that period. You could arrange with exchangers in other parts of the world of interest to you, to use your vacation home during your absence. You would then use those banked exchanges in the future when it is more convenient for your travel scheduling. In practical terms, it does not create an issue in most cases whether you are using someone's primary residence or vacation home or both. With enough lead time, flexibility in scheduling when they are going to be away on vacation is easy to arrange.

Another option to extend your range of attractive offerings is to make arrangements with friends or relatives with vacation homes or even primary homes, to make their homes also available as part of a package of potentially available offerings. This is helpful for exchangers who want to do some travelling in your province or other parts of Canada, for example. In exchange, you could ask them to do likewise. You will find the availability of two or more properties as an enticing menu offering is becoming more common on exchange websites.

Home Exchange Websites and Catalogues

When you are considering how to offer your vacation property or primary home for exchange purposes, and see what offerings exist that might interest you, there are several options available.

As most people throughout the world are computer literate and use the Internet as their primary source of research information, the most popular option is using a home-exchange website. There are many companies in Canada, the U.S., and internationally that provide this type of matchmaking service. Refer to the Appendix under Helpful Websites for some of the most popular exchange sites.

These exchange websites are automated and generally restrict access to fellow exchange members only, but not always. There is often an annual fee to become a member, which is nominal and ranges from about $75 to $200 or more, depending on the features that you select. Possibly you want to profile both your primary residence and vacation home, with separate profiles. There is usually a discounted fee for a second listing. The way it works is that you are automatically notified through your email when someone is interested in doing an exchange with you. You take the communication from there, and either decline or start exploratory discussions. Many of the exchange websites use a member exchange email address that is then sent to your personal email address, to avoid or minimize your being spammed, where the general public might have access to the exchange site. You can then choose to use your own email address or not. In some sites, only members can see the email address that you have given.

Many home exchange sites have additional features available for you to offer if you wish, such as vacation rentals, long-term exchanges, home-sitting, simultaneous or non-simultaneous options, homestays (e.g., stay in the house with the owners as their house guests for a few days or a week), etc.

To find companies who do online home exchanges, you can do a Google search under "home exchanges," "home swaps," "house exchanges," etc. If you rent out your vacation home, and are listed on various owner-direct rental sites, many of those sites also have a feature that you can display on your listing to show your home's availability for exchanges. To optimize your marketing and odds of finding an attractive match, consider listing your home on two, three, or more exchange sites. Although all exchange sites have listings throughout the world, some may be more heavily weighted in listings from certain parts of the world than others.

Some of the larger online home exchange companies also have seasonal catalogues with their listings, since those print catalogues pre-dated, of course, the online format. In most cases, you have a choice of including your listing in the catalogue or online or both, with prices adjusted accordingly. Most people have their listing online only, as it gives a searcher instant gratification and can sort based on interests, location, dates, etc. However, for the modest extra cost, having your listing in the catalogue could enhance your marketing.

What Information Is in the Home Exchange Listing?

When you check out the various online sites, you will see they have similar user-friendly formats, with template fields and prompts for you to complete, so that there is consistency and ease of navigation and comprehension for the viewer. All the main exchange sites have a place for photos of your home; sometimes up to 12 or more photos can be uploaded. Using high-quality digital photos is important to enhance the look and feel of your home, and make it more inviting to the prospect. You can put brief descriptions under the photos in many cases.

The sites have a description of your property, which you provide, plus a checklist of home features and amenities, and features of the geographic area and location, and distance from the closest major city or airport or train station. Your listing will also state the various locations that you wish to travel to, at what times of the year, and the duration of exchange. In some cases, people state they are open to offers, available at any time of the year, by scheduling arrangement. You can also state whether you are interested in simultaneous or non-simultaneous exchanges, and whether you have your primary home as well as vacation home available, and whether you have a car available. You could also list other recreational craft you have available for use, such as boats, canoes, kayaks, bikes, etc.

Your listing also sets out the owner's conditions, such as no pets, no smoking, no children, how many exchanges you have done in the past, your occupation, languages spoken, contact information, etc.

It does not take long to input your site information, and you can easily modify it any time you want, in real time. If you have a website, you can link to that site from your listing.

Passive or Active Marketing

Once your listing is online and/or in the catalogue, you can either wait until the world metaphorically knocks your door down with compelling exchange offers, or you can take the initiative yourself. If you have a vacation home in a well-known and desirable location, you will get exchange offers. However, it is important to set up your own online initiative to ensure you find potential exchanges in the location of interest to you. Once you are a member of an exchange site, you can search by the country, city, or geographic area you want to visit, and see who has listings there. If any listing seems attractive to you, it will say where prospective exchangers want to go and when. If there is a geographic match of interest, that is a good start. If not, you can contact them anyway and sell them on why they should exchange with you.

If you get offers that are not timely for your interest, reply courteously that the time is not right for you, but keep them on your computer in an organized fashion in case you want to contact them in the future. If you get offers that don't interest you, simply send a courteous but straightforward reply.

It is a good technique to prepare an interesting overview letter for those you want to exchange with or who contact you for an exchange. Some exchange websites have more space than others for descriptive narrative. Your overview letter can give more information that might help persuade interested parties, such as what you and your family do, your interests, what you are looking for in an exchange, and the attractive features and amenities of your home and general area that make it an interesting place to visit.

Exchanging Without a Car

Many home exchanges include the use of a car. If you are comfortable with this, you can include your car as part of a simultaneous exchange, or lend one of your cars (if you have more than one) for a non-simultaneous exchange. Insurance implications are discussed on the next page.

There are circumstances, however, where including a car is not necessary or desirable. The exchange family may have their own car, or decide to rent one because they want to travel throughout the province or into another province. If an exchange is your primary residence in a major city, or your vacation home is in a major resort area, a car may not be needed if public transportation is adequate, or if the beach or centre of town is within walking distance. If you are exchanging with someone located in downtown Paris, Rome, London, or New

York, you may find that a car is not desired anyway, since parking can be difficult or expensive, and public transportation is more convenient.

If you are not including a car in your exchange arrangement, make sure you emphasize this in your listing or subsequent letter to a prospective exchanger.

Insurance Coverage

You want to make sure that your primary home, vacation home, and automobile insurance covers any accident, theft, or fire, if you are exchanging with someone else. If you have a vacation home with rental coverage, you should be fine. If you are usually the sole user of your vacation home, and do not carry rental insurance, or are exchanging with your primary residence, you should check with your insurance company and policy. It is likely that your policy will cover use of your home by guests for shorter periods, but for extended periods there could be notification and approval protocols in advance required by your insurance company.

If you are also exchanging the use of your car, check with your insurance broker to ensure that you will be covered if someone else is using it.

Confirm your conversations with your insurance broker in writing to make sure there is no misunderstanding and request confirmation of the desired coverage—you don't want to rely on the broker's verbal assurances alone. Each insurance company is different and each policy is different, so don't assume anything.

You also want to check how you will be covered while using an exchange car in another country. Will your car and homeowner personal liability insurance coverage apply, or will you be covered by the policy of the exchange owner? Make sure these issues are clarified in advance in writing. Be prepared for discrepancies between insurance laws, policies, and practices in different countries. You don't want to run the risk of not being insured if you have an accident in another country. The results could be financially devastating.

Getting Expanded Personal Liability Protection

It is prudent to extend the third-party liability protection on the use of your personal car to at least $5 million, and preferably up to $15 million if you can. The premiums are reasonable, and it is cheap money for peace of mind. You can imagine the risk if you had a car accident using the exchange guest's car or even your own car with a home exchange in the United States, and someone were seriously injured. An additional line of protection is to extend your personal liability protection under your homeowner policy to the maximum allowable by paying an extra premium, up to $10 million if you can. Again, these premiums tend to be modest, relative to the protection that covers you for anyone suing you personally. Make sure you understand the fine print of the coverage and any exclusions, deductibles, limitations, etc.

Also check into your insurance coverage for your primary residence when you are away for more than 30 consecutive days, and no one else is staying at your home. Again, policies vary, but most state that the insurance risk is greater when there is no one home for an extended period of time. They require certain protections in order for your coverage to protect you if there is a claim. Confirm the requirements in writing after your conversation.

You should go through an insurance broker who can compare rates of all relevant companies for you, so that you can short-list the companies that could meet your needs and compare policy coverage and premium rates. It is normal to receive a pro-rata refund of the balance of any insurance policy if you have pre-paid it for the year and cancel it before expiry. For more detail on insurance options, refer to Chapter 11: Insurance Issues and Strategies.

Some exchange companies have an exchange cancellation insurance option. It normally is a fund for the purpose of compensating members who suffer last-minute exchange cancellations, due to illness, personal crisis, etc., by their exchange partners. If you have already made financial commitments, such as booking flights, and your exchange arrangement is cancelled, you will consequently require accommodation such as a hotel, motel, or bed and breakfast at your destination. If you pay a set amount into a fund, the funds are pooled and available to members during that calendar/membership year, on a pro-rated basis, depending on the number and amount of claims in that time period. There is normally a maximum limit on the amount of compensation (e.g., up to $4,000), which could be total or partial. There are various conditions associated with these types of compensation funds, so make sure you obtain specific details in advance.

Documentation to Sign with Exchangers

Several of the major home-exchange websites have template documentation for you to print off and use if desired. Some examples are a home exchange agreement setting out the key terms, and an automobile exchange agreement. These documents would include issues such as responsibility for breakage of items, payment of the insurance claim deductible, or the minimum amount before an insurance claim would be made, etc.

Long-term Exchanges

You might want to exchange for several months or much longer in a particular area. Possibly a specific location is required for business or personal reasons. If you had your family with you, living in a hotel room could be a bit limiting or stressful after a while. You could give a potential exchanger the option of using your primary residence as well as vacation home. For example, there could be artists or writers who might welcome the opportunity to stay in a relaxing resort or metropolitan area for creative stimulation.

If you are exchanging for an extended stay, discuss in advance how to deal with expenses such as utilities. It is not uncommon in this scenario for the exchange parties to reimburse each other for the utility expenses, especially if they might be disproportional. For example, air conditioning or other utility usage such as propane or natural gas might be more expensive in one country than another.

Preparing Your Home for Your Exchange Guests

Once you have your exchange arranged, you want to ensure that your home is ready for your new guests. If you frequently rent your vacation home, you are probably prepared for this routine. However, the common protocol for home-exchange guests tends to be a bit more personal. Here are some basic tips to maximize the enjoyment of your guests. Chances are that you will receive a reciprocal welcome procedure, especially if your exchange guests are experienced with the exchange lifestyle.

- √ Describe your home accurately in your listing and in all correspondence. You want your home-exchange partners to be pleasantly surprised, not disappointed, when they arrive. Always be upfront about the existence of pets, and whether they will be removed and cared for by others, or whether you would like your exchange guests to care for them.

- √ Leave your home clean. You probably do anyway. Standards of cleanliness vary and people's expectations can vary, but at a minimum you should make sure that floors are vacuumed and mopped, refrigerator emptied, stove and oven free from grease, shower and bath free of mould and grime, and surfaces dust free.

- √ Leave sufficient clean sheets and towels, toilet paper, tissues, soap, shampoo, etc.

- √ Don't leave paperwork or bills hanging around. Clear away enough of your personal belongings to leave space on shelves, in closets, and in drawers so that your guests can easily empty their suitcases, arrange their things in bedrooms and bathrooms, and feel at home. Any items that are precious or breakable, which might cause you worry, should be stored in a locked "no go" area of your house.

√   Compile a clear and useful "Guide to Your Home and Surroundings." Include local tourist information and maps, your favourite restaurants and prices and maybe menus, and household notices about the use of electrical appliances, pool maintenance, pet and plant care (if applicable), and when the rubbish is put out.

√   Compile an emergency phone number list, including a local contact number for a family member, relative, friend, or friendly neighbour whom the guest can contact if there are any questions or problems.

√   Have an exchange contract to avoid any misunderstandings and to clarify who pays for what in terms of telephone, electric bills, insurance deductibles in case of accidents, replacement of staple goods, such as flour, sugar, seasonings, payment for cleaning service at end of the stay, etc. Normally, you make arrangements for your own cleanup after the guests have gone to meet your own high standards of cleanliness.

√   Leave sufficient food for a first meal—just a snack to keep them going until they have time to go shopping. Leaving a fresh bouquet of flowers is always appreciated and creates a welcoming environment. It is a nice touch to leave a small gift of welcome, such as a bottle of local wine or local maple syrup. It is always a pleasant surprise to experience the thoughtfulness of the home exchanger, especially at the end of a long journey.

√   Before leaving your exchange residence, remember to put things back where you found them, and leave the house organized and clean. This will be a welcome sight when your exchange partners arrive back home. Leaving a thank-you card, along with a small gift, is also a thoughtful gesture.

Trade or Barter Exchange

You have likely heard of bartering networks, barter trades, or contra deals. The concept is simple: people exchange one commodity (goods or services) for another (similar goods or services of equal value), or obtain a credit for the fair market value of a good or service, to be used in the future. It can be a formal or informal process.

Informal Trade Exchange

In this format, someone with a product or service will utilize various mediums to exchange their offering for something of equal value or similar value, or a combination of things for equal value. One medium would be weekly publications frequently published in larger towns and cities.

There are quite a few trade types of websites on which you can post without charge or for a nominal fee. Some are located in local geographic areas. Others are Canada-wide or international in scope. Your products or services are listed under relevant categories, and you can see what others are offering. You put a price point on your offering, and make your own arrangements for the exchange. This could be the use of your cottage for a week or a long weekend, for something else of equal value of interest to you. The website is just the clearinghouse medium; it is not involved in the process.

You might wonder why some websites offer this service for free. The reason is that some sites use the free exchange functionality as a loss leader, and up-sell other types of products or services that are provided for a fee. Alternatively, they may just want to drive a lot of traffic to their site on an ongoing and increasing basis, and then generate revenue through Google or similar type of ad click-through revenue.

You can find out the availability of the above types of sites by doing a Google search using various relevant keywords, such as "bartering," "barter clubs," "trade exchanges," "trade exchange networks," etc.

Formal Trade Exchange

Over the past 20 years or so, the practice of bartering for goods or services has evolved into a sophisticated and fully automated system of commerce proliferated by independent or franchised member-only barter clubs, in which credit units possessing a notional monetary unit value have become a medium of exchange. In this type of system, which is a form of trade dollar currency, commodities of different value can be exchanged, resulting in a debit or credit to the account of the member.

Some of these trade-exchange companies cater primarily to small business owners, as well as individuals. The sophistication and technology has prompted many businesses to increase their sales, efficiency, and profitability. With the trade dollar concept, members can buy or sell goods and services without any of the traditional restraints imposed by needing the perfect match and comparable product values. The trade-exchange company is in effect acting as a bank, and tracks accounts and transactions using a system similar to that used by credit-card issuers.

A member can go online through a secure account and purchase airline tickets, packaged vacations, a week or more at a vacation or resort property, legal services, cars, computers, consulting services, or any multitude of products or services. The trade-exchange company provides monthly statements of usage, and charges a fee for any exchange. This is generally under 10% of the value of the trade. The members quote retail value for their products and services. An example of an established barter company in Canada is Trade Exchange Canada. Their website is www.tecvan.ca.

It is common for the larger barter companies to be part of a network of barter companies throughout the world. This is an important issue to inquire about at the outset, as you may wish to have the flexibility of using your "trade dollars" on a "dollar for dollar" basis outside your immediate geographic area. For example, let's say you want to travel to New Zealand, Australia, and the Cook Islands and use your "trade dollars" in those locations for accommodation, car rentals, meals, activities, tourist attractions, etc.

You can see a how the formal barter option could be enticing to consider for your vacation property. If you already rent it out seasonally, periodically, or full time, you are familiar with the process of having other people use your home for revenue-generation purposes. There could be times in the "shoulder" rental season (that is, the period between peak and off-peak periods), or when you are not using your property for your personal needs, when there is limited or no demand for a normal rental. Or possibly you want to consider making your property available at peak or other high demand times. In these situations, you might wish to use the barter system for a "rental." You would set the best retail rate you believe you could obtain for your vacation home, e.g., for a week or two weeks, or long weekend, and dollar credits accordingly. Of course, you may prefer to rent out the property for old-fashioned cash instead. In that case, refer to the discussion on rental management in Chapter 16: Professional or Owner-Direct Rental Management. Also check out the website www.homebuyer.ca.

Tax Implications of the Bartering Process

You should obtain customized tax advice in your given circumstances in advance. However, in general terms, here is an overview of how your friends at the Canada Revenue Agency (CRA) look at it.

In brief, if you make an arm's-length transaction (e.g., not dealing with family or relatives), and the barter exchange is of equal value, there is generally no net income to be declared. However, if you are offering goods or services that are of a kind generally provided by you in the course of earning income in your business or profession, the value of those services should be brought into your business income. Some examples are if you are offering consulting services or legal services, or customarily rent out your vacation property.

In the above scenario, you are supposed to declare the income in your tax return, and charge GST on your service or product, assuming that you are required to have a GST number (i.e., if you earn more than $30,000 per year in your business). Refer to Chapter 10: Tax Issues and Strategies, for more detail. The GST portion would be collected separately as cash from the person utilizing your commodity, and not as part of the barter credit/debit system. If you are running a business generating revenue from your vacation property, you could claim related expenses, of course, such as the cost of the trade exchange transaction commission. In addition, the value of the product or service that you use your trade dollar credit to acquire would be an expense, assuming that it relates to your business use in some fashion. When all the dust settles, one could off-set the other, so you have generated a financial benefit from your vacation home that otherwise would not have occurred.

16 Professional or Owner-Direct Rental Management

Whether you are renting your vacation home full time, seasonally, or periodically, you will find this chapter has lots of creative ideas to improve your bottom line.

Effective revenue property management is a vital part of making the maximum amount of profit on a recreational property with a minimum amount of stress and risk. Property management has many objectives, but the primary one is to attain the highest possible cash flow, net income, and property value. This is done by using successful management techniques. These in turn will give you the best return on your investment. Other objectives, which are fundamental to achieving the primary objectives, include making the right type of management decisions to result in ideal renters, few vacancies, maximum revenues, and minimal expenses. In addition, the maintenance of the property at its optimal condition is part of those general objectives.

Many novice landlords eventually put their rental properties up for sale, frequently at a loss, when it otherwise would not have been necessary. This is likely due to the lack of property management knowledge and skills. Difficulties often arise because the investor gets tired of the chronic frustration, stress, and time involved in dealing with problems such as disruptive renters, payment problems, vacancies, vandalism or damage to property, negative or sporadic cash flow, tenant disputes or complaints, neighbours' complaints, and high repair and maintenance costs. All of these, however, can be addressed through good management techniques and practices.

This chapter will assist you in attaining your personal objectives of stress-free vacation property management and avoidance of the common pitfalls. The following sections will cover types of rental management such as professional management and owner-direct rentals, as well as keeping records. It will also cover how to save on expenses and increase the income from your revenue property.

After reading this chapter, you may want more information on how to profitably rent your vacation home. If so, consider taking the recreational property seminar offered throughout Canada by the National Real Estate Institute Inc. Check out www.homebuyer.ca for details.

Criteria for Deciding on the Type of Rental Management

The initial decision that you make regarding the form of management will be largely determined by the size of the property, the type of property, the frequency of short-term tenants, your interest and experience in rental management, and the time you have available. If you are purchasing a vacation condominium in a resort area, you may not have any choice in the rental management. It could be that you are required to put your condo unit into a rental pool for a minimum number of days per year, at set commission rates. (This was discussed in some detail in Chapter 3: Types of Recreational Real Estate under the condominium option.)

There are essentially two main forms of property management: professional property management and self-management or owner-direct rentals. A hybrid variation of these alternatives may also be used.

Professional Rental Management

Many owners of resort condos, recreational chalets, cottages or cabins, absentee owners, or inactive owners use a professional management company. These companies tend to be very experienced at residential property management and have many systems and procedures for efficient operation of their support function. You can use as many or as few of the services as you need. The types of services and benefits provided could include:

√   experienced staff

√   computerized accounting, bookkeeping procedures, and management systems

√   access to suppliers who can provide bulk-buying discounts and good service

√   arranging for housekeeping services (including laundry) between guest rentals

√   careful selection of, and contracting out for, competent tradespeople for repair or general maintenance service, subject to a limit beyond which any expenditure would require your written authorization

√ finding and selecting short-term tourist accommodation renters, displaying your accommodation on their website, negotiating rental contracts with property use and care provisions, using forms supplied or approved by you and your lawyer (e.g., conditions that you might set, such as limit on number of guests, no smoking, no noise after 10 p.m., no pets, no children, etc.)

√ monitoring tenant problems and evicting them if necessary if they are in breach of the terms of the rental agreement

√ being available 24/7 for emergencies

√ collecting rental money in advance, as well as a security deposit

√ arranging for staff to do a "meet and greet" of your short-term renters on arrival, and checking for any damage after they depart

√ paying all bills on your behalf

√ maintaining all necessary records

√ sending you a monthly statement on the rental of your vacation property

√ ensuring that the grounds and buildings are maintained properly if a house or cottage.

One of the key benefits of using a professional rental management company is that such a company will provide the continuity of management to ensure a consistent level of quality. Professional management fees can range from 5% to 50% or more of the gross monthly revenue from the property, depending on the nature of services provided. Like any highly competitive business activity, fees are negotiable. It is important to give the management company guidelines in writing, as well as to incorporate them in the overall management contract. Make sure you have your lawyer review the contract before you sign it.

There are two main forms of professional property management arrangements:

Property Management Company You Have the Autonomy to Select

In this scenario, you own your own vacation home that is not covered by a rental pool agreement. This includes single-family houses, as well as resort condos. You can select who you want and the services you want, and negotiate the commission fee to be charged. There are many types of fee or commission arrangements available, as you will see when you do your comparative and competitive research.

Check out the company thoroughly and ask for references from vacation property owners of other properties being managed. Look in the Yellow Pages or on the Internet under "Property Management" companies in the geographic locale of your vacation property.

Property Management Company You Are Obligated to Use

In this example, you have bought a resort condo, or fractional interest condo that is part of a rental pool contract. As part of your purchase agreement, you would be required to make your property available for a set number of days each year for tourist rentals. You would be permitted to use the condo yourself for a pre-set number of days, or you could choose to leave them in the rental pool instead to generate more revenue.

In the type of arrangement just described, you are required to deal with a property management company that is contracted by the project development. That way, there is consistency of service, marketing, and systems. However, you are required to pay the fees and commissions that have been negotiated by the developer or development for the condo project. In some cases, these can be as high as 40% or more, depending on what services are being offered.

Self-managed or Owner-direct Rentals

The self-management alternative is attractive to many owners, due to the potentially higher net revenue. It is not necessary in a self-management situation that the owners themselves clean the grounds, cut the grass, shovel the snow, do the gardening, and sweep the driveways. In does mean, though, that the owners, or a representative of the owners, would have to be directly involved in supervising the performance of these types of services. Frequently the jobs are done by firms under contract.

Clearly, there are cost savings to managing the property yourself, but not everyone is suited for it. Ask yourself how much free time you have and are prepared to spend. For example, if you are retired or semi-retired, you may be able to comfortably manage several vacation properties. Even if you work full time, if you manage your time well and are an efficient and effective landlord, you may be capable of managing several properties successfully.

You also have to look realistically at your skills and interest in doing minor repairs and maintenance. In addition, consider whether you really enjoy dealing with short-term tenants and their problems, and have the patience, temperament, and personality to do so. If not, maybe one of your family members does.

Another reason for self-management or on-site management, if you purchase a house with a year-round tenant suite in it, is that the property may be outside a tourist area, so there may be difficulty in obtaining the services of a professional rental management company.

Remember, in terms of real estate management, you can involve yourself as little or as much as you want. It comes down to personal choice and circumstances and desire for profit. Although it is easier to have someone else assume the management responsibilities, there will be a cost factor. You may wish to work at it on a part-time basis and have the right tenant or contract service assist on matters such as minor cleanup, cutting the lawn, and watering the plants.

On-site, Year-round Tenant Help with Services

If you have a chalet in a resort area, for example, you might have or consider a one- or two-bedroom suite option that you would rent to a year-round tenant for security and revenue. They could provide some of the services for you, either as part of the rental agreement, or for a discounted rent, or for extra money. Many tenants would probably be willing to perform basic tasks without the benefit expected, if the duties were minor and seasonal in nature. Everyone is unique in his or her motivations, needs, and wishes.

If you have a year-round tenant, you could also utilize the tenant for meeting and greeting your short-term guests who are renting your property for a weekend or week or two. They could do a walk-through with the house renter and check the place for any damage when the renter leaves. Your year-round tenant could also do the laundry and clean-up after the renter leaves. This on-site flexible option could be an attractive feature to consider, if the recreational property circumstances permit it, and tenant personality and maturity are suited to it. If you do have an arrangement for services by your year-round tenant, make sure that you have it clearly confirmed in writing, so there are no misunderstandings. If the tasks are to be considered as part of the tenancy agreement, e.g., minor duties that could be seasonal in nature, make sure a description of those tasks is included in the tenancy agreement.

The Owner-direct Option: Tips for Marketing and Managing Your Rental

A website is now the key portal to marketing your vacation home. The majority of prospective renters do their primary research over the Internet, shortlist their favourite accommodation options, submit a booking request, receive booking confirmation, and pay the money to complete the deal—all on the Internet. This being the case, there are many strategies to successfully market using this powerful sales tool of the Internet. The system you adopt for your vacation rentals will make all the difference in your revenue—from not covering your costs or just breaking even, to having positive cash flow or even making a lot of money.

In the vacation rental business, the vast number of resorts and the many quality levels available means that you'll be up against a lot of competition. The following highlights some of the key issues you need to consider to be competitive and attract clientele:

Select the Right Website Advertising for Your Needs

There are five main types of vacation owner-direct website options to consider, or possibly using a combination of them to optimize your exposure to your target groups:

√ *Listing Portal Sites*

The main function of these sites is to act as a clearinghouse and matchmaker between those seeking general vacation home rental accommodation and those providing it. These sites do extensive marketing to try to rank as high as possible on search engines, to capture people typing in intuitive, descriptive keywords. The sites generally provide the key information that people are looking for, such as location, property description, features, number of beds, amenities, local attractions, testimonials, rental rates, additional charges or restrictions, contact information, map locators, as well as photos that you can easily upload yourself. Sometimes there is the option of a 360-degree virtual tour of your vacation home, to provide a more graphic feeling for your place. Most portal sites permit a link to your personal website if you have one, which is highly recommended.

Some portal listing sites are free, or have a two- to three-month free trial period. Most charge an annual, semi-annual, or monthly fee. Those offering free listings have to make money somehow, and tend to generate revenue either through advertising, such as Google type of ads where revenue is generated by the number of clicks to other websites, or affiliate links to other sites where the listing site receives a percentage of what you buy through that site (e.g., books), or ads for local businesses in the area.

√   *Specialized Sites*

These sites tend to cater to specific types of target groups of vacation property renters. Some examples are people interested in specific recreational activities (e.g., golfing, skiing, or fishing), or pet owners or sun seekers.

√   *Service Sites*

These are sites that offer customized features for vacation property owners who are marketing their property. Sometimes these are included as part of your listing portal or specialized sites, and sometimes you need to have a link through your personal website. The most common examples of these sites are those that have mapping features such as Mapquest or Google, or calendar features that show your rental availability, or sites that provide electronic payment options for those renting your accommodation, such as Paypal. Many listing and specialty sites include an option of using their credit card services for people renting. You pay a commission for all transactions, and possibly a service fee. Many people want the convenience of using a credit card for payment.

√   *Home Exchange Sites*

Home exchanging is a very popular lifestyle option, as discussed in the previous chapter. Many home exchange sites also have the feature of listing your home for vacation rentals.

√   *Personal Sites*

There are many benefits of having your own personal website to personalize your vacation property. Even though you could be listed with several listing or specialized websites, a link to your personal website allows you to paint a more interesting picture of your property to make it stand out, and provide a lot more detailed information. You want your personal website to be your key selling tool. You can use website space for your site through your Internet Service Provider (ISP), or register your own domain name and find a company to host your site. There are many advantages of owning your own domain name, including branding your site name by making the site distinctive, interesting, and memorable. Another advantage is control over your site and the consistency of your image.

You can design, build, and maintain your own site, or hire a web designer to do this for you. There are many advantages to hiring a professional after you have done your competitive market research of great websites, and checked the portfolios of sites developed by designers you are considering. You can have your site designed so that you can easily make any changes to the text yourself, and manage the domain content. Alternatively, you can pay the designer to make any changes. You should consider the pros and cons before you have the website built, so that you can incorporate the features and functions that you want to use in the foreseeable future. Many domain registration sites also offer you the option of building your own site using a wide range of customized templates that are user-friendly to develop and maintain. Examples of these domain registration sites are www.godaddy.com, and www.networksolutions.com. There are many others. When building your site, either through template programs or customized design, ask for candid and constructive feedback for improvement from friends, relatives, and business colleagues. For maximum impact, you want to fine-tune your site in a beta version before you officially launch it to a highly competitive world.

It is inexpensive to register and renew a domain name. It can range from $15 to $30 annually to register and renew, depending on the domain registration company that you use, and type of domain you register. It is a very competitive marketplace, so comparison shop. In Canada, the common suffix for a domain is ".ca" to denote the Canadian marketplace. A ".com" domain is still universally known and recognized. The key factor is the distinctiveness of the domain you select so that it is descriptive and memorable at the same time. For example, if you had a vacation home in Whistler, British Columbia, you could decide to register a domain such as www.whistlerchalet.ca. (But don't try to register that domain name, as I've already beat you to it!)

When you have your own website, you want to use as many common keywords as possible in your text, to enable a higher ranking on the search engines. These engines are constantly trawling the Internet to search for keywords in websites. Do your own research of which websites are ranked the highest, by doing a Google search, for example, of keywords.

Contact Information

It is easy for people to communicate with you through your website. You can add as many email addresses on as you wish for specific purposes, and set your

computer to put the different emails into separate folders for easier organization (e.g., jane@muskokacottageforrent.ca or booknow@muskokacottageforrent.ca).

People like to be able to make telephone contact. You can obtain a 1-800
toll-free number, but many people have unlimited long-distance plans, so it is
generally not an impediment if you don't have a toll-free number. If you are
showing your phone number, show your area code and the hours to phone
in your time zone. You could also have a separate number than your regular
phone number, so that it can go into voice mail automatically during nighttime
hours, in case people are phoning from different countries.

Most people make their decision based on the quality and content of your
website and the emotional and visual responses evoked by the images. If people
want to ask questions, they tend to do so in an email. Depending on the type of
vacation property you own, the value and demand for it, and the frequency that
it is rented throughout the year, you may want to have a policy of phoning the
prospective renter first to talk to them before you make a commitment. This
personalizes your vacation property and gives you an opportunity to screen
your prospective renters, as well as ask any questions you have. It is a good
policy to require a security deposit in advance for any damage, the amount
depending on the type of property you own.

Photos

The cliché that a picture is worth a thousand words is especially true when it
comes to vacation property rentals. People want to be sure the vacation home
is going to meet their needs and expectations. You can have enticing content
descriptions, but they have to be balanced by compelling photos that provide
an immediate sense of an inviting place. Generally, the more photos of the
home's highlights, the better. Take external views and selective inside images of
the kitchen, living room, bedrooms, and bathrooms.

Most people own digital cameras, and many feel confident that they can
capture the essence of their vacation home. However, in many cases, you are
further ahead to utilize the services of a professional photographer experienced
in taking photos of vacation homes. The cost can be modest compared to the
benefits. Of course, you can write off the expense against revenue. The quality
of photographic equipment, the wide-angle lens, the experienced eye, the sense
of composition, and the intuitive sense of the right lighting and impact make
the skills of a professional photographer worthy of serious consideration. The

best test is to look at vacation property websites that have used professional photographers. You can tell the difference in an instant.

You may wish to consider the benefits of also having a virtual 360-degree tour of your vacation property. This would not be instead of, but in addition to, your photos. You are likely familiar with the concept. It puts the viewer in a position of being in different rooms of your property, as if walking through the home, and looking out the windows. If you think your property has unique features or stunning views, you may wish to consider this option.

As in any selection of professional services, comparison shop to find a photographer, and use the rule of thumb of obtaining a minimum of three quotes in writing.

Pricing and Conditions

How you price your vacation home is critical to the response you will get. You need to start by determining, as realistically as possible, the rates you need to charge, and the rates that your particular vacation property will bear. Many factors come into play, including your break-even point (anticipated expenses minus necessary revenue to balance them); rates for comparable vacation properties in terms of size, features, quality, age, and location; market conditions; and seasonal variations in rates (high, moderate, shoulder, low demand times, as well as holiday periods).

You should have your rates clearly shown on your listing or website, including any special rates during low-demand or shoulder seasons, and any financial incentives you have. For example, you may offer four nights for the price of three, or larger discounts for longer stays. You should also spell out other conditions and expenses, so that you have full disclosure. You don't want your prospective renter to be taken by surprise when they are doing their budgeting and comparison shopping. Typical extra expenses would include taxes, such as federal, provincial, and local hotel tax if applicable. It could also include a housecleaning fee, extra fee for pets if they are allowed, and extra cost per person if there is more than a certain number of people, up to a maximum number. It is common and prudent to have a security deposit for any damage or missing inventory. This could be from $200 to $2,000 or more, depending on the quality of the property and other factors.

Conditions could include a minimum stay, no one renting under 25 years of age, no group rentals for parties, no noise after a set time (e.g., between 10 p.m. and 7 a.m.), maximum number of people sleeping on the property, no smoking, no pets, no use of boats while drinking, etc.

Requests for Use by Friends and Family

Friends, and possibly relatives, have probably asked if they could use your property. It can sometimes be an awkward situation. The dynamics can be sensitive. Your friends may assume that they can use your home for free. Given that you have ongoing costs associated with owning your vacation home, you would be indirectly subsidizing your friends' vacation! The other issue is that if you are renting your vacation home as a full-time enterprise, or have seasonal or periodic rentals, you could be losing potential revenue.

The best way to deal with these types of scenarios is to have a policy. It makes it more comfortable and businesslike. You could say that your priority is rentals to cover your overhead and investment, but that you would be pleased to let your friends use the property during the slow periods, or at your cost, or at a discounted rate. You should also build in the housekeeping costs that could be incurred when your friends depart their stay. The reason is that cleaning standards vary: cleanliness may be in the eye of the beholder, but you need to maintain your own standards for the next guests who walk through the door.

Dealing with and Pre-empting Problems

When renting a vacation property, there are many different types of potential problems that could arise. However, you can anticipate and therefore try to pre-empt most of them. You need to put your mind to your policy on such issues as:

- √ cancellations (have a variable penalty based on amount of time of notice)
- √ complaints (weather, condition of property, noise nearby)
- √ telephone long-distance charges (advisable to get a long-distance block on your phone)
- √ withholding deposits (basis for your right to do so and what is covered)
- √ major or minor damage caused by renter (costs to be taken from deposit, with tenant being liable for any shortfall)
- √ theft (have an inventory list agreed to in advance; costs to be taken from deposit)
- √ smoking, having pets, or allowing too many people to stay in the home, in breach of the rental agreement (right of owner to evict the renter and keep all or part of the deposit for that breach).

Rental Agreement

It is very important that you put your relationship with your renter in writing. You want the agreement to cover all the core issues and potential problems, as well as your rights if any conditions of the agreement are breached by the tenant. Through research of other rental properties online, try to determine the standard expectations or precedents set by others, then modify an agreement to reflect your situation. After you have done that, take a draft to your lawyer and ask for candid feedback on preparing an agreement that will legally protect you. Stipulate that your renter must review and sign this agreement before they can use the property. Make sure you use the services of a lawyer with expertise in real estate law and contracts. You will be better protected with streetsmart advice.

Use and Care Policy

Part of the rental agreement should be your use and care policy for using the property. This can be referenced and attached as a schedule to the main agreement if you prefer. It could set out requirements such as no shoes to be worn inside the house (to avoid marking hardwood floors or carpets), to not leaving the gas fireplace on when no one is at the home (for fire safety reasons). The document could also include use and care provisions for appliances, vacuum cleaner, television, etc.

You can see that there are lots of matters to consider if you are to maximize your revenue, enjoyment, and investment, and minimize your expenses, stress, and risk.

Keeping Records

Records must be kept regardless of whether you rent the property yourself or pay a professional management company to do so. If a rental management company is used, they should have detailed records of revenue, and should make these records available to you. If you are renting out your vacation property yourself, records such as bank deposit books, invoices, receipts, contracts, and other documents should be kept. It is important to develop systems for recording and filing the various types of records, so they can be retrieved and examined quickly and efficiently.

Accurate records should be kept for both external and internal reasons.

External Reasons for Keeping Records

√ Government regulations—federal government departments have rules and regulations related to record keeping. For example, Canada Revenue Agency (CRA) requires you to pay income tax on net revenue income. If CRA decides to conduct an audit, you will need to produce your records for review.

√ Raising financing from a bank or any other lending source.

√ Attracting potential investors for your revenue property.

√ Selling the property.

√ Meeting insurance company requirements for a loss claim.

Internal Reasons for Keeping Records

√ Keeps you better informed about the financial position of your investment.

√ Makes it easier to complete accurate income tax returns with supporting receipts for expenses.

√ Provides the basis for evaluating the condition, efficiency, and operation of the revenue property.

√ Reminds you when creditor obligations are due.

√ Provides an opportunity for comparing budget goals with historical records and future projections.

√ Provides the basis for preparing cash flow, income and expense projections, and break-even analyses to enable you to improve your cash management and revenue operational position.

√ Prepares for eventual sale of the property.

Keeping the Canada Revenue Agency Happy

The *Income Tax Act* requires that you keep your records and books in an orderly manner at your place of business or your residence, as CRA may request this material at any time for review or audit purposes.

You are required to maintain business records and supporting documents for at least six years from the end of the last taxation year to which they relate. If you filed your return late for any year, records and supporting documents must be kept for six years from the date you filed that return. CRA permits computer storage of records, as long as those records provide adequate information to verify taxable income.

Typical Financial Records

Some examples of typical financial records to be maintained manually or on a computerized program are as follows (not all will be applicable in your situation):

- √ sales journal
- √ cash receipts journal
- √ accounts receivable ledger
- √ accounts payable journal
- √ cash disbursements journal
- √ credit purchases journal
- √ credit sales journal
- √ payroll journal
- √ general synoptic ledger.

Some of the non-financial records include documents relating to personnel, equipment, inventory, and tenants.

Record-keeping Systems and Equipment

The equipment and systems that a vacation property investor uses for record keeping can range from simple, inexpensive, manual procedures to more complex computer systems. You should ask your accountant to recommend the most efficient record-keeping system for your type of operation. There are some excellent software programs available, and some that are geared for real estate investors and rental property management.

Saving on Expenses

Part of making money from your rental property is ensuring that you save money wherever possible. Here are some of the steps you can take to offset expenses:

- √ appealing a high property tax increase to the property assessment authority

√ hiring tenants who will handle maintenance, such as snow removal, gardening, and minor painting

√ utilizing government subsidy programs for insulation, energy efficiency, gas conversion, etc.

√ buying supplies in bulk

√ getting at least three competitive bids for any major expense, such as landscaping, painting, and renovating

√ reviewing present property insurance coverage and premiums regularly, and getting competitive quotes

√ reviewing property management contract and commissions regularly, and getting competitive quotes

√ employing your children or other family members, at fair market rates, to do necessary cleanup and odd jobs at your vacation property if appropriate and necessary, thereby keeping the money in the family. If you are self-managing your vacation property rentals, you could also employ family members for marketing, database management, website maintenance, competitive research, bookkeeping, records management, etc.

√ enforcing warranties and contracts to ensure quality service or operation.

PART VI

Outward Bound

Buying Vacation Property in the United States and Abroad

Are you planning to become a snowbird by buying a home outside Canada and living part-time in the United States, Mexico, or abroad for up to six months a year? Do you live near the American border and are you thinking about buying a vacation home in the United States? Are you thinking of buying a vacation home as a revenue investment in a resort area outside of Canada? If any of these scenarios apply to you, there are special issues and cautions you need to consider.

If you live in the United States part-time and own property there, tax- and estate-planning can become quite complex because you could be affected by both U.S. and Canadian tax laws. In the United States, for example, you could be liable under certain circumstances for income tax, capital gains tax, estate tax, and gift tax.

The following overview provides general guidelines only; competent professional tax advice is essential. Laws are always in a state of flux. The discussion in this chapter should help you better communicate with your professional advisors. Refer as well to Chapter 5: Selecting Your Advisors.

It cannot be overstated how important it is to obtain skilled professional tax and legal advice from professionals in Canada and the United States, or experts with combined cross-border experience, with respect to U.S. property purchases. The same caution applies when buying in other countries. Advance planning is critical to minimize stress and taxes and maximize peace of mind. The strategies and documentation are highly technical.

There is an excellent publication available for Canadians who own or are thinking of owning U.S. vacation or investment property. It is written by an expert on U.S. property and tax and estate issues. It is called *Brunton's U.S. Tax-letter for Canadians*. It is available by subscription and contains a lot of helpful information and analysis. For further information and the website, refer to the Appendix under Helpful Websites.

This chapter will discuss the following: determining if U.S. tax laws affect you, renting or selling U.S. property, paying U.S. and Canadian taxes on death, strategies for reducing taxes on U.S. vacation property, and tax information exchange between the United States and Canada.

For an extensive discussion of buying, owning, renting, or selling a vacation home in the United States or Mexico, and the relevant tax- and estate-planning considerations, refer to my book *The Canadian Snowbird Guide: Everything You Need to Know about Living Part-time in the U.S.A. and Mexico.*

Do U.S. Tax Laws Apply to You?

Even though you are a Canadian citizen and only living in the States periodically or part-time, you could still be subject to U.S. taxation. Even if you are not required to pay U.S. tax, you could be subject to various U.S. filing requirements. The Canada-U.S. tax treaty includes provisions that will affect you. Since changes can occur at any time, be sure to get current professional tax advice.

Resident vs. Nonresident Alien Tax Status

If you are a Canadian resident who spends part of the year in the United States, you are considered by the Internal Revenue Service (IRS) as a "resident alien" or a "nonresident alien" of the United States for tax purposes. It is important to know which category you fall into, as there are considerable tax implications. For example, resident aliens are generally taxed in the United States on income from all sources world-wide, which of course would include Canadian income. Nonresident aliens are generally taxed in the United States only on income from U.S. sources. Not all nonresident aliens have to file.

Internal Revenue Service (IRS) Shares Information with the Canada Revenue Agency (CRA)

The ability of the IRS and the CRA to exchange data on Canadian and U.S. taxpayers by computer increased dramatically as a result of requirements for certain Canadians to have a U.S. taxpayer identification number (ITIN).

When you apply for your ITIN, you must provide some brief but very personal information to the IRS. This includes your name, your name at birth, if different, and your address in Canada. Post office boxes and "care of" addresses are not allowed. Your date and place of birth are asked for, along with your sex, your father's complete name, and your mother's maiden name. In addition, you are asked for your passport number and U.S. visa number, if any.

You are also asked for your Canadian social insurance number. You can imagine the potential cooperation between the IRS and the CRA this facilitates. The IRS has a fast, computerized cross-referencing capability between your U.S. and Canadian taxpayer numbers. Information on certain U.S. tax-related activities in which you are involved, as outlined in the next section below, can be transmitted to the CRA by computer, giving the CRA your name, your Canadian address, and your Canadian social insurance number.

The IRS Has Your Number

Do you ever wonder what the IRS might know about your U.S. activities? The IRS potentially has a wide variety of information on individuals having U.S. income, U.S. property, or involved in a U.S. financial transaction. For example: If you purchase U.S. real estate, your name and address are recorded in the local county property records. When you sell your U.S. real estate, another entry is made in the county records. Information on both of these transactions is readily available to the IRS if it wishes to obtain it.

√ If you *sell* U.S. real estate, the closing agents (i.e, the lawyer, title insurance agent, etc.) must complete an IRS form, and submit it to the IRS along with a copy to you. This form includes your name, address, and the sale price of your property. The IRS can use the form to determine if you have filed a U.S. tax return.

√ If you *sell* U.S. real estate to an American citizen and take back a mortgage, a notation of the interest paid to you must be made on the American's tax return.

√ If you *rent out* your U.S. real estate, another IRS form may be generated. The rental agent is required to complete an IRS form and submit it to the IRS along with a copy to you. The form lists your name, Canadian address, and the rental income you received. Again, the IRS can use this form to determine if you have made the proper U.S. filing.

√ If you receive certain types of interest or dividends from U.S. sources (e.g., a U.S. bank account), an IRS form is also filed with the IRS.

√ If you receive pension income from U.S. sources, an IRS form may also be generated and sent to the IRS.

As mentioned, all the information available to the IRS can also be given to the CRA.

Rental Income From U.S. Real Estate

You may be renting out your U.S. property on a part-time or full-time basis. As a nonresident alien, you are subject to U.S. income tax on the rental income.

Tax on Gross Rental Income

The rents you receive are subject to a 30% withholding tax, which your tenant or property management agent is required to deduct and remit to the IRS. It doesn't matter if the tenants are Canadians or other nonresidents of the United States, or if the rent was paid to you while you were in Canada. The Canada-U.S. tax treaty allows the United States to tax income from real estate with no reduction in the general withholding rate. As rental income is not considered to be effectively connected, it is subject to a flat 30% tax on gross income, with no expenses or deductions allowed.

You need to file an IRS form for a U.S. Nonresident Alien Income Tax Return, showing the gross rental income and withholding tax. Your tenant or property management agent must withhold the tax and complete various IRS forms.

Tax on Net Rental Income

As 30% of gross income is a high tax rate, you may prefer to elect to pay tax on net income, after all deductible expenses. This would result in reduced tax and possibly no tax. The IRS Code permits this option, if you choose to permanently treat rental income as income that is effectively connected with the conduct of a U.S. trade or business. You could then claim expenses related to owning and operating a rental property during the rental period, including mortgage interest, property tax, utilities, insurance, and maintenance. You can also deduct an amount for depreciation on the building. However, the IRS only permits individuals (rather than corporations) to deduct the mortgage or loan interest relating to the rental property if the debt is secured by the rental property or other business property. If you borrow the funds in Canada, secured by your Canadian assets, you would not technically be able to deduct that interest on your U.S. tax return. Obtain strategic tax-planning advice on this issue.

Selling Your U.S. Real Estate

If you are a nonresident alien, any gain or loss that results from a sale or disposition of your U.S. real estate is considered to be effectively connected with a U.S. trade or business. The purchaser or agent of the purchaser is generally required to withhold 10% of the gross sale price at the time the sale transaction is completed and the balance of payment is made. The 10% holdback is to be forwarded to the IRS.

Waiver of Withholding Tax

If you anticipate the U.S. tax payable would be less than the 10% withheld, you can apply to the IRS in advance to have the withholding tax reduced or eliminated. You would complete a withholding certificate. If the 10% was paid, you would still be entitled to a refund if it was greater than the amount due, once you have filed your U.S. tax return.

You may be exempt from withholding tax completely if the purchase price is less than $300,000 (US) and the buyer intends to use the property as a residence at least one-half of the time it is used, over the subsequent two-year period. The buyer does not have to be a U.S. citizen or resident or use the property as a principal residence. To obtain this type of exemption, the buyer needs to sign an affidavit setting out the facts related above. If the purchase price is over $300,000 (US) or the buyer is unwilling or unable to sign the affidavit, you can request the waiver of withholding tax discussed previously.

Avoiding the U.S. Gift Tax

One might think that as a nonresident alien of the United States you could give anything to your spouse, children, or other family members, and the IRS would not have any jurisdiction. The laws, however, are not that simple. You may have U.S. gift tax to pay if you give real property or tangible personal property located in the United States to another person.

There is a $12,000 (US) annual exemption per recipient, meaning you can give a total of $12,000 per year to as many different people as you wish, without being subject to gift tax. If the recipient is your spouse, and not a U.S. citizen, the annual exemption is $120,000. If the recipient spouse is a U.S. citizen, as a general rule you can give unlimited amounts without gift tax—but exceptions apply for both exemptions. Consult your tax advisor.

The gift tax rates are the same as the estate tax rates, but the actual amount of the gift tax may be higher because there generally are no tax credits or deductions for gift tax purposes. Subject to these exemptions, the rules are as follows:

Real Estate and Gifting

If you own U.S. real estate directly and give it to another person, U.S. gift tax will generally be payable. Alternatively, if you buy real estate jointly with another person (other than your spouse) and the two of you make unequal contributions to the purchase price, gift tax may be payable. If you made equal contributions, there would not be any gift tax payable.

If you purchase real estate jointly with your spouse and make unequal contributions, beware when you sell the property. If the sales proceeds are not distributed to the two of you in proportion to your original contributions, gift tax may apply.

Suppose, at the time of purchase, the title to the property was placed entirely in the name of your spouse (or other family member) but the funds to make the purchase came solely from you. Gift tax may apply since you bought the property for the other person.

U.S. Taxes on Death

If you are a Canadian nonresident living part-time in the United States, you will be taxed at your death for any assets you hold in the United States by both U.S. and Canadian authorities. Assets would include real estate.

U.S. Estate Tax

U.S. federal estate tax is based on the fair market value of the U.S. asset on the date of the owner's death. There may be state estate taxes as well, depending on the state, ranging from zero to 10% or more of the federal estate tax. Under the Canada-U.S. tax treaty, you can claim foreign tax credits on U.S. estate tax paid against deemed disposition capital gains income taxes owed in Canada. Naturally, you would convert the amount paid in U.S. dollars to the Canadian equivalent. In the past, you could not do the above; therefore you were effectively subjected to double taxation on the same assets by each country.

Canadian Capital Gains Tax

Although Canada does not have an estate or death tax as such, in effect it does because the *Income Tax Act* deems that you have disposed of your assets at the time of your death and taxes you on any capital gains on your assets, whether they are in Canada or the United States. As mentioned above, you would now be able, under the Canada-U.S. tax treaty, to offset any U.S. federal tax paid against any Canadian capital gains tax due relating to those same assets in the United States. However, the benefit of this change should be kept in perspective.

Canada only taxes on 50% of the capital gains of the U.S. property, that is, the difference between the purchase price and the deemed value of the property or asset at the time of death. If the amount of the appreciation of the U.S. property is small, the benefit of applying the U.S. tax paid will be equally small. U.S. estate taxes can go up to 55% and are applied against the gross value of the property. If a complete exemption from U.S. tax was not possible and you had to pay U.S. estate tax, the amount paid could significantly exceed the offset against Canadian tax due, resulting in a large but unusable U.S. tax credit.

With proper tax planning, Canadian residents can defer Canadian capital gains tax on death by leaving the property to a spouse or spousal trust.

The Tax Impact of Dying in the United States

The impact depends on various factors. If you are a seasonal resident only of the United States and have no assets in that country, then only the CRA will be involved. The CRA requires a deemed disposition of all your assets, i.e., any capital gain as of your date of death is taxed. If you have assets in the United States, you need to file with the IRS and there could be federal and state death taxes payable. However, for the U.S. federal tax, you would normally be eligible for protection under the Canada-U.S. Tax Treaty, which has various exemptions. In addition, Canada may allow a foreign tax credit for the amount that you paid the IRS to be offset against any amount that you would owe for capital gains tax to the CRA for the same asset.

As you can see, competent cross-border tax advice is necessary.

There are U.S. Tax Treaty exemptions, such as a pro-rated unified credit that is allowed under the Treaty (based on U.S. assets, divided by the total assets, X unified credit). This often produces a significant sheltering from U.S. estate tax. Also, this credit is doubled when property passes to a spouse. Speak to an expert on U.S. and Canadian tax laws to strategically plan what will work the best in your situation.

Strategies for Reducing U.S. Estate Tax on Your U.S. Property

There are many strategic techniques to accomplish the objective of reducing, delaying, or eliminating U.S. tax. It is beyond the scope of this book to discuss them in detail. If you want a comprehensive discussion, read the latest edition of my book *The Canadian Snowbird Guide: Everything You Need to Know about Living Part-time in the U.S.A. or Mexico*. Also check out the website www.snow-bird.ca. Here are the main options, all of which have pros and cons that need to be customized to your specific situation and needs. The options are: claiming your Canadian primary residence exemption, joint ownership of property with your spouse or family members, sale and leaseback, disposing of U.S. property prior to your death, buying term life insurance, keeping your U.S. real estate in a Canadian holding company, giving the property to your beneficiaries during your lifetime, and leaving your U.S. property to a qualified domestic trust.

Buying a Vacation Home in Countries Other than the United States

The previous section discussed the implications and challenges of buying a vacation home in the United States. In relative terms, U.S. purchases are easier and less complicated than buying vacation property in countries such as Mexico, any of the Caribbean countries, Portugal, and elsewhere. That is because there is a well-established protocol for dealing with Canada-U.S tax issues. The greater the distance from Canada, and the less developed the area, the more challenges you need to deal with, for example: legal issues, national and local laws, and regulations about foreign ownership, financing, exchange rates, crime, political stability, local attitudes towards foreigners, quality of medical services, medical insurance, security, tax issues, renting your vacation home from afar or having a local agent, your rights and obligations in the country as a foreigner, etc.

If you are considering buying abroad, here are some general cautions you need to consider.

Do Your Due Diligence Research Thoroughly

This is a critical step. Fortunately, in the age of the Internet, you can do a great deal of your primary research from the comfort of your own home. Once you have worked up a checklist of questions that you want answered, you can then go to the local consulate of the country that you are interested in going to. You can also speak with the Canadian government department dealing with information and assistance for Canadians abroad. Seeking legal and tax advice on the implications of your situation—from both Canadian advisors and advisors in the country of interest to you—is very important.

The federal government has an excellent, information-rich website to assist Canadians in getting a reality check on other countries and the steps that need to be taken. Go to www.voyage.gc.ca, which is operated by Foreign Affairs and International Trade Canada. This site provides information on: country profiles, current issues, travel reports, travel warnings, publications, maps, traveller's checklist, dual citizenship, Canadian consular services, Canadian government offices abroad, taking medical supplies, supplemental health insurance, tourist visas, registrations of Canadians abroad, laws and regulations in other countries, and much more.

You can contact the Canadian consulate in the geographic area closest to the location where you are considering buying a vacation property and ask for candid feedback on the range of issues that you need to deal with, for example, learning to speak the language reasonably well to communicate effectively with the locals, etc. Alternatively, maybe you are thinking of buying in an international resort where the English language is commonly spoken.

You also need to check on any immunizations that are required for diseases endemic or indigenous to the area where you are planning to buy a vacation home.

Once you decide you want to explore the pros and cons more seriously, you should visit the area first hand. Maybe you already have done so many times, which is why you have considered buying a vacation property there. Once you have thoroughly done your advance research, make a realistic list of pros and cons of buying a vacation home outside of Canada or the United States. You may want to rent a home or apartment in the area of your interest as a long-term stay for up to six months before you make up your mind. That option is popular and has been made affordable in many countries in order to attract Canadians who like to spend the winter months in a warm climate.

After your research is concluded, you need to do a risk/reward assessment, and then think about it a second time. You want to keep your life simple, as well as keep your financial security intact.

Review Chapter 4: Finding the Right Recreational Property, and use the contents of that chapter as a guideline for your research as well.

Political Uncertainties

If you buy a property in a country where the political situation is tenuous, or there is a history of instability or a polarized society, that presents a whole host of additional problems. In a nutshell, it is not worth the hassle to consider buying in that environment. If this scenario is even remotely relevant to your situation, proceed with great caution.

Foreign Laws

In addition to the foreign laws regarding property ownership, you also want to become thoroughly acquainted with the laws and regulations of the country, and what your rights are as a nonresident and non-citizen. If you are renting a property, there are many other issues you need to deal with.

Financing

Getting financing for nonresidents is not an option in most foreign countries. You will have to arrange your own financing in Canada, through a home-equity loan on your own home, or by adding an additional mortgage on to it, in order to pay for the vacation property outside Canada or the United States.

Owning Rental Properties Abroad

Owning a property in your own name in another country may not be possible. The first thing you need to find out is whether non-citizens or nonresidents are permitted to own property. Some countries do not allow you to own property unless you are a citizen, or you can't own property on the ocean, although inland purchases may be allowed. Sometimes a way around any restriction is to buy a property through a local resident whom you know, or through an agent, such as a law firm, on your behalf. All these options involve increased risk for obvious reasons. The less direct control you have, the more risk. Special permits could be required, as well as fees, taxes, etc.

Get a legal opinion from several lawyers in the area who are familiar with real estate law and foreign ownership. The Canadian consulate in the area could be a source of referral for legal advice and could provide other cautions.

Renting for Income

If you own a vacation home in Canada that is located a long distance from your primary residence, it can be a logistical challenge, especially if you are arranging rentals from afar. If you own a vacation home in a foreign country, the challenges can be compounded considerably. You will need to rely on others, e.g., property agents or lawyers, to look after your interests. The more people assisting you, the less net revenue you receive. It can also be more difficult to rent in a foreign country, unless you own a luxurious villa in an international resort area in high demand.

You would also need to check on the local and national tax laws in the country where the property is located, and the cost of filing tax returns. As mentioned in the previous section of this chapter on renting in the United States, the Canada Revenue Agency will require you to annually disclose, in your tax return, your world-wide income from all sources.

Expert Legal and Tax Advice

If you are thinking of renting out a vacation home in Canada or the United States, you need to have expert tax advice. If you are thinking of renting out a vacation home or buying or selling one abroad, you really need to make sure you have talented and objective legal and tax advice.

As you can see, there are considerable complications, implications, and cautions when buying vacation real estate outside Canada. Refer to the Appendix under Helpful Websites for further information, and check out www. snowbird.ca and www.homebuyer.ca. If you are interested in seminars on buying vacation property outside Canada, refer to www.homebuyer.ca.

CHAPTER 18

Selling Your Recreational Property

Selling is an integral part of the real estate process, whether your vacation home is used for personal use or revenue investment. Most of the emphasis in discussions of real estate is on buying and managing. Many people treat the selling process casually without a full appreciation of the skills and techniques that should be used. They may rely blindly on the experience of their realtor to get the top price. If you don't know how to maximize the selling price, you could minimize your potential capital gain. With that in mind, this chapter will give you some constructive tips and suggestions.

There are many questions you have to ask yourself before deciding to sell, including the reasons for selling, the timing, price, terms, and benefits. You also have to consider how you will sell, including selecting and negotiating with a realtor, a lawyer, and the buyer.

The key topics that will be covered in this chapter include determining when to sell, preparing to sell your property, the different types of listing agreements, and the potential disadvantages of selling the property yourself. Refer again to Chapter 5: Selecting Your Advisors, regarding finding a real estate agent. For a detailed discussion about preparing your home inside and out for sale, refer to my books, *Making Money in Real Estate, Real Estate Investing for Canadians for Dummies*, and *101 Streetsmart Condo Buying Tips for Canadians*.

Determining When to Sell

One of the critical decisions of any recreational property owner is deciding when to sell. There are many factors that would suggest a sale is appropriate. The following factors could justify a decision to sell, whether you are using your vacation home for personal use only or as a rental investment property:

√ market is reaching its peak in terms of upward momentum of sales

√ appreciation of the property is plateauing or starting to decline

√ income is plateauing if revenue property

√   return on investment is decreasing

√   capital expenditures will increase

√   tax shelter or tax benefits are declining

√   financial needs have been met

√   you are interested in other priorities or opportunities

√   area is not economically healthy; it is either stagnating or declining

√   reached appropriate stage in original strategic holding period

√   reduction in net operating income

√   if an investor, you are getting frustrated with property management problems.

In short, monitor the market and your investment regularly. Anticipate problems and act accordingly.

Preparing to Sell Your Property

Once you have made the decision to sell, there are other issues you have to deal with. These would include the following:

Timing

The optimal rule here is to sell when everyone else is buying, although this is not always possible. The best time for selling a recreational property is generally in the spring or summer.

Pricing

The property has to be priced right for the market—without emotion and based on objective assessment or value. It is normal to determine the ideal price and then add another 5% to 10% or more for negotiating margin, depending on the market at the time, and the type of property.

Documents

Prepare all necessary documents for the realtor or purchaser. For example, if a mortgage is assumable without qualification and has an attractive interest rate, get a copy of the mortgage. If you have a vacation revenue property, get all the financial and other records for a purchaser to review.

Financing

If you have an assumable mortgage or you are prepared to take a first or second mortgage back in terms of vendor financing, clarify the terms.

Professional Advice

Depending on the nature of your property, obtain advice from your tax accountant and lawyer with regard to pricing, apportioning value, and timing.

Tax Implications

This is a big factor for recreational property, as has been discussed in the chapters on tax and estate planning.

Select a Realtor

Most experienced real estate investors utilize realtors extensively. Make certain your realtor is experienced in selling the type of recreational real estate in your specific geographic area. Of course, you can try to sell the property yourself through various home-selling websites. There are pros and cons of this approach to consider.

Competition

Check out similar properties for sale and the positive or negative features about your own property relative to others you have reviewed.

Promotion

Have your realtor advertise and promote the property as extensively as possible. This would usually be done through a Multiple Listing Service (MLS) website, the realtor's own website and contact list, an open house for public viewing, an open house for realtor viewing, newspaper advertising, and lawn signage. There are many other types of marketing techniques. Ask the realtor to confirm in writing, before you commit yourself, what their marketing plan will be for your property.

Make the Property Attractive

First impressions are lasting, so give your property special "curb appeal."

Set Terms

Determine what your best deal and bottom-line position will be and why. The purchaser will attempt to negotiate the best deal, so be prepared. Although the points on making the offer are designed from the purchaser's perspective, they will give you a good idea on which matters to counter-offer.

Calculate Closing Costs

Determine what you will net after all costs and before taxes. For example, you might have a three- or six-month penalty clause in your fixed-term mortgage for prepayment. There would be an exception, of course, if the purchaser assumes the mortgage.

Disadvantages of Selling the Property Yourself

You may be tempted to sell the property yourself. There is primarily only one reason for doing so, and that is to save the expense of a real estate commission. The only other motivation could be a personal challenge or learning experience, or because the market is a hot seller's market. But basically, the desire to save money is the main motivator. And you may indeed save money. On the other hand, the saving could be an illusion. Depending on the nature of the property, the market at the time, the specific realtor you are considering, and the real estate company involved, you can negotiate a reduced real estate commission. The problem with a reduced commission structure, though, is that if you want the property listed on the MLS, other realtors will see the reduced commission involved, and may not be motivated to spend time attempting to sell it when they can make a higher commission on other properties.

Here are some general disadvantages of selling a property yourself as opposed to using a carefully selected and experienced realtor. The comments apply whether you are selling your recreational second home or vacation investment property. The following remarks are not intended to dissuade you from attempting to sell your own property, but to place the process in a realistic perspective. In the end, you will have to balance the benefits and pitfalls and make up your own mind, as in any business or financial decision.

Inexperience

If you don't know all the steps involved, from the presale operation to completing the deal, you could make mistakes that will be costly to you. If you use a realtor who knows the market well in your community, you can capitalize on making the correct decisions.

Emotional Roller Coaster

Many people, especially with personal-use recreational property, tend to get emotionally involved in the selling process because of the direct interaction with the prospective purchasers. For example, vendors can experience frustration if prospective buyers reject the house, if there are negative comments or fault-finding, if they don't like the personalities of prospective buyers, or people who negotiate aggressively on the price. These one-on-one direct dynamics or comments can sometimes be taken personally and therefore be a cause of stress.

If you use a realtor to act as an agent, you rarely (if ever) meet the prospective purchaser directly, either before the agreement of purchase and sale is signed, or before or after closing. This degree of anonymity reduces stress.

Time Commitment

To sell the home yourself, you have to hold open houses and show your property at times that may not necessarily be convenient for you. In addition, you will have to spend time preparing the ad copy and staying at home to respond to telephone calls or people knocking on the door.

If you use a realtor, you will be able to save time by not having to be around when the property is shown or to answer phone calls. The realtor does all that for you as inquiries go directly to the realtor.

Expense, Nature, and Content of Advertising

Costs include any daily or weekly newspaper classified and/or box ads, as well as a lawn sign. You would pay for these yourself. In addition, you may not know what specific types of advertising would be appropriate for your type of property, how to write ad copy that would grab the attention of a reader and prospective purchaser, or how to identify and emphasize the key selling features of your property.

If you use a realtor, he or she pays for all the advertising costs. The nature and amount of advertising is negotiated at the time the listing agreement is signed. Not only could you get listed in the MLS book, which normally comes out weekly and is circulated to all member realtors, you could also be on the MLS computer database, which is accessible to all realtors on the Internet through the MLS website or through the real estate company website. Your property could also be advertised in daily and/or community newspapers, plus in special weekly real estate newspaper publications, which are available in most major cities. In addition, your realtor can show your property to realtors at an open house once the property is listed. All the techniques described are various forms of advertising. There are many more. An experienced realtor should also know how to write good ad copy and accentuate the key selling features of your property.

Limited Market Exposure

The previous point covered the comparative differences in market exposure in terms of advertising that you do yourself and the types of advertising a realtor could do for you. There is obviously a direct correlation between the nature and degree of market exposure and the end price. Clearly, self-advertising has limited exposure.

Potential Legal Problems

The prospective purchaser may supply you with his own agreement of purchase and sale. This contract may have clauses and other terms in it that could be legally risky, unenforceable, unfair, or otherwise not beneficial to you. You may not recognize these potential problems or risks. In addition, you could end up agreeing to take back a mortgage (vendor take-back mortgage) when it would not be necessary or wise, or to accept a long-term option or other legal arrangement that could be risky.

If you use a realtor, the realtor should recognize those aspects of the agreement that are unfair, unenforceable, or unclear, and advise you accordingly. The importance of having a real estate lawyer protect your interests before signing an agreement of purchase and sale is mentioned several times throughout this book. It is an inexpensive investment for protection and peace of mind.

Lack of Familiarity with the Market

You may not have a clear idea of exactly what a similar property in your market is selling for, or the state of the real estate market at that point. This can place you at a distinct disadvantage. For example, if you are unrealistic in your pricing and have limited advertising exposure, you could literally price yourself out of the market. Prospective purchasers may not even look, let alone make an offer. You may eventually sell your property, but only after several price reductions and after a long period. Naturally, of course, this depends on the market and the nature of your property.

If you use a realtor, he or she should be familiar with the market in your area, especially if you carefully select a realtor who is experienced with your type of residential property and knows your geographic area well. The pricing and overall marketing strategies recommended would therefore be customized for market conditions and general saleability.

No Pre-screening of Prospective Purchasers

You would not generally know the art of pre-screening prospects in terms of which questions to ask them over the phone. The end result is that you could waste your time talking to people over the phone or showing people through the house who are not and never will be serious prospects. You could also end up accepting an offer from someone who does not realistically have a chance of financing the house, or who asks for unrealistic time periods for removing purchaser conditions, which effectively would tie up your property during that time.

A realtor can pre-screen the potential prospects over the phone or in person to limit a potential waste of time for you. When the offers are finally presented, you will have more serious prospects involved.

Offer Is Not Necessarily the Best

Once an offer is on the table, you may think that offer is the best possible one from that prospective purchaser, or any purchaser, and therefore may accept it. That price may not be the best price at all. You may have started too low or too high for your initial asking price based on emotion or needs (not reality); you may have received a "low-ball" offer from the purchaser that was never intended to be accepted but was designed to reduce your expectations; you may not have strong negotiating skills and may be influenced by a prospective purchaser to close a deal that undervalues the property.

If you use a realtor, the realtor should be able to eliminate all the above problems. The realtor would normally provide the following services: do the initial research and set the original asking price realistically and objectively, depending on the market conditions, nature, and condition of the property, etc.; recognize a "low-ball" offer as a tactical ploy, and attempt to find out the reasons for the offer and whether the prospect was a serious one; suggest to you how to deal with offers in terms of counter-offers; know what negotiating skills to use in a given situation, and use them on your behalf; and know how to use effective closing skills.

Lack of Negotiating Skills

This problem was referred to in the previous point. You may lack any negotiating or sales skills, and as a consequence the price and terms you eventually settle for may not be as attractive as they otherwise could be.

If you use a realtor who is experienced and competent in selling your type of property in your area and who has a successful track record, you will benefit from that realtor's astute use of professional negotiating and sales skills. Another advantage is that the prospective purchaser will be dealing with your realtor, and you will probably never personally meet the purchaser before or after you accept the offer and the deal closes. Removing yourself from direct interaction with the prospective purchaser and using an agent instead enhances your negotiating position and the effective use of strategies.

Purchaser Wants Discount in Price Equal to Commission Saved

When you attempt to sell privately, it is not uncommon for the prospective purchaser to determine what the fair market value is, and then ask to have an additional discount equal to the real estate commission you are saving. The primary reason why prospective purchasers are attracted to a "For Sale by Owner" is the prospect of getting a better deal than a property listed with a realtor due to the commission otherwise built into the sale price. The primary reason why you are selling the property yourself is to save the full amount of any commission otherwise payable, hence the problem.

A compromise may be possible whereby the price is further reduced by 50% or 75% of the commission saved. Again, in practical terms, it is normally an illusion to think that you will save the full amount of the commission. The other related issue is that if you save on a commission (say, $5,000) after the purchaser saves an additional $5,000 on the purchase price (e.g., splitting the commission saving), would you not have a lingering doubt that you could have netted more if you had listed through a realtor and with MLS?

If you use a realtor, the above problem, of course, will not occur. Also, there is a good chance a realtor's efforts will result in a higher selling price for your property. Statistically, if you had listed it and had greater market exposure, better pricing, and a realtor who had applied more experienced real estate negotiating and selling skills than you possess, a higher sale price would be achieved.

Tough to Sell in a Buyer's Market

In a buyer's market—where there is a substantial supply of property but limited demand), buyers are very price sensitive, negotiate aggressively because they want the best deal, and have the time to be selective after comparing what is available in the market. You are at a disadvantage if you don't get all the exposure possible and use all the negotiating and selling skills available. You could wait a long time before finally selling, and the market could go down further by that time in a declining sale market.

If you use a realtor, whether the market is a buyer's or seller's market, for the reasons outlined in this section, the statistical odds are that you would benefit, in general terms, in your net sale proceeds.

The above summary of the key points shows that there are distinct benefits to selling through a realtor who is experienced and carefully selected. Of course, there are exceptions in certain situations where you may choose to sell yourself, but you have to be very aware of the disadvantages and pitfalls. Most people who invest in recreational properties realize the benefits of using a realtor and do so as a business decision, whether for buying or selling.

The Listing Agreement

The real estate listing agreement is usually a partially pre-printed form with standard clauses and wording. The balance of the agreement, completed by the agent and the vendor, covers the specific information with respect to the property being offered for sale and the nature of the contractual bargain between the agent and vendor. Because the listing agreement is a binding legal contract, you should be very cautious about signing it without fully understanding the implications of what you are signing. If in doubt, get advice from your lawyer beforehand. The following section covers the general contents of, and the types of, listing agreements.

Contents of a Listing Agreement

A listing agreement performs two main functions. First, you are giving the real estate agent the authority to act on your behalf to find a purchaser for your property. The agreement sets out the terms and conditions of this agency relationship, including the commission rate or method of compensation for the agent's services, the length of time of the appointment, when and how the fee or commission is earned, how and when it will be paid to the agent, and what the property marketing program will be.

A second feature of the listing agreement sets out the details of the property being offered for sale. All pertinent details should be set out, including civic and legal address, list price, size of property, description of the type of property, number and size of rooms, number of bedrooms, type of heating system, main recreational features, and other amenities. Any chattels (e.g., appliances, draperies and drapery track, carpeting) or extra features that are to be included in the list price should also be set out.

You should also insert other particulars in the listing agreement relating to the property for sale, including details of existing financing, the balance on the mortgage, the amount of monthly payments, and the due date on the mortgage. Any other mortgages should be listed as well. Annual property taxes should be set out, as well as any liens, rights of way, easements, or other charges on the property.

Once you have come to an agreement on all the terms and you are satisfied with them, the agreement is signed and witnessed and you receive a copy.

Types of Listing Agreements

There are three basic types of agreements that you may wish to consider when listing your property with a real estate agent: open, exclusive, and multiple listing.

Open Listing

In an open listing, the real estate agent does not have an exclusive right to find a purchaser for the property; you can sign any number of open-listing agreements with as many different agents as you wish. Only the agent who sells the property earns a commission. The problem with an open listing is that many realtors don't spend a great deal of time on such a listing because of the owner's lack of commitment to a specific realtor, and the lack of assurance that they will ever receive a commission on the sale of the property, despite spending a lot of time trying to find a buyer. This is because so many other realtors could also be looking for purchasers.

Open listings are more common in commercial sales than in residential sales, and in any event you should obtain legal advice before signing such an agreement, if you are considering such an option. To protect yourself, make sure that the agreement is in writing and the terms clearly spelled out. Commission rates could be similar to the "exclusive listing" below.

Exclusive Listing

In this situation, the vendor gives to the real estate agent an exclusive right to find a purchaser for the property. This right is given for a fixed period. The real estate agent is automatically entitled to receive a commission whether someone else sells the property, the vendor sells the property, or the property is sold at some future point to someone who was introduced to the property by the real estate agent during the listing period. The duration of an exclusive listing is normally 30, 60, or 90 days. In many ways the shorter the time period, the more energetically the realtor will have to work to achieve the sale. You can always extend the listing if you are satisfied with the realtor's performance and service. The typical range of commission is between 4% and 5% on the first $100,000, and 2.5% thereafter. If it is raw land, a 10% commission is common. Commissions can vary and are generally negotiable, depending on the circumstances. Do your comparison shopping of your options thoroughly.

Multiple Listing

With a multiple listing, a realtor is given an exclusive listing, in effect, for a fixed period of time, but also the right to list the property with the Multiple Listing Service (MLS). This computerized database is available to all members of the real estate boards who participate in the MLS. In practical terms, this constitutes almost all real estate companies; the entire real estate network becomes like a group of subagents for the sale of your property. If another agent finds a buyer, the selling company and the listing company will split the commission equally. Multiple listings are generally offered for a minimum of 60 days, but this is negotiable. Typical commission rates vary between 5% and 7% on the first $100,000, and 2.5% thereafter. Commissions are generally negotiable, depending on the circumstances. Again, do your comparison shopping of your options thoroughly.

Now that you have finished this final chapter in the book, congratulations! Your dream of owning a recreational property is now within reach. Whether you are deciding to buy for personal enjoyment or a family retreat, as a revenue investment or for a future retirement home, the many benefits of owning a vacation home are worth the effort to attain that goal.

With the insights and knowledge you have attained through this book, you are well-equipped to make the acquisition process go smoothly, and make the ownership experience a pleasurable one.

If you would like to obtain more real estate information or be notified of seminars in your geographic area on buying recreational property, please refer to my website: www.homebuyer.ca.

Best wishes on your future recreational property purchase!

Appendix

Helpful Websites

Here are some websites to assist you in your information and contacts research before you buy a recreational property, be it a cottage, house, or condominium.

General Information

Google Internet search	www.google.ca
National Real Estate Institute Inc.	www.homebuyer.ca
Canadian Estate Planning Institute Inc.	www.estateplanning.ca
Canadian Enterprise Development Group Inc.	www.smallbiz.ca
Canadian Retirement Planning Institute Inc.	www.retirementplanning.ca
Canadian Snowbird Institute Inc.	www.snowbird.ca

Real Estate Listings

Multiple Listing Service	www.mls.ca

Housing Surveys and Stats

Royal LePage Survey of Canadian Houses Prices	www.royallepage.ca
Royal LePage Recreational Property Survey	www.royallepage.ca
Century 21 Recreational Property Survey	www.century21.ca
Canadian Mortgage and Housing Corporation	www.cmhc.ca
National Real Estate Institute Inc.	www.homebuyer.ca

Professional Associations

Appraisal Institute of Canada	www.aicanada.ca
Canadian Association of Home and Property Inspectors	www.cahpi.ca
Canadian Home Builders' Association	www.chba.ca

The Royal Architectural Institute of Canada	www.raic.org
Canadian Bar Association	www.cba.org
Canadian Institute of Chartered Accountants	www.cica.ca
Certified General Accountants Association of Canada	www.cga-canada.org
Canadian Institute of Mortgage Brokers and Lenders	www.cimbl.ca
Canadian Real Estate Association	www.crea.ca
Financial Advisors Association of Canada	www.advocis.ca
Financial Planners Standards Council of Canada	www.cfp-ca.org
Insurance Brokers Association of Canada	www.ibac.ca
Canadian Life and Health Insurance Association	www.clhia.ca

Cross-Border Financial Planning/Tax Planning

| International Tax Services Group | www.ustax.ca |
| Brunton's U.S. Taxletter for Canadians | www.taxintl.com |

Mortgage Insurance, Title Insurance, and Credit Reports

Canadian Mortgage and Housing Corporation	www.cmhc.ca
Genworth Financial Canada	www.genworth.ca
Equifax Canada	www.equifax.ca
First Canadian Title Insurance	www.firstcanadiantitle.com

Federal Government

Canadian Mortgage and Housing Corporation	www.cmhc.ca
Statistics Canada	www.statcan.ca
Bank of Canada	www.bankofcanada.ca
Canada Revenue Agency	www.cra-arc.gc.ca

Provincial Governments—Condominium Legislation

Alberta	www.gov.ab.ca
British Columbia	www.fin.gov.bc.ca
Manitoba	www.gov.mb.ca/cca
New Brunswick	www.gov.nb.ca
Newfoundland and Labrador	www.gov.nf.ca
Northwest Territories	www.gov.nt.ca

Nova Scotia	www.gov.ns.ca/snsmr
Nunavut	www.nunavut.com
Ontario	www.cbs.gov.on.ca
Prince Edward Island	www.gov.pe.ca
Saskatchewan	www.saskjustice.gov.sk.ca
Quebec	www.soquij.qc.ca
Yukon	www.gov.yk.ca

New Home Warranty Programs

Alberta New Home Warranty Program	www.anhwp.com
Association provinciale des constructeurs d'habitations du Québec	www.apchq.com
Atlantic New Home Warranty Program	www.ahwp.org
British Columbia Homeowner Protection Office	www.hpo.bc.ca
Manitoba New Home Warranty Program	www.mbnhwp.com
New Home Warranty Program of Saskatchewan	www.nhwp.org
Ontario New Home Warranty Program	www.newhome.on.ca

Private Warranty Programs

London Guarantee Insurance Company	www.londonguarantee.com
National Home Warranty Programs	www.nationalhomewarranty.com
Residential Warranty of Canada Inc.	www.reswar.com
Wylie-Crump Limited	www.wyliecrump.com

Condominium Associations

The Canadian Condominium Institute	www.cci.ca
Condominium Homeowners Association of B.C.	www.choa.bc.ca
Vancouver Island Strata Owners Association	www.visoa.bc.ca

Tourism Associations

National	www.canadatourism.com
Alberta	www.tourismalberta.com
British Columbia	www.hellobc.com
Manitoba	www.tourismmanitoba.ca

New Brunswick	www.tourismnewbrunswick.ca
Newfoundland and Labrador	www.newfoundlandandlabradortourism.com
Northwest Territories	www.explorenwt.com
Nova Scotia	www.novascotia.com
Nunavut	www.nunavuttourism.com
Ontario	www.ontariotravel.net
	www.tourism.gov.on.ca
	www.ontariotourism.com
	www.tourismontario.com
	www.ontariooutdoor.com
Prince Edward Island	www.tourismpei.com
Saskatchewan	www.sasktourism.com
Quebec	www.bonjourquebec.com
Yukon	www.travelyukon.com

Cottage Associations

National:
Canadian Coalition of Provincial Cottagers'
  Associations   www.cottager.org

Alberta:
Alberta Urban Municipalities Association   www.munilink.net

British Columbia:
Floating Home Association Pacific/Canada   www.floathomepacific.com

Manitoba:
Manitoba Association of Cottage Owners   http://maco.clickusfirst.com

Ontario:
Federation of Ontario Cottagers Association   www.foca.on.ca
Baptiste Lake Association   www.baptistelake.org
Big Rideau Lake Association   www.brla.on.ca
Gloucester Pool Cottagers Association   www.gloucesterpool.ca
Lake of Bays Association   www.loba.ca
Lake of the Woods District Property
  Owners Association   www.lowdpoa.com

Muskoka Lakes Association	www.mla.on.ca
Rondeau Cottagers' Association	www.rondeaucottagers.ca
Temagami Lakes Association	www.tla-temagami.org

Saskatchewan:
Provincial Association of Resort
  Communities   www.parcs-sk.com

Canadian Cottage and Resort Magazines

Cottage   www.cottagemagazine.com
*Western Canadian Resorts, Vacation
  Homes and Investment Properties*   www.resortsmag.com
Cottage Life   www.cottagelife.com
The Cottager   www.thecottager.mb.ca

Vacation Rental Websites

(many also have vacation/home exchange option)

www.resortac.com	www.craigslist.com
www.alluradirect.com	www.cottageportal.com
www.cyberrentals.com	www.greatrentals.com
www.greatrentals.com	www.holiday-rentals.uk.com
www.holiday-rentals.com	www.lakerentals.com
www.vacationrentals.com	www.ownerdirect.com
www.vacationvillas.net	www.shorevacations.com
www.vrbo.com	www.srbo.com
www.perfectplaces.com	www.digsville.com

Vacation/Home Exchange Websites

(many also have vacation rental option)

www.exchangehomes.com	www.trading-homes.com
www.homeexchange.com	www.sunswap.com
www.homeinvite.com	www.seniorshomeexchange.com
www.homelink.ca	www.craigslist.com
www.intervac.ca	www.tecvan.ca

CHART 1: Determining the Real Estate Cycle

	A	B	C	D
Values	Depressed	Increasing	Increasing	Declining
Rents	Low	Increasing	Increasing	Declining
Vacancy Level	High	Beginning to Decrease	Low	Increasing
Occupancy Level	Low	Increasing	High	Decreasing
New Construction	Very Little	Increasing	Booming	Slowing
Profit Margins	Low	Improving	Wildest	Decline
Investor Confidence	Low	Negative to Neutral	Positive	Slightly Negative
Media Coverage	Negative and Pessimistic	Positive and Encouraging	Positive and Optimistic	Negative and Pessimistic
Action	Buy	Second best Time to buy	Sell	Buy

CHECKLIST 1: Recreational Property Assessment Checklist

1. This assessment checklist has many of the essential features to look for when evaluating a recreational property house (cottage, chalet, cabin, etc.), apartment condominium, or townhouse condominium (100% owned, fractional interest, or timeshare, etc.).

2. Not all the categories are necessarily applicable in your individual case. Terminology in some instances can vary from province to province.

3. On the line provided, indicate your rating of the listed factor as one of the following: excellent, good, poor, available, not available, not applicable, further information required. Sometimes only yes or no responses are required. This will help you in your research and provide objective clarity for each property you are seriously considering.

A. General Information

Location of property   _____

Condition of neighbourhood   _____

Condition of property   _____

Upkeep required of property   _____

Age of property   _____

Type of property   _____

Zoning of property   _____

Zoning of surrounding areas   _____

Nightly rentals permitted in property   _____

Nightly rentals permitted in surrounding areas   _____

Prospect for future increase in value   _____

Prospect for future change of zoning   _____

Traffic density in area   _____

Proximity and number of neighbouring properties   _____

Land boundaries clearly marked and surveyed   _____

Crime stats and nature of crime in area   _____

Risk of forest fire or other natural disaster   _____

Full-time or volunteer fire department and proximity of
   firehalls and hydrants   _____

Annual weather patterns (sun, snow, rain, etc.)   _____

Special Features:

Lakefront   _____

Riverfront (risk of flooding?)   _____

Oceanfront _____

Lakeview _____

Riverview _____

Oceanview _____

Mountainview _____

Proximity to body of water _____

Recreational Amenities:

Nature of amenities _____

Private and cost of use if applicable _____

Public and cost of use if applicable _____

Proximity of:

Schools _____

Churches _____

Shopping _____

Recreation _____

Entertainment _____

Parks _____

Children's playgrounds _____

Public transportation _____

Highways _____

Hospital _____

Police department _____

Fire department _____

Ambulance _____

Neighbours _____

Access, Water and Sewage:

Accessibility of property—drive, fly, boat, ferry, etc. _____

Availability for use—year-round or seasonal _____

Municipal sewage piping system _____

Sewage holding tank (pump-out required and cost) _____

Septic field _____

Municipal water supply _____

Well water—quality and supply _____

Cost to drill well _____

Other forms of water supply   _____
Garbage removal or other forms of disposal   _____

Taxes:
Provincial   _____
Municipal/Local   _____
How taxes assessed and primary revenue source   _____
Maintenance fees/assessments (if condominium)   _____

Property Restrictions:
Easements   _____
Rights of way   _____
Restrictive covenants of builder or developer   _____
Restrictive covenants of local government   _____
Local zoning bylaw restrictions (e.g., nightly rentals not
   permitted, no mobile homes on property, no other
   buildings to be constructed, seasonal use only, etc.)   _____
Condo bylaw restrictions   _____
Condo property management restrictions   _____
Condo rental pool restrictions   _____
Pending local tax or development changes and impact   _____
Other   _____

Quietness of:
Neighbourhood   _____
Condo complex   _____
Individual condominium unit   _____
House   _____

Condominium Development:
Percentage of units that are owner-occupied (if
condominium)   _____
Percentage of units that are rented out (if condominium)   _____
If next to commercial or tourist centre, is access to
   residential section well controlled?   _____
Is adjacent commercial/tourist development being
   planned?   _____
Size of development related to your needs (small,
   medium, large)   _____

Development compatible with your lifestyle   _____

Style of development—adult-oriented, children,
   retirees, etc.   _____

Age of development, in years   _____

Rental of Your Recreational Property

Seasonal nightly renters permitted?   _____

Are you required to put your condo in rental pool when
   not in use?   _____

Are you required to use a specific property management
   company for any rentals and what is their
   commission/fee?   _____

If you are relying on rental revenue and you are required
   to use a specific property management company, what
   marketing program do they have, and what is their
   historical track record of net revenue for your unit?   _____

If you are required to be in a rental pool, are the expenses
   fair and fairly apportioned?   _____

If you are not required to be in a rental pool for your
   condo, and not required to use a specified property
   management company, how do you propose to market
   your condo or other property, e.g., through owner-direct
   Internet sites, etc.?   _____

B. Exterior Factors

Privacy:

Roadway (public street, private street, safety for children) _____

Sidewalks (adequacy of drainage)   _____

Driveway (public, private, semi-private)   _____

Privacy   _____

Garage:

Reserved space (one or two cars)   _____

Underground garage   _____

Automatic garage doors   _____

Security   _____

Adequate visitor parking   _____

Housing Construction:

Construction material (brick, wood, stone) _____

Siding (aluminum, vinyl, wood, other) _____

Condition of paint _____

Other _____

Roof:

Type of material _____

Age _____

Condition _____

Balcony or Patios:

Location (view, etc.) _____

Privacy _____

Size _____

Open or enclosed _____

Landscaping:

Trees _____

Shrubbery, flowers _____

Lawns _____

Automatic sprinklers _____

Condition and upkeep of exterior _____

C. Interior Factors

Security:

Intercom system _____

Medical alert system _____

Fire safety system (fire alarms, smoke detectors, sprinklers) _____

Burglar alarm system _____

General Safety:

TV surveillance _____

Controlled access _____

Pre-wired for television and telephone cable _____

Lobby:

Cleanliness _____

Decor   _____
Security guard   _____

Public Corridors:
Material used   _____
Condition   _____
Plaster (free of cracks, stains)   _____
Decor   _____

Access:
General accessibility   _____
Number of stairwells   _____
Elevators   _____
Wheelchair accessibility   _____

Storage Facilities:
Location   _____
Size   _____
Cost   _____
Adequacy (if you have lots of toys, e.g., boats, skidoos,
    snowmobiles, kayaks, canoes, dirt bikes, quads, etc.!)   _____

Heating and Insulation:
Insulation: (The R factor is the measure of heating and
cooling efficiency; the higher the R factor, the more efficient)
R rating in walls (minimum of R-19; depends
    on geographic location)   _____
R rating in ceiling (minimum of R-30; depends
    on geographic location)   _____
Heat pumps   _____
Windows (insulated, storm, screen)   _____
Air conditioning   _____
Heating (gas, electric, hot water, oil)   _____

Temperature Controls:
Individually controlled   _____
Convenient location   _____

Plumbing:

Functions well   _____

Convenient fixtures   _____

Quietness of plumbing   _____

Suitable water pressure   _____

Utility Costs:

Gas   _____

Electric   _____

Other   _____

Other:

Laundry facilities (private or public)   _____

Soundproofing features   _____

D. Management of Condominium

Condominium management company   _____

Owner-managed   _____

Resident manager   _____

Management Personnel:

Front desk   _____

Maintenance   _____

Gardener   _____

Trash removal   _____

Snow removal   _____

Security (number of guards, hours, location, patrol)   _____

E. Condominium Corporation

Experience of directors of corporation   _____

Positive or negative relationship between owners and
    condo council or board of directors, and other owners   _____

Any litigation history of condo corporation?   _____

Any upcoming special assessments or other anticipated
    maintenance/repair expenses in near future?   _____

Average age of other owners   _____

Percentage of renters vs. owner-occupiers   _____

Is condo still covered by a New Home Warranty program? _____

Condo unit monthly maintenance fees   _____

Condo contingency/reserve fund balance   _____

F. Recreation Facilities (if condominium)

Clubhouse   _____

Club membership fees (included, not included)   _____

Sports:

Courts (tennis, squash, racquetball, handball, basketball) _____

Games room (ping-pong, billiards)   _____

Exercise room   _____

Bicycle path/jogging track   _____

Organized sports and activities   _____

Children's Playground:

Location (accessibility)   _____

Noise factor   _____

Organized sports and activities (supervised)   _____

Swimming Pool:

Location (outdoor, indoor)   _____

Children's pool   _____

Noise factor   _____

Visitors' Accommodation   _____

G. Individual Unit (if condominium)

Location in complex   _____

Size of unit   _____

Is the floor plan and layout suitable?   _____

Will your furnishings fit in?   _____

Is the unit exposed to the sunlight?   _____

Does the unit have a scenic view?   _____

Is the unit in a quiet location (away from
  garbage unit, elevator noise, playgrounds, etc.)?   _____

Accessibility (stairs, elevators, fire exits)   _____

Closets:
Number   _____
Location   _____

Carpet:
Colour   _____
Quality/texture   _____

Hardwood floors, condition   _____

Living Room:
Size/shape   _____
Windows/view   _____
Sunlight (morning, afternoon)   _____
Fireplace   _____
Privacy (from outside, from rest of condo)   _____

Dining Room:
Size   _____
Accessibility to kitchen   _____
Windows/view   _____

Den or Family Room:
Size/shape   _____
Windows/view   _____
Sunlight (morning or afternoon)   _____
Fireplace   _____
Privacy (from outside, from rest of condo)   _____

Laundry Room:
Work space available   _____
Washer and dryer   _____
Size/capacity   _____
Warranty coverage   _____

Kitchen:
Size   _____
Eating facility (table, nook, no seating)   _____

Floors (linoleum, tile, wood)   _____

Exhaust system   _____

Countertop built in   _____

Countertop material   _____

Work space   _____

Kitchen cabinets (number, accessibility)   _____

Cabinet material   _____

Sink (size, single, double)   _____

Sink material   _____

Built-in cutting boards   _____

Oven (single, double, self-cleaning)   _____

Gas or electric oven   _____

Age of oven   _____

Microwave (size)   _____

Age of microwave   _____

Refrigerator/freezer (size/capacity)   _____

Refrigerator (frost-free, ice maker, single/double door) _____

Age of refrigerator   _____

Dishwasher (age)   _____

Trash compactor/garbage disposal   _____

Pantry or storage area   _____

Is there warranty coverage on all appliances?   _____

Bedrooms:

Total number of bedrooms   _____

Master Bedroom:

Size/shape   _____

Privacy (from outside, from rest of condo)   _____

Closets/storage space   _____

Fireplace   _____

Floor and wall covering   _____

Master Bathroom (En Suite):

Size   _____

Bathtub   _____

Whirlpool tub/Jacuzzi   _____

Shower   _____

Steam room   _____
Vanity   _____
Sink (single, double, integrated sink bowls)   _____
Medicine cabinet   _____

Bathrooms:
Total number of bathrooms   _____
Complete, or sink and toilet only?   _____

Fractional Ownership of Condo:
What are conditions of personal use and rentals?   _____
What are monthly maintenance costs?   _____

H. Legal and Financial Matters
Project documents (e.g., disclosure/declaration)
   received and read (if new condominium)   _____
Bylaws received and read (if condominium)   _____
Rules and regulations received and read
   (if condominium)   _____
Financial statements received and read
   (if condominium or revenue-generating property)   _____
Condo council minutes, and annual general
   meeting and special general meeting minutes
   over past two years received and read
   (if condominium or revenue-generating property)   _____
No litigation or pending litigation   _____
No outstanding or pending special assessments   _____
No pending repairs, or leaky condo problems   _____

Other documents (list):
_____   _____
_____   _____
_____   _____
_____   _____

All above documentation (as applicable) reviewed
   by your lawyer and legal advice on potential
   purchase obtained   _____

Financial statements reviewed by your accountant
   and tax advice on investment obtained   _____

All assessments, maintenance fees, and taxes detailed   _____

Condominium corporation insurance coverage
   adequate   _____

Restrictions acceptable (e.g., pets, renting of unit,
   number of people living in suite, children, etc.) for
   rental condo   _____

All verbal promises or representations of sales
   representative or vendor's agent that you are relying
   on written into the offer to purchase   _____

If you are buying a property with other parties, agreement
   on use, repairs, expenses, and sale, etc., prepared and/or
   reviewed by your lawyer in advance of any purchase
   and acceptable to you   _____

If you are buying a property for rental purposes,
   periodically or full-time, rental documents prepared
   by your lawyer, along with security deposits, etc.   _____

If you are buying a property you would like to pass
   on to your children on your death, tax planning
   strategic advice obtained in advance from a qualified
   tax expert (lawyer or accountant, i.e., CGA or CA) as
   to the best tax-saving options available to you
   (e.g., trusts, etc.)   _____

Your will is current and prepared by a lawyer (don't do a
   "do-it-yourself" will)   _____

Other

_____   _____
_____   _____
_____   _____
_____   _____

CHECKLIST 2: Preparing for a Mortgage

A. Ask Yourself These Questions

1. Is your income secure? _____

2. Will your income increase or decrease in the future? _____

3. Are you planning on increasing the size of your family (e.g., children, relatives) and therefore your living expenses? _____

4. Will you be able to put aside a financial buffer for unexpected expenses or emergencies? _____

5. Are you planning to purchase the property with someone else? _____

6. If the answer is yes to the above question, will you be able to depend on your partner's financial contribution without interruption? _____

7. If you are relying on an income from renting out all or part of your purchase, have you determined:

   • If city zoning and use bylaws permit it? _____

   • If the condominium corporation bylaws permit it? _____

   • If the mortgage company policies permit it? _____

8. Have you thoroughly compared mortgage rates and features so that you know what type of mortgage and mortgage company you want? _____

9. Have you determined the amount of mortgage that you would be eligible for? _____

10. Have you considered the benefits of a pre-approved mortgage? _____

11. Have you considered talking to a mortgage broker? _____

12. Have you considered assuming an existing mortgage? _____

13. Have you considered the benefits of a portable mortgage? _____

14. Have you considered having the vendor give you a mortgage? _____

15. Have you determined all the expenses you will incur relating to the purchase transaction? (See Checklist 3) _____

16. Have you completed your present and projected financial needs analysis (income and expenses)? _____

17. Have you completed the mortgage application form, including net worth statement (assets and liabilities)? _____

B. Ask the Lender These Questions

Interest Rates

18. What is the current interest rate? _____

19. How frequently is the interest calculated? (semi-annually, monthly, etc.) _____

20. What is the effective interest rate on an annual basis? _____

21. How long will the lender guarantee a quoted interest rate? _____

22. Will the lender put the above guarantee in writing?   _____
23. Will you receive a lower rate of interest if the rates fall before you
    finalize your mortgage?   _____
24. Will the lender put the above reduction assurance in writing? _____
25. Will the lender show you the total amount of interest you will have to
    pay over the lifetime of the mortgage?   _____

Amortization

26. What options do you have for amortization periods? (10, 15 years, etc.) _____
27. Will the lender provide you with an amortization schedule for your loan
    showing your monthly payments apportioned into principal and interest? _____
28. Have you calculated what your monthly payments will be, based on each
    amortization rate?   _____
29. Are you required to maintain the amortized monthly payment schedule if
    annual pre-payments are made, or will they be adjusted accordingly? _____

Term of the Mortgage

30. What different terms are available? (6 months, one, two, three, five years, etc.) _____
31. What is the best term for your personal circumstances?   _____
32. What are the different interest rates available relating to the different terms? _____

Payments

33. What is the amount of your monthly payments (based on amortization period)? _____
34. Are you permitted to increase the amount of your monthly payments, if you
    want to, without penalty?   _____
35. Does the lender have a range of payment periods available, such as weekly,
    bi-weekly, monthly, etc.?   _____
36. What is the best payment period in your personal circumstances? _____

Prepayment

37. What are your prepayment privileges?
    • Completely open?   _____
    • Open with a fixed penalty or notice requirement?   _____
    • Limited open with no penalty or notice requirement?   _____
    • Limited open with fixed penalty or notice requirement?   _____
    • Completely closed?   _____
    • Some combination of the above?   _____
38. What amount can be prepaid and what is the penalty or notice required, if
    applicable?   _____

39. How long does the privilege apply in each of the above categories, if applicable? _____

40. When does the prepayment privilege commence? (six months, one year, anytime, etc.) _____

41. Is there a minimum amount that has to be prepaid? _____

42. What form does your prepayment privilege take—increase in payments or lump sum? _____

43. Is your prepayment privilege cumulative (e.g., make last year's lump sum prepayment next year)? _____

Taxes

44. How much are the property taxes? _____

45. Does the lender require a property tax payment monthly (based on projected annual tax), or is it optional? _____

46. Does the lender pay interest on the property tax account? If yes, what is the interest rate? _____

Mortgage Transaction Fees and Expenses

47. What is the appraisal fee? Is an appraisal necessary? _____

48. What is the survey fee? Is a survey necessary? _____

49. Will you be able to select a lawyer of your choice to do the mortgage work? _____

50. Does the lender charge a processing or administrative fee? _____

51. Does the lender arrange for a lawyer to do the mortgage documentation work at a flat fee, regardless of the amount of the mortgage? _____

52. Does the lender know what the out-of-pocket disbursements for the mortgage transaction will be? _____

53. Does the mortgage have a renewal administration fee? How much is it? _____

Mortgage Assumption Privileges

54. Can the mortgage be assumed if the property is sold? _____

55. Is the mortgage assumable with or without the lender's approval? _____

56. What are the assumption administrative fees, if any? _____

57. Will the lender release the vendor from all personal obligations under the terms of the mortgage if it is assumed? _____

Portability

58. Is the mortgage portable; i.e., can you transfer it to another property that you may buy? _____

CHECKLIST 3: Real Estate Purchase Expenses Checklist

In addition to the actual purchase price of your investment, there are a number of other expenses to be paid on or prior to closing. Not all of these expenses will be applicable. Some provinces may have additional expenses.

Type of expense	When paid	Estimated amount
Deposits	At time of offer	_____
Mortgage application fee	At time of application	_____
Property appraisal	At time of mortgage application	_____
Property inspection	At inspection	_____
Balance of purchase price	On closing	_____
Legal fees re property transfer	On closing	_____
Legal fees re mortgage preparation	On closing	_____
Legal disbursements re property transfer	On closing	_____
Legal disbursements re mortgage preparation	On closing	_____
Mortgage broker commission	On closing	_____
Property survey	On closing	_____
Property tax holdback (by mortgage company)	On closing	_____
Land transfer or deed tax (provincial)	On closing	_____
Property purchase tax (provincial)	On closing	_____
Property tax (local/municipal) adjustment	On closing	_____
Goods and services tax (GST) (federal)	On closing	_____
New Home Warranty Program fee	On closing	_____
Mortgage interest adjustment (by mortgage company)	On closing	_____
Sales tax on chattels purchased from vendor (provincial)	On closing	_____
Adjustments for fuel, taxes, etc.	On closing	_____
Mortgage lender insurance premium (CMHC or GEM)	On closing	_____
Condominium maintenance fee adjustment	On closing	_____
Building insurance	On closing	_____
Life insurance premium on amount of outstanding mortgage	On closing	_____
Moving expenses	At time of move	_____

Utility connection charges	At time of move	_____
Redecorating and refurbishing costs	Shortly after purchase	_____
Immediate repair and maintenance costs	Shortly after purchase	_____
House and garden improvements	Shortly after purchase	_____
Other expenses (list):		
_____	_____	_____
_____	_____	_____
_____	_____	_____
TOTAL CASH REQUIRED		$_____

CHECKLIST 4: Vacation Property Sharing and Use Agreement Checklist

Note: The first item in your Sharing and Use Agreement should state that the draft agreement will be reviewed by an independent lawyer and accountant, for legal and tax implications, before signing takes place.

- Date of agreement   _____
- Address of property   _____
- Owners' names and contact information, including emergency numbers   _____
- Description of cottage owners (family, business partners, etc.)   _____

Ownership

- How property is held (joint tenancy, tenancy in common, other)   _____
- Percentage ownership of each owner   _____
- Purpose of property ownership (personal use only, investment, investment/personal use, etc.)   _____
- Long-term goals (temporary arrangement, long-term commitment, speculation, etc.)   _____
- Policy on future property sale if any   _____
- Formula for owners wanting to sell their equity interest (e.g., in the event of illness, disability, divorce, etc.)   _____
- Formula if one owner wants to buy out the other owner(s)   _____
- Property evaluation methods if future sale, or owner is to be bought out   _____
- Policy on parting of the ways, setting out all possible scenarios   _____
- Policy on wills: all owners to have current wills drawn up by a lawyer to avoid future legal and estate problems   _____
- Formula for buying out deceased owner's interest (e.g., right of first refusal by remaining owners, valuation criteria and method of payment, and option of payment over time)   _____
- Policy that individual owners will not encumber the property (e.g., mortgage, etc.)   _____
- Assets of vacation property owners itemized (e.g., boats, equipment), and ownership clarified (group or individual)   _____
- Policy on future capital contributions (circumstances when required, amount and form, apportionment of contribution among owners, etc.)   _____

Insurance

- Property insurance (e.g., coverage, limits, deductibles, premiums, etc.)   _____
- Policy on a limit before an insurance claim will be made   _____

- Policy on how accidents will be dealt with (e.g., if an owner or guest of an owner breaks a window, is that owner responsible for replacing the window?) _____
- Life insurance: life insurance on each owner to be sufficient for purchase of other owners' interest in the event of death _____

Governance

- Decision-making (majority or unanimous), and methods to resolve an impasse _____
- Policy on resolving disputes in general _____
- Policy on regularity of meetings (e.g., annually or semi-annually, over the phone or in person) to discuss, re-evaluate, and record priorities (e.g., re-surface driveway vs. purchase a new oven, etc.) _____
- Policy on elections of president, secretary, etc. _____
- Meeting agendas and minutes (responsibility and circulation) _____
- Bank accounts (naming your accounts, signing authority on cheques, etc.) _____
- Policy on borrowing money, amounts, purpose, and procedures _____
- Responsibility for ledgers and bookkeeping _____
- Annual estimate of costs and budgeting of expenses for maintenance, upkeep, improvements, supplies, etc., as well as contingency buffer for unexpected and emergency expenses; method of timing of owners paying into expense fund _____

Maintenance, Repairs and Day-to-Day Use

- Maintenance schedule, including who, when, and how the maintenance will be done (e.g., owners do it themselves, hire a contractor, work weekends, etc.) _____
- Maintenance schedule/plan for spring cleaning and preparing for off-season _____
- Opening-up checklist _____
- Closing-down checklist _____
- Maintenance procedures for each visit/user _____
- Policy on renting chalet to others, including friends or relatives (e.g., can teenage children use the property on their own, and limit on number of people staying in cottage at any one time) _____
- Fairness formula for owners or friends using the cottage more than others if applicable (e.g., percentage of expense adjustment) _____
- Policy with regard to pets _____
- Policy with regard to parties and drinking _____
- Rules, regulations, and use policy manual for guests, renters, etc. _____
- Policy with regard to using boats or other equipment at the cottage (e.g., replenishing fuel, minimum age of pilot, etc.) _____

- Booking procedures (double booking, collection, time limits, reminders, bumping, first come first served) _____
- User fees (when and what to charge, security deposit, responsibility for loss or damage) _____
- Checking-in checklist _____
- Checking-out checklist (e.g., cleaning up, restocking supplies used, laundry procedures, damage notification, etc.) _____
- Emergency phone numbers _____
- Phone numbers of trades to be called in emergency (e.g., plumber, electrician) _____
- First aid kit (and replenishment policy) _____
- Fire extinguishers _____
- Smoke/fire alarms _____
- Quiet hours _____
- Policy on smoking inside cottage _____
- Log book of daily occurrences (e.g., breakages, mice running around, use of boats, repairs done or needing to be done, etc.) _____
- Guest comment book _____
- Website (password access for communication among owners) _____
- Meal-planning checklist _____
- Pantry and cottage staples (basic stock and replacement policy, and checklists) _____
- Fairness policy on cooking for guests _____
- Laundry (with or without washing machine); policy on guests using owners' laundry or bringing their own (e.g., for saving on water use, laundry detergent, etc.) _____
- Security (keys, number and policy about access and use) _____
- Storage (shared and non-shared) _____
- Designation of a specific room and/or certain amount of closet space for each owner's personal items _____
- Policy on how interior decorating will be done, what the priorities are, and how decisions will be made _____
- Donations (cash or in kind) _____
- Gardening _____
- Bird feeders _____
- Garbage removal _____
- Recycling _____
- Energy savings policy _____
- Environment care policy _____
- Water use _____
- Other (list) _____

Glossary

ACB: See *Adjusted cost base* below.

Acceleration clause: Usually written into a mortgage to allow the lender to accelerate or call the entire principal balance of the mortgage, plus accrued interest, when the payments become delinquent.

Adjusted cost base (ACB): The value of the real property established for tax purposes. It is the original cost plus any allowable capital improvements, plus certain acquisition costs, plus any mortgage interest costs, and less any depreciation taken.

Administrators: In Quebec, those persons the co-ownership has appointed to act as administrators of the immovables. Equivalent to a *board of directors* or *condominium council*. The administrators are responsible to the co-proprietors and are entrusted with the conservation of the immovables and the maintenance and administration of the common portions.

Agreement of purchase and sale: A written agreement between the owner and a purchaser for the purchase of real estate on a predetermined price and terms.

Amenities: Generally, those parts of the condominium or apartment building that are intended to beautify the premises and that are for the enjoyment of occupants rather than for utility.

Amortization: The reduction of a loan through periodic payments in which interest is charged only on the unpaid balance.

Amortization period: The actual number of years it will take to repay a mortgage loan in full. This can be well in excess of the loan's term. For example, mortgages often have 5-year terms, but 25-year amortization periods.

Analysis of property: The systematic method of determining the performance of investment real estate using a property analysis form.

Appraised value: An estimate of the fair market value of the property, usually performed by an appraiser.

Assessment fee: Also referred to as maintenance fee. A monthly fee that condominium owners must pay, usually including management fees, costs of common property upkeep, heating costs, garbage-removal costs, the owner's contribution to the contingency reserve fund, and so on. In the case of time-shares, the fee is normally levied annually.

Assumption agreement: A legal document signed by a homebuyer to assume responsibility for the obligations of a mortgage made by a former owner.

Balance sheet: A financial statement that indicates the financial status of a condominium corporation or apartment building, or other revenue property, at a specific point in time by listing its assets and liabilities.

Base rent: The fixed rent paid by a tenant. This is separate from any rent paid as a result of extra charges or percentage rents.

Blended payments: Equal payments consisting of both a principal and an interest component, paid each month during the term of the mortgage. The principal portion increases each month, while the interest portion decreases, but the total monthly payment does not change.

Board of directors: The directors of the condominium corporation formed under provincial legislation. Sometimes called just "the Board." In Quebec, the responsibilities of the "administrators" are generally the same as those for the board of directors in other provinces. Directors may have personal liability exposure.

Budget: An annual estimate of a condominium corporation or apartment building's expenses and the revenues needed to balance those expenses. There are operating budgets and capital budgets. (See also *Capital budget*.)

Buildings: The buildings included in a property. In the case of a condominium purchase, this usually refers to the parts that are divided into the units and the common area.

Canada Mortgage and Housing Corporation (CMHC): The federal Crown corporation that is governed by the *National Housing Act*. CMHC services include providing housing information and assistance, financing, and insuring home purchase loans for lenders.

Canada Revenue Agency (CRA): The current name of the former Revenue Canada.

Canadian Real Estate Association (CREA): An association of members of the real estate industry, principally real estate agents and brokers.

Capital budget: An estimate of costs to cover replacements and improvements, and the corresponding revenues needed to balance them, usually for a 12-month period. Different from an operating budget.

Capital gain: Profit on the sale of an asset that is subject to taxation.

Capital improvements: Major improvements made to a property that are written off over several years rather than expensed off in the year in which they are made.

Capitalization rate (CAP): The percentage of return on an investment when purchased on a free-and-clear or all-cash basis.

Charge: A document registered against a property, stating that someone has or believes he or she has a claim on the property.

Closing: The actual completion of the transaction acknowledging satisfaction of all legal and financial obligations between buyer and seller, and acknowledging the deed or transfer of title and disbursement of funds to appropriate parties.

Closing costs: The expenses over and above the purchase price of buying and selling real estate.

Closing date: The date on which the sale of a property becomes final and the new owner takes possession.

CMHC: See Canada Mortgage and Housing Corporation.

Collateral mortgage: A loan backed up by a promissory note and the security of a mortgage on a property. The money borrowed may be used for the purchase of a property or for another purpose, such as home renovations or a vacation.

Common area: The area in a condominium project that is shared by all of the condominium owners, such as elevators, hallways, and parking lots.

Common area maintenance (CAM): The charge to owners to maintain the common areas, normally due on a monthly basis.

Common expenses: Expenses incurred by the condominium corporation in carrying out the duties and responsibilities as specified in the project documents, i.e., in the declaration.

Common funds: Funds (such as a contingency/reserve fund) held by the corporation or administrators of the co-ownership of the immovables, but belonging to the unit owners.

Common interest: The proportional interest in the common elements belonging to a unit owner. (See also *Unit proportion*.)

Condominium: A housing unit to which the owner has title and of which the owner also owns a share in the common area (elevators, hallways, swimming pool, land, etc.).

Condominium corporation: The condominium association of unit owners incorporated under some provincial condominium legislation, automatically at the time of registration of the project. It is called a strata corporation in British Columbia. Under each of the provincial statutes, it will differ from an ordinary corporation in many respects. The condominium corporation, unlike a private business corporation, usually does not enjoy limited liability, and any judgment against the corporation for the payment of money is usually a judgment against each owner. The objects of the corporation are to manage the property and any assets of the corporation, and its duties include effecting compliance by the owners with the requirements of the Act, the declaration, the bylaws, and the rules.

Condominium council: The governing body of the condominium corporation, elected at the annual general meeting of the corporation. Similar to a *board of directors* (see above).

Condominium legislation: The legislation enacted by the provinces and territories to permit both individual and shared ownership of portions of multi-unit developments. Describes what a condominium is, how one is created, and how it must be administered. Provinces may from time to time make significant changes to their legislation. For reliable guidance, the reader should always refer to the most recent provincial legislation and seek the advice of a real estate lawyer.

Condominium management: The firm or individual responsible for managing and maintaining the physical and financial administration aspects of a condominium. Hired by the board of directors.

Condominium plan: In certain provinces, a plan which is registered and which in essence describes the total project and each of the units in it. (See also *Declaration* and *Description*.)

Contingency fund: See *Reserve fund.*

Conventional mortgage: A mortgage loan that does not exceed 75% of the appraised value or of the purchase price of the property, whichever is less. Mortgages that exceed this limit generally must be insured by mortgage insurance, such as that provided by CMHC and Genworth Financial.

Conversion: The changing of a structure from some other use, such as changing a rental apartment to a condominium apartment.

Conveyancing: The transfer of property, or title to property, from one party to another.

Co-operative: A form of ownership in which the individual "owner" has a share in the co-operative, which body actually owns the property. The "owner" has the right to live in a housing unit by means of a lease but does not own the actual unit.

Co-proprietor: In Quebec, a condominium unit owner. The actual form of ownership is called co-ownership.

Corporation: The condominium association of unit owners incorporated under some provincial condominium legislation automatically at the time of registration of the project. It is called a strata corporation in British Columbia. Under each of the statutes it will differ from an ordinary corporation in many respects. The corporation, unlike a private business corporation, does not enjoy limited liability, and any judgment against the corporation for the payment of money is also a judgment against each owner. The objects of the corporation are to manage the property and any assets of the corporation, and its duties include effecting compliance by the owners with the requirements of the Act, the declaration, the bylaws, and the rules.

CRA: Canada Revenue Agency.

Debt service: Cost of paying interest for the use of mortgage money or other borrowed funds.

Declaration: The document used in some provinces under the condominium legislation, and which, upon registration, submits the project to the provisions of the Act and creates the condominium. It is called a condominium plan in some provinces, and a strata plan in British Columbia. In Quebec it is known as the declaration of co-ownership.

Deductions: The expenses that Canada Revenue Agency allows you to deduct from your gross income.

Deed: This document conveys the title of the property to the purchaser. Different terminology may be used in different provincial jurisdictions.

Depreciation: The amount by which you write off the value of your real estate investment over the useful life of the investment. Does not include the value of your land.

Description: In some provinces, the document which is registered simultaneously with the declaration and which defines the total project and describes each unit. It sets out those parts of the condominium development that are to be privately owned, and those areas that are to be owned in common by the owners.

Destruction: A legal concept. When a condominium project is seriously damaged, the owners must decide whether or not to rebuild it. If they decide the latter, the project undergoes destruction, is destroyed, a legal process which divides the condominium corporation's assets among its owners. In certain circumstances condominium owners can also "destroy" a corporation even if it has not been damaged.

Development: The building or buildings and the land upon which they are situated. Sometimes used interchangeably with *project* (see below).

Disclosure statement: A series of documents prepared by the developer and issued to proposed unit purchasers describing the property, and containing a budget statement for a set period immediately following the registration of the condominium. Until the purchaser receives a copy of the current disclosure statement, the agreement of purchase and sale can be voided by the purchaser in most provinces.

Down payment: An initial amount of money (in the form of cash) put forward by the purchaser. Usually it represents the difference between the purchase price and the amount of the mortgage loan.

Encumbrance: See *Charge*.

Equity: The difference between the price for which a property could be sold and the total debts registered against it.

Equity return: The percentage ratio between your equity in the property and the total of cash flow plus mortgage principal reduction.

Escrow: The holding of a deed or contract by a third party until fulfillment of certain stipulated conditions between the contracting parties.

Estoppel certificate: A written statement requested by the prospective purchaser of a resale unit. The estoppel outlines whether or not all maintenance fees and other payments to be made by the current unit owner are up to date. In addition, it outlines other important financial or legal considerations. Sometimes referred to as a *Status certificate.*

Exclusive portion: In Quebec, the parts of the immovables owned by and reserved for the private use of the individual proprietor. (See also *Unit.*)

Estate: The title or interest one has in property such as real estate and personal property that can, if desired, be passed on to survivors at the time of one's death.

Fair market value: The value established on real property that is determined to be one that a buyer is willing to pay and a seller is willing to sell.

Fee simple: A manner of owning land, in one's own name and free of any conditions, limitations, or restrictions.

Financial statements: Documents that show the financial status of the condominium corporation, apartment building, or other revenue property at a given point in time. Generally includes income and expense statement and balance sheet.

Fiscal year: The 12-month period in which financial affairs are calculated.

Floating-rate mortgage: Another term for variable-rate mortgage.

Fixed-rate mortgage: This is the conventional mortgage that normally has a term of from one to 10 years, and is amortized over 20 to 40 years.

Foreclosure: A legal procedure whereby the lender obtains ownership of, or right to sell, the property following default by the borrower.

Fraction: In Quebec, an exclusive portion and a share of the common portions under the Civil Code. Each co-proprietor has an undivided right of ownership in the common portions. His or her share in the common portions is equal to the value of the exclusive portion of his or her fraction, in relation to the aggregate of the values of the exclusive portions.

Fractional ownership: Where you own a fraction or portion of the property. This format is most common in resort areas, and normally involves from one-quarter to one-tenth ownership of a condominium or a house.

GE Mortgage Insurance Canada: See *Genworth Financial*.

Genworth Financial Canada: A private insurer in Canada that insures high-ratio mortgages.

High-ratio mortgage: A conventional mortgage loan that exceeds 75% of the appraised value or purchase price of the property. Such a mortgage must be insured.

Immovables: In Quebec, in reference to condominiums, all the land and buildings comprising the condominium project.

Income, gross: Income or cash flow before expenses.

Income, net: Income or cash flow after expenses (but generally before income tax).

Interest averaging: The method of determining the overall average interest rate being paid when more than one mortgage is involved.

Interim financing: The temporary financing by a lender during the construction of real property for resale, or while other funds are due in.

Legal description: Identification of a property that is recognized by law, and that identifies that property from all others.

Lessee: The tenant in rental space.

Lessor: The owner of the rental space.

Letter of intent: Used in place of a formal written contract with a deposit. The prospective purchaser informs the seller, in writing, that he or she is willing to enter into a formal purchase contract upon certain terms and conditions if they are acceptable to the seller.

Leverage: The use of financing or other people's money to control large pieces of real property with a small amount of invested capital.

Lien: A claim for the payment of money against a unit or a condominium corporation.

Limited common elements: Those common elements whose use is restricted to one or more condo unit owners or, conversely, those which are not available for use by all unit owners. These areas are often referred to as exclusive-use areas.

Limited partnership: An investment group in which one partner serves as the general partner and the others as limited partners. The general partner bears all of the financial responsibility and management of the investment. The limited partners are obligated only to the extent of their original investment plus possible personal guarantees.

Listings, exclusive agency: A signed agreement by a seller in which he or she agrees to co-operate with one broker. All other brokers must go through the listing broker.

Listings, multiple: (See also *Multiple listing service*.) A system of agency/subagency relationships. If Broker A lists the property for sale, "A" is the vendor's agent. If Broker B sees the MLS listing and offers it for sale, "B" is the vendor's subagent.

Listings, open: A listing given to one or more brokers, none of whom have any exclusive rights or control over the sale by other brokers or the owner of the property.

Maintenance fees: Fees for the upkeep of a project based on a unit owner's percentage share of operating and administrative costs of the condominium corporation. (See *Assessment fee*.)

Management agreement: A contract between representatives of the condominium corporation and a management company to provide management services for the project's day-to-day operation, and also to provide overall administrative services.

Marginal tax rate: That point in income at which any additional income will be taxed at a higher tax rate.

MLS: See *Multiple listing service*.

Mortgage: The document that pledges real property as collateral for an indebtedness.

Mortgage, balloon: A mortgage amortized over a number of years, but which requires the entire principal balance to be paid at a certain time, short of the full amortization period.

Mortgage, constant: The interest rate charged on a mortgage consisting of both the rate being charged by the lender and the rate that represents the amount of principal reduction each period.

Mortgage, deferred payment: A mortgage allowing for payments to be made on a deferred or delayed basis. Usually used where present income is not sufficient to make the payments.

Mortgage, discounted: The selling of a mortgage to another party at a discount or an amount less than the face value of the mortgage.

Mortgage, first: A mortgage placed on a property in first position.

Mortgage, fixed-rate: This is a conventional mortgage, with payments of interest and principal. Fixed terms with a fixed rate can vary from six months to 10 years or more.

Mortgage insurance: This is insurance provided by the lender as an option for the borrower. It would pay out the balance outstanding on your mortgage, in the event of your death.

Mortgage, interest only: Payments to interest only are made. There is no principal reduction in the payment.

Mortgage, points: The interest rate charged by the lender.

Mortgage, second: A mortgage placed on a property in second position to an already existing first mortgage.

Mortgage, variable: This is a mortgage with an interest rate that fluctuates with the Bank of Canada interest rate. You pay the interest, with optional pay-down on the principal. Different from a fixed-rate mortgage. See above.

Mortgage wraparound: Sometimes called an all-inclusive mortgage. A mortgage that includes any existing mortgages on the property. The buyer makes one large payment on the wraparound and the seller continues making the existing mortgage payments out of that payment.

Mortgagee: The lender.

Mortgagor: The borrower.

Multiple listing service (MLS): A service licensed to member real estate boards by CREA. Used to compile and disseminate information by publication and computer concerning a given property to a large number of agents and brokers.

National Housing Act **(NHA) Loan:** A mortgage loan that is insured by CMHC to certain maximums.

New Home Warranty Program (NHWP): New Home Warranty Program, which is provincial in nature and provides warranty protection for new homes.

NHA: The federal *National Housing Act*.

Offer to purchase: The document that sets forth all the terms and conditions under which a purchaser offers to purchase property. This offer, when accepted by the seller, becomes a binding agreement of purchase and sale once all conditions have been removed.

Operating budget: An estimate of costs to operate a building or condominium complex and corresponding revenues needed to balance them, usually for a 12-month period. Different from a capital budget.

Operating costs: Those expenses required to operate an investment property, generally excluding mortgage payments.

Option agreement: A contract, with consideration, given to a potential purchaser of a property, giving him or her the right to purchase at a future date. If he or she chooses not to purchase, the deposit to the seller is forfeited.

Personal property: Property in an investment property, such as carpeting, draperies, refrigerators, etc., that can be depreciated over a shorter useful life than the structure itself.

Phantom mortgage: A technique developers of new condo units may use to compensate for the legal requirement to pay interest on the purchaser's deposit toward the purchase price. Comes into operation once a unit purchaser enters into interim occupancy pending the registration of the condominium by the developer. Under the condominium legislation of some provinces, the developer can charge an "occupant rent," which consists of common expenses for the unit, an estimate of municipal taxes for the unit, and interest on any mortgage the purchaser is required to assume or provide under the terms of the agreement of purchase and sale.

A vendor (developer) take-back mortgage, payable on demand, is inserted in the agreement. The demand is normally made at the time of closing or within seven days; the mortgage is therefore "phantom." By inserting this provision, the developer obtains the right to charge interest on the balance of the purchase price, which could be more than the amount the developer has to pay the purchaser in interest on the deposit money. Since the legal enforceability of a given phantom mortgage might be questionable, legal advice should be obtained.

PI: Principal and interest due on a mortgage.

PIT: Principal, interest, and taxes due on a mortgage.

Prepayment penalty: A penalty charge written into many mortgages that must be paid if the mortgage is paid off ahead of schedule.

Principal: The amount you actually borrowed, or the portion of it still owing on the original loan.

Project: The entire parcel to be divided into condo units and common elements.

Project documents: The documents required to create a condominium, including, where such are applicable in the provincial jurisdiction, the declaration, the plan, the description, and the bylaws.

Prospectus: A written presentation prepared by the developer that outlines material facts about the offering to induce offers from prospective purchasers.

Property manager: A manager or management company hired to run an investment property for the owner.

Purchase-and-sale agreement: See *Agreement of purchase and sale.*

Pyramiding: The process of building real estate wealth by allowing appreciation and mortgage principal reduction to increase the investors' equity in a series of ever larger properties.

Resident manager: An individual, usually living in the building, who handles all day-to-day problems in the building.

Rescission: That period of time following the sale during which the buyer can change his or her mind, cancel the purchase agreement, and get a refund of funds paid on deposit. It varies from province to province from approximately three to 30 days.

Reserve fund: A fund set up to cover major condo repair and replacement costs or other unforeseen expenditures. In many provinces a percentage of all monthly maintenance fees must be put toward the reserve fund, and it is non-refundable. A healthy fund should make special assessments unnecessary.

Rules and regulations: Rules that the board adopts respecting the use of the condo common elements and units to promote the safety and security of owners and property.

Sale/leaseback: The tenant (owner) in a building sells the building to an investor and leases it back for a period of years.

Schedule of interests upon destruction: A schedule showing the proportionate amounts of the land and assets of a condominium corporation due to the individual strata lot owners upon the destruction of the corporation. (See *Destruction.*)

Special assessment: An assessment above and beyond the monthly assessment, which the condominium council (for larger expenditures, generally 75% of the strata corporation members) may decide to levy for a special purpose, e.g., building a sauna or swimming pool. Primarily for unexpected or unbudgeted expenses.

Special resolution: A resolution generally requiring approval of 75% of the condominium unit owners. Required for granting easements, acquiring or disposing of common property, or passing bylaws, etc.

Status certificate: See *Estoppel certificate.*

Statutory bylaws: Bylaws of the corporation set out as schedules to the Condominium Acts of various provinces. Automatically in force when the Act is invoked until repealed or amended by a new provincial statute.

Strata corporation: In British Columbia, equivalent to the term *condominium corporation.*

Strata lot: Term used in British Columbia to describe property subject to individual ownership. Similar to *unit* (see below).

Strata plan: Term used in British Columbia. (See *Declaration* and *Description.*)

Sub-lease: The tenant (lessee) leases part of his or her premises to another user.

Tax shelter: The tax write-off possible through the depreciation benefits available on investment real estate ownership.

Time value of money: The value of a future sum of money if it is paid today. Usually there is a discount factor as you would be getting the benefit of the money today even though it is not due until some time in the future.

Timeshare: The traditional concept of prepaying for a "right to use" a property for a period of a week or longer, generally in a tourist or resort area. This could include exchange privileges for accommodation in other areas. Normally this does not involve any equity ownership. The ability to sell your "use week" is very limited if you tire of it, or can't use it.

Title: Generally, the evidence of right that a person has to the possession of property.

Title insurance: This insurance covers the purchaser or vendor, in case of any defects in the property or title that existed at the time of sale, but were not known about until after the sale. It could also cover subsequent issues, such as identity fraud relating to the property title.

Trust account: The separate account in which a lawyer or real estate broker holds funds until the real estate closing takes place or other legal disbursement is made.

Trust funds: Funds held in trust, either held as a deposit for the purchase of real property or to pay taxes and insurance.

Undivided interest: An individual condominium owner's partial interest in the project's common property that is not defined by boundaries but is an abstraction.

Unit (1): In all provinces, except British Columbia and Quebec, each part of the project subject to individual ownership. In Ontario this comprises not only the space enclosed by the unit boundaries, but all material parts of the land within the space at the time the declaration and description are registered. In British Columbia, called *strata lot,* and in Quebec, *exclusive portion.*

Unit (2): Normally refers to the rental suite or that part of a condominium owned and occupied or rented by the owner.

Unit entitlement: The share of a condominium owner in the common property, common facilities, and other assets of the strata corporation.

Unit factor: In some provinces, the share ownership in the common elements separate from the unit. The same factor also relates to voting rights and contribution towards common expenses. (See *Unit proportion.*)

Unit proportion: Generally, the proportion of the total common expenses for which a condominium unit holder is responsible.

Useful life: The term during which an asset is expected to have useful value.

Vacancy allowance: A projected deduction from the scheduled gross income of a building to allow for loss of income due to vacant apartments or other rental units.

Value, assessed: The property value as determined by local, regional, or provincial assessment authority.

Variable-rate mortgage: A mortgage in which the interest rate varies with the prime rate fixed by the mortgage company, which is in turn based on the prime rate of interest set by the Bank of Canada weekly. Generally is one or more percentage points lower than the conventional fixed-rate mortgage.

Vendor: A person selling a piece of property.

Vendor take-back: A procedure wherein the seller (vendor) of a property provides some or all of the mortgage financing in order to sell the property. Also referred to as vendor financing.

Zoning: Rules for land use established by local governments.

Index

A

accountant, 77–79
accounting fees, 142
actual disposition, 139
adjusted cost base (ACB), 139, 175
administration (condominium), 26
advertising (selling), 142, 245
advisors
    accessibility, 71
    accountant, 77–79
    communication, 71
    compatibility, 70
    confidence, 70
    criteria for selecting, 69–72
    experience, 70
    fees, 71–72
    home inspector, 80–83
    insurance broker, 83–85
    integrity, 71
    lawyer, 75–77
    mortgage broker, 79–80
    qualifications, 69
    realtor, 72–75
    references, 71–72
    trust, 71
agency disclosure, 72
agreement of purchase and sale, 124–129
all-risk comprehensive insurance, 30
"all risks" insurance, 150
alter ego trust, 178
Amazon Books, 50–51
amortization, 91
animals, 65
annuity (charitable remainder trusts),
   181–182
apartment (condominium), 26
appearance, 61
appreciation (property), 22, 172
assessed value of property, 131, 132
Association of Home and Property
   Inspectors, 81
assumable mortgage (selling), 245

B

Baby Boomers, 12
balanced market, 11
bare-land condominium, 27

barter exchange, 208–211
bartering
    and GST, 211
    networks, 208–211
    tax implications, 210–211
barter trades, 208–211
Better Business Bureau, 38, 46, 82
boats (owner-direct rentals), 222
boundaries, 65
Brunton's U.S. Tax-letter for Canadians, 231
Budd, John, 161, 169, 185
builders, 38–39
building lot (condominium), 26
building schemes, 63–64
buyer's market, 11

C

Canada Mortgage and Housing Corporation,
   50, 51–52, 79, 90, 91, 92, 94
Canada Revenue Agency, and IRS, 232
Canada-U.S. tax treaty, 232, 234, 236, 237
Canadian Bar Association, 76
Canadian consulate, 239
Canadian Homebuilders' Association, 50
cancellation insurance (home exchange), 206
capital beneficiaries, 177
capital cost allowance (CCA), 142
capital expenses, 142, 143
capital gains, 132, 139, 172, 175, 177
capital gains tax
    and charitable remainder trust, 182
    and estate planning, 171, 178, 179
    and fair market value, 183
    and investment real estate, 19
    and principal residence, 18
    U.S., 236-237
    when to pay, 183–184
capital losses, 19
car insurance (home exchange), 205
cash-surrender value (life insurance), 157
certified financial planner, 77
certified general accountant, 78
Chapters/Indigo, 50–51
charitable memorial endowment, 183
charitable remainder trusts, 181–182
chartered accountant, 78
chattels, 128

child as property owner, 172–175
climate, 62
closed mortgage, 91
closing costs (selling), 246
closing date (vacation rental property), 106
collateral mortgage, 90–91, 97
commercial property taxes, 13
commission
    as negotiable, 246, 253
    in purchase and sale agreement, 129
    real estate investment property, 143
    and realtor, 250–251
common elements (condominium), 26, 57
common expenses (condominium), 29–30
common property (condominium), 29–30
community cycle, 10
competition (selling), 245
computer-related expenses, 143
computer storage (records), 225–226
conditional offer, 82
conditions
    to benefit purchaser, 126–127
    to benefit vendor, 127
    for condominiums, 127
    and deposit, 124
    owner-direct rentals, 222
    in purchase and sale agreement, 125–129
    for revenue property, 127
    vacation rental property, 106
condominium
    advantages, 32–33
    bare-land, 27
    and common elements, 26
    contingency reserve fund, 29–30
    defined, 25–27
    disadvantages, 33–34
    expenses, 28–32, 143
    freehold, 26
    insurance, 30–31
    investing in, benefits, 34
    leasehold, 26
    lease payments, 31
    maintenance, 29–30
    management and administration, 26
    management fees, 31–32
    and ownership rights, 26
    property tax, 28–29
    and provincial legislation, 26
    recreational, 27
    rental pool, 28–29
    repair and maintenance, 31
    resort, 27–28
    special assessment, 30
    stratified format, 27
    structural forms, 26
    unit, defined, 26
    utilities, 31
    and vertical dimension, 27
condominium association websites, 257
condominium homeowner's package
    insurance, 31
construction liens, 129
construction materials, 57–58
construction mortgage, 91
contingency reserve fund (condominium),
    29–30
contra deals, 208–211
conventional mortgage, 89–90
co-proprietorship, 26
corporation as property owner, 180
Cottage, 50, 187
cottage associations, 55
cottage association websites, 258–259
Cottage Life, 50, 187
The Cottager, 50
counter offers (selling), 246
courses, real estate, 50
credit report websites, 256
curb appeal (selling), 245

D
death tax (U.S.), 236, 237
deemed disposition, 139, 171, 172, 175, 178,
    179
defects, 129
deposit
    explained, 124–125
    vacation rental property, 104–105
depreciation, 19
design, 58
detached (condominium), 26
developers, 9
development stage, 60
discretionary trust, 179
documents (selling), 244
dogs, 157
do-it-yourself will, 164
domain names, 219–220
domain registration sites, 220
donating to charity, 181–183
donation tax credit, 182
"doubling up," 140
dual agency agreement, 73
duplex (condominium), 26
dying intestate, 163
dying in U.S., 237

E

easement, 63

economic climate, 14, 60

education, 144

electronic communication expenses, 143

enduring, defined, 194

enduring power of attorney, 166

equity, 17–18, 20

estate liability, 184–185

estate planning

    buying property in child's name, 174–175

    and capital gains tax, 183–184

    and charity, 181–183

    and corporation, 180

    explained, 170

    and future tax liabilities, 180

    and investment tax, 184

    and joint partner trust, 177–178

    and liability, 184–185

    and life insurance, 180

    and life interest, 178–179

    and magazines, 186–187

    objectives, 170

    perspectives for, 170–171

    and power of attorney, 161

    and principle residence exemption, 171–172, 179

    and probate tax, 184

    and remainder interest, 178–179

    selling property to child, 173

    strategies, 171–180

    tips checklist, 185–186

    transferring property to child, 172–173

    transferring property to family trust, 176–177

    transferring property to trust, 175–176

    and vacation property, 171

estate tax (U.S.), 236

exchange cancellation insurance, 206

exclusive listing (selling), 253

exemption formula, 139

exemption fraction, 140

expenses (condominium), 28–32

F

fair market value (FMV)

    and capital gains tax, 183

    and estate planning, 172, 175, 178, 179

    and GST rebate, 135

family trust (estate planning), 175–176

farmland, 136

federal government websites, 256

federal taxes, 13, 133–148

fee simple, 27, 44, 46

Financial Advisors Association of Canada, 84

financial and tax planning websites, 256

financial needs, 108

financial status, 108

financing (selling), 245

financing terms (vacation rental property), 106

finder's fee, 144

fire, 154

fire department, 54

fire hydrants, 154

first mortgage, 93

fixtures, 128

Foreign Affairs and International Trade Canada, 239

foreign vacation property

    financing, 240

    political uncertainties, 239–240

    property laws, 240

    renting out, 240–241

    researching, 238

    tax returns, 241

forgery, 129

formal trade exchange, 209–210

fractional ownership, 46

fraud, 129

freehold condominium, 26

freehold ownership, 121

furs, insuring, 150

G

general information websites, 255

Genworth Financial Canada, 79, 90, 91, 92

gifting, 175

gift of beneficial ownership, 175

gifts in kind, 182

gift tax (U.S.), 235–236

Globe and Mail, 49–50

goods and services tax. *See* GST

Google, 51, 219

government restrictions, 64

ground rights, 64

group rentals (owner-direct rentals), 222

GST

    farmland, 136

    land, 136

    new home, 134–135

    owner-built home, 135

    principal residence, 134

    property, 133–134

    rebate, 133, 134–135

    renovated home, 135–136

resale home, 134
residential dwelling, 134

H
harmonized sales tax (HST), 133
health care directive, 167
health care proxy, 167
high-ratio financing, 19
high-ratio insurance, 92
high-ratio/insured mortgage, 90
"home," 134
homebuilders' association, 55
home business income, 19
home exchange
    active marketing, 204
    with car, 205
    catalogues, 202–204
    documentation for, 206
    listing, 203
    long-term, 207
    passive marketing, 204
    preparing for, 207–208
    trade or barter, 208–211
    websites, 202–204, 219, 259
    without car, 204–205
home inspectors
    checklist for hiring, 83
    and conditional offer, 82
    finding, 82–83
    and new homes, 81
    and older homes, 81–82
    qualifications, 80–81
    selecting, 80–83
    services, 81–82
    as source of information, 55
home office insurance, 158
homeowner's grant, 131–132
house, building yourself, 39–40
housecleaning fee (owner-direct rentals), 222
house exchanges, 199–211
house insurance, and long absence, 206
The Housing Market Outlook, 52
housing surveys websites, 255

I
income beneficiary, 181–182
income tax, 136–148
Income Tax Act, 138, 177, 186, 225, 236
inflation, 23
informal trade exchange, 209
insurance, 149–159
    "actual cash value," 151
    condominium, 30–31

deductible, 154–155
and depreciation, 151
discounts, 155
and earthquakes, 150
"fine print," 150
and fire, 154
and floods, 150
full replacement value, 152
for home exchanges, 205, 206
home office, 158
inflation allowance, 153
life, 157
and long absence, 206
mortgage, 157
"new for old" coverage, 151
personal liability, 156–157
premiums, 153–155
property, 149–153
real estate investment property, 144
and renovations, 152
rental, 158
and risk, 127–128
risk factors, 153–155
and "spread of risk," 153
and theft, 154
title, 158–159
and weather, 154
insurance broker, 83–85
Insurance Brokers Association of Canada, 31, 84
interest, 144
interest rates, 12, 93
Internal Revenue Service, 232
Internet, 51
Internet Service Providers, 219
interval ownership, 44
investment income property, 18
investment partnerships
    assessing risks, 114–115
    buying others out, 115
    compatibility, 112
    contribution, 114
    control, 113–114
    documenting, 115–117
    expertise, 111
    getting out of, 115
    goals and objectives, 111
    legal structure, 113
    liability, 113
    liquidity, 112
    losses, 115
    management, 112
    percent of investment, 114

pitfalls, 117–118
profits, 115
taxes, 114
types, 115
investment real estate, 19, 20–21
investment value, 17–24
IRS, and Canada Revenue Agency, 232
IRS Code, 234

J
jewellery, insuring, 150
Joint Centre for Bioethics, 167
joint ownership, 122–124
joint tenancy, 122

K
key words (websites), 220

L
land, 14, 23, 136
landscaping, 144
lawn signs (selling), 245
lawyer
    finding, 76–77
    and mortgage financing, 76
    referral service, 76
    selecting, 75–77
lawyer-prepared will, 164–166
layout, 58
leasehold condominium, 26
leasehold interest, 121–122
lease payments (condominium), 31
legal advice, 241
legal expenses, 145
life insurance, 157, 180
"life interest" (charitable remainder trusts),
    182
life interest (estate planning), 178–179
lifetime capital gains exemption, 172
"liquidated damages," 124
listing agreement, 251–254
listing portal sites, 218–219
living will, 167
loan value (life insurance), 157
local business cycle, 10
local fire department, 54
local homebuilders' association, 55
Local Housing Now, 52
local taxes, 131–132
location, 14, 56
lot size, shape, 61
"love money," 96–97

M
magazines, 50
magazine websites, 259
maintenance
    condominium, 29–30
    real estate investment property, 145
management (condominium), 26, 30, 31–32,
    59
manufactured homes, 43–44
Mapquest, 219
market assessment, 9
market value of property, 172
memorial scholarships, 183
merger, 128–129
mill rate, 131
minimum stay (owner-direct rentals), 222
MLS, 52, 53, 72, 245, 253
mobile home, 42–43
mobile home park (condominium), 26
money, insuring, 150
mortgage
    approval, 79
    assumable, 90
    from business loan, 95
    closed, 91
    complex, 80
    conditions, 90
    defaulting on, 93
    from family, 96–97
    financing, 76
    frequency of payment, 92
    from friends, 96–97
    hierarchy, 93
    and high-ratio insurance, 92
    nsurance, 157
    interest calculations, 91–92
    interest rate, 91–92
    length of term, 91
    negotiating, 99
    open, 91
    payments, 145
    pre-approved, 93–94
    on recreational property, 92
    simple, 80
    terms, 91–92
    types, 89–91
mortgage broker, 79–80, 94
mortgage insurance, 157
mortgage insurance websites, 256
motor vehicle expenses, 145
multi-ownership, 44
multiple listing (selling), 253

Multiple Listing Service (MLS), 52, 53, 72, 245, 253
municipal property taxes, 13, 28–29
municipal services
    building inspector, 54
    fire department, 54
    planning department, 53
    police department, 54
    tax department, 53–54
municipal taxes, 131–132

N
National Housing Observer, 52
National Post, 49–50
National Real Estate Institute Inc., 24, 50, 187
negative debt financing, 18
negotiating, 99–106
    and mortgage, 99
    preparation, 99–100
    tips, techniques, 104–106
neighbourhood value, 58
neighbours, 55
new home, and GST, 134–135
New Home Warranty Program, 38, 81
new home warranty websites, 257
new property, legislation for, 125
newspapers, 49–50, 54
noise, 56, 222
nonresident aliens, 232, 234–236

O
office expenses, 146
online home exchange, 202–204
open house (selling), 245, 248
open listing (selling), 252–253
open mortgage, 91
operating costs (condominium), 29
owner-built home, and GST, 134–135
owner-direct rentals
    conditions, 222
    contact information, 220–221
    keeping records for, 224–226
    marketing and managing, 218–227
    photos, 221–222
    prices, 222
    and problems, 223
    rental agreement, 224
    requests for free use, 223
    saving on expenses for, 226–227
    and tenant help, 217
    use and care policy, 224
    website advertising, 218–220
owner-direct rental sites, 202

owner powers of attorney, 193–194
ownership of property, 172–180
ownership rights (condominium), 26
owners *vs.* tenants, 58–59
owner wills, 193–194

P
parking, 57
partition, 123
penalties, 146
perception of area, 60
personal guarantee, 90
personal income tax return, 132
personal information record, 167–168
personal liability insurance
    and alcohol, 156
    for condominium owner, 30
    for home exchange, 205–206
    and pets, 157
    and "slip and fall," 156
    and swimming pool, 157
    and tenants, 157
"personal property," 150
personal websites (rentals), 219–220
pets, 157, 222
photos (owner-direct rentals), 221–222
political factors, 15
population trends, 60
positive cash flow, 18
possession date, 128
pre-approved mortgage, 93–94
prepackaged house, 39–40
preparation (selling), 244–246
price
    recreational property, 57
    vacation rental property, 105
pricing, 222, 244
principal residence
    and capital gains, 139
    disclosing to CRA, 139
    and estate planning, 175
    exemption formula, 139–140
    and GST, 134
    and seasonal residence, 138
    and tax advantage, 18
    and vacation property, 138
    vs. home, 138
principal residence exemption, 137–140, 171–172, 179
privacy, 56
private warranty websites, 257
probate fees, 178
probate tax, 184

professional advice (selling), 245
professional associations websites, 255–256
professional rental management, 214–216
promissory note, 90, 173
promotion (selling), 245
property as security, 19
property insurance
    basis of claim settlement, 151
    bylaws, 151–152
    conditions, 152
    contents coverage, 153
    deductible, 152
    exclusions, 150–151
    guaranteed replacement cost, 151
    how much to buy, 152–153
    and inflation allowance, 150
    insured perils, 150
    replacement cost, 151
    special limits, 150
property management companies, 215–216
property management (rentals), 213–227
property ownership, 121–129
property purchase tax, 132–133
property tax
    comparing, 59
    condominium, 28–29
    local, 131–132
    real estate investment property, 146
provincial government websites, 256–257
provincial taxes, 13, 132–133
proximity, 62
"public accountant," 78
public image, 14
public trustee, 163
purchase-and-sale agreement, 124–129
pyramiding, 20

R
raw land, 40–42
real estate
    agents, 53, 246–251
    boards, 52
    buying with others, 110–118
    commission (selling), 246, 250–251
    and community cycle, 10
    cycle, 12
    firms, 52
    as investment, 17–24
    and local business cycle, 10
    market, 9–10, 11
    market types, 11
    price factors, 11–15
    surveys, 52

real estate investment property
    accounting fees, 142
    advertising, 143
    and capital cost allowance, 142
    capital expenditures, 143
    and capital expenses, 142
    and capital gains, 141
    commissions, 143
    computer-related expenses, 143
    condominium expenses, 143
    and current expenses, 142–147
    education, 144
    electronic communication expenses, 143
    fees, 143
    finder's fee, 144
    and flipping, 141
    and income, 141
    insurance, 144
    interest, 144
    landscaping, 144
    legal expenses, 145
    maintenance, 145
    mortgage payments, 145
    motor vehicle expenses, 145
    office expenses, 146
    and original intent, 141
    penalties, 146
    property taxes, 146
    record keeping, 147–148
    repairs, 145
    salaries, 146
    tax return preparation, 146
    travelling expenses, 145, 146–147
    utilities, 147
    vacant land, 147
    wages, 146
real estate listings websites, 255
real estate newspapers, 50
realtor
    and agency disclosure, 72
    benefits, 74–75
    and commission, 75
    and confidentiality, 73
    how to find, 73–74
    and MLS, 72
    selecting, 72–75
    selling, 245
reason for selling, 62, 243–244
record keeping
    checklist, 226
    and computer storage, 225–226
    equipment, 226
    for owner-directed rentals, 224–226

real estate investment property, 147–148
reasons for, 225
and Revenue Canada, 225
for self-managed rentals, 224–226
systems, 226
recreational real estate
appreciation, 22
donating to charity, 181–183
equity build-up, 22
flexibility, 23–24
general information, 49–51
goals and objectives for, 107
and inflation, 23
as investment, 17–24
and land, 23
and leverage, 19–20
reasons for selling, 101–102
risk, 20–22
selecting, 49–68
specific information, 51–55
tax advantages, 18–19
types, 25–46
remainder interest, 178–179
renovated home, and GST, 135–136
rental income
accrued method, 148
allowable expenses, 148
from U.S., 233, 234
as write-off, 18–19
Rental Income Guide, 136–137
rental insurance
for home exchange, 205
for vacation home, 158
rental management, 213–227
choosing type of, 214
companies, 31–32
professional, 214–216
Rental Market Reports, 52
rental pool (condominium), 28–29
rental property
demand for, 59
general features and factors, 55–63
information sources, 49–55
plan for buying, 65–66
special considerations, 63–65
vacation, finding, 66–68
rent controls, 13–14
repair and maintenance (condominium), 31
repairs (real estate investment property), 145
replacement-cost insurance, 30
representation agreement, 167
resale home, and GST, 134
resident aliens, 232

residential dwelling, and GST, 134
"residential property," 134
resort timesharing, 44–46
restrictions (use), 63
retirees, 12
return on investment, 17–18
revocable trusts, 176
right of survivorship, 122, 123
right of way, 63
right to use (timeshare), 44–46
risk
and insurance, 127–128
and interest rates, 93
minimizing, 20–22
row house (condominium), 26
RRIF, 185
RRSP
designating beneficiaries, 185
and mortgage, 89, 94–95

S
salaries (real estate investment property), 146
same-sex partners, 178
seasonal catalogues (home exchanges), 203
seasonal factors (real estate prices), 15
seasonal residence, 138
second mortgage, 93
security deposit (owner-direct rentals), 222
self-assessment, 107–108
self-directed RRSP, 95
self-managed rentals, 216–227
conditions, 222
contact information, 220–221
keeping records for, 224–226
marketing and managing, 218–227
photos, 221–222
pricing, 222
and problems, 223
rental agreement, 224
requests for free use, 223
saving on expenses for, 226–227
and tenant help, 217
use and care policy, 224
website advertising, 218–220
seller's market, 11
selling vacation investment property
closing costs, 246
competition, 245
curb appeal, 245
documents, 244
financing, 245
listing agreement, 251–254
preparation, 244–246

pricing, 244
professional advice, 245
promotion, 245
and realtor, 245
reasons, listed, 243–244
setting terms, 246
taxes, 245
timing, 243–244
without an agent, 246–251
selling your own property
advertising, 247–248
assessing offers, 249–250
in buyer's market, 251
and commission, 250–251
and emotion, 247
expense, 247–248
and experience, 246–247
market exposure, 248
and market knowledge, 248–249
and negotiating skills, 250
potential legal problems, 248
screening purchasers, 249
and time, 247
Semi-Annual Survey of Recreational Home Prices, 52
semi-detached (condominium), 26
seminars, real estate, 50
services, 61–62
service websites (rentals), 219
settlors, 176, 177
shared use of property, 191–197
shared vacation plan, 44
shareholder loan, 95–96
single-family house, 35–39
single family house (condominium), 26
single-purpose corporation, 180
"slip and fall," 156
smoking (owner-direct rentals), 222
social insurance number (Canada), 233
sole ownership
freehold, 121
leasehold interest, 121–122
types, 121–122
special assessment (condominium), 30
specialized websites (rentals), 219
spousal transfers, 140
spouses, 178
stack townhouse (condominium), 26
standard clauses (listing agreement), 251
Statistics Canada, 51, 60
storage, 57
subdivision (condominium), 26
subject clauses, 125–129
to benefit purchaser, 126–127

checklist, 125–126
for condominiums, 127
for revenue property, 127
"subject to" clauses, 124
"substantial renovations," 135, 136
summer resort condominium, 27
"supply," 133
supply and demand, 12
Survey on Recreational Home Prices in Canada, 52
sustaining power of attorney, 166
swimming pool, 157

T
"taxable event," 183
tax advantages, 18–19
tax advice, 241
taxes, 13, 131–148, 245
tax laws (U.S.), 232
tax on net rental income (U.S.), 234
taxpayer identification number (U.S.), 232–233
tax return preparation, 146
tenancy in common, 122–124
tenants, 157
tenants *vs.* owners, 58–59
term life insurance, 157
terms (selling), 246
The Cottager, 187
theft, 154
timeshares, 44–46
timing (selling), 243–244
title insurance, 129, 158–159
title insurance websites, 256
toll-free numbers, 221
topography, 61
tourism association websites, 257–258
trade exchange, 208–211
trade shows, 51
transfer of title document, 174
transferring property ownership, 172–180
transportation, 61
travelling expenses, 145, 146–147
trust accounts, 124, 125
trust as owner, 175–178
trust declaration, 174
trustees, 176
"21-year deemed disposition rule," 176, 179

U
undivided share, 123
unit entitlement, 29
U.S. estate tax, 180
U.S. filing requirements, 232

U.S. Nonresident Alien Income Tax Return, 234
U.S. pension income, 233
U.S. property, 231–238, 241
U.S. taxes, 231–238, 241
U.S. tax laws, 232
U.S. Tax Treaty, 237
"used residential property," 134
"useful life," 179
utilities, 31, 147
utility taxes, 132

V
vacant land, 147
vacation investment property
    abroad, 238–241
    barter networks, 199–211
    buying abroad, 238–241
    checklists for, 196
    and death of owner, 193–194
    and dispute resolution, 195
    estate liability, 184–185
    estate planning for, 171–180
    as exchange option, 200–201
    exchanges, 199–211
    and family feuds, 170–171
    joint ownership, 170–171
    joint tenancy, 192–193
    legal advice, 241
    long-term goals, 194
    maintenance schedule for, 195
    managing as business, 191–197
    non-simultaneous exchanges, 201–202
    owner powers of attorney, 193–194
    owner wills, 193–194
    probate tax, 184
    reasons for selling, 102–104
    rules for use of, 196
    run as business, 195
    selling, 243–254
    selling or buying out of, 194
    shared use, 191–197
    simultaneous exchanges, 201–202
    tax advice, 241
    taxation on death, 184
    tenancy in common, 192–193
    in U.S., 180, 231–238, 241
    written use agreement, 192–197
vacation ownership (timeshares), 44
vacation property
    and "doubling up," 140
    and estate planning, 171
    and Google search, 67

    jointly owned, 140
    and MLS, 67
    newspaper ads, 67
    and owner, 68
    as principal residence, 138
    and real estate agent, 66–67
    tax exemption for, 140
vacation rental websites, 259
"vendor's disclosure statement," 82
vendor take-back mortgage, 248
volunteer fire department, 154

W
wages, 146
warranties, 125–129
waste disposal, 65
waterfront restrictions, 64
weather, 154
Western Canadian Resorts, Vacation Homes and Investment Properties, 50, 187
whole-life plan, 157
wildlife, 65
will
    basic (checklist), 162–163
    contents, 162–163
    do-it-yourself, 164
    dying without, 163
    and estate planning, 171
    and joint ownership, 122
    and lawyer, 164–166
    living, 167
    and personal information record, 167–168
    and powers of attorney, 166–167
    preparing, 163–164
    reason for, 161–162
    "standard form," 164
    and tenancy in common, 123
    updating, 162
winter resort condominium, 27
withholding certificate (U.S.), 235
withholding tax, 234
withholding tax (U.S.), 235
work orders, 129
written use agreement
    how property is held, 192–193
    and legal and tax advice, 196–197
    for vacation investment property, 192–197

Z
zoning, 59–60, 129

Reader Feedback and Seminars

Your candid feedback and constructive suggestions for improvement in future editions of this book would be most welcome.

If you would like to provide feedback, be on a mailing list for a free email newsletter, or be kept informed about any upcoming seminars in your area relating to real estate in Canada, please visit the website at www.homebuyer.ca.

If you would like further information about real estate investment in Canada, including seminars, books, and consulting, please contact:

National Real Estate Institute Inc.
3665 Kingsway, Suite 300
Vancouver, BC   V5R 5W2
E-mail: institute@homebuyer.ca

Or visit the website at www.homebuyer.ca

About the Author

Douglas Gray, B.A., LL.B., formerly a practising real estate and business lawyer, has extensive experience in all aspects of real estate, mortgage financing, and acting for clients buying or developing recreational property. He has acted on behalf of buyers, sellers, developers, investors, lenders, borrowers, tenants, and landlords. He also has wide experience as a personal investor in real estate for more than 35 years, as well as being a landlord of many properties.

His career morphed from practising law to being a consultant, columnist, speaker, and author of 23 bestselling books, some of which are published in up to 10 foreign-language editions. He has written nine books on real estate.

Doug has personally experienced the joys of the recreational property lifestyle. He grew up in Victoria. His parents owned two waterfront recreational homes on Langford Lake, about a half-hour drive away. One house was built from scratch on a large tract of land; the other was an older cottage bought a few lots down, and then substantially renovated. Doug's childhood was enriched by pleasurable times spent at the cottage with family, relatives, and friends.

Doug has since bought two recreational properties for personal pleasure in Whistler. One lot was bought 35 years ago, when Whistler was still in its infancy, for $7,000. The current value of that lot is now about $1.5 million. Unfortunately, Doug sold the lot a year after he bought it to help pay for law school tuition! Fast-forward to 1994, when he bought a three-quarter-acre lot in Whistler. He acted as the general contractor on building a luxury chalet there. The chalet is used for lifestyle enjoyment, revenue from selected rentals (there is also a year-round tenant suite in the back), home exchanges with people throughout the world, and capital gains appreciation.

Doug lives in Vancouver, British Columbia.

His website is www.homebuyer.ca. His chalet site is www.whistlerchalet.ca.